Case Book to accompany

basic marketing

A GLOBAL-MANAGERIAL APPROACH

ELEVENTH CANADIAN EDITION

KENNETH B. WONG
Queen's School of Business
Queen's University

STANLEY J. SHAPIRO
Simon Fraser University
(Professor Emeritus)

WILLIAM D. PERREAULT
University of North Carolina

E. JEROME McCARTHY
Michigan State University

Selected Cases updated by
ALGIS JUZUKONIS
Seneca College of Applied Arts and Technology

 **McGraw-Hill Ryerson**

Toronto Montréal Boston Burr Ridge, IL Dubuque, IA Madison, WI New York
San Francisco St. Louis Bangkok Bogotá Caracas Kuala Lumpur Lisbon London Madrid
Mexico City Milan New Delhi Santiago Seoul Singapore Sydney Taipei

Case Book to accompany
Basic Marketing: A Global-Managerial Approach
Eleventh Canadian Edition

ISBN: 0-07-095234-5

2 3 4 5 6 7 8 9 10 TRI 0 9 8 7 6 5

Printed and bound in Canada.

Care has been taken to trace ownership of copyright material contained in this text; however, the publisher will welcome any information that enables it to rectify any reference or credit for subsequent editions.

Vice President, Editorial and Media Technology: Patrick Ferrier
Sponsoring Editor: Kim Brewster
Marketing Manager: Kim Verhaeghe
Supervising Editor: Joanne Murray
Senior Production Coordinator: Jennifer Wilkie
Printer: Tri-Graphic Printing

<u>Case Book to accompany Basic Marketing 11/e: Table of Contents</u>

Cases

Guide to the Use of these Cases

Cases can be used in many ways. The same case can be analyzed several times for different purposes.

The main criterion for the order of these cases is the amount of technical vocabulary—or text principles—needed to read the case meaningfully. The first cases are "easiest" in this regard. This is why an early case can easily be used two or three times—with different emphasis. Some early cases might require some consideration of product and price, for example, and might be used twice, perhaps regarding product planning and, later, pricing. In contrast, later cases, which focus more on price, might be treated more effectively after the price chapters are covered.

In some of the cases, we have disguised certain information—such as names or proprietary financial data—at the request of the people or firms involved in the case. However, such changes do not alter the basic substantive problems you will be analyzing in a case.

Please note that Wong/Shapiro/Perreault/McCarthy, *Basic Marketing* 11/e provides video selections that correspond to each chapter. These are available for both student and instructor use. The synopsis of each video case, in addition to video streaming, discussion questions and answers can be found in both the Instructor's Manual and on the Student and Instructor Online Learning Centres. Please visit: www.mcgrawhill.ca/college/wong.

Instructors may also order VHS cassettes of these video cases for in-class use. Please contact your local i-Learning Sales Specialist for a complimentary copy.

---

1   Marketing a Web Site*

Designing commercial Web sites is a relatively simple business to enter with few competitive barriers preventing newcomers from giving it a try. After all, designers only really need a good computer, a proper software package, and a place to work. However, artistically and creatively motivated designers may find it somewhat difficult to find clients. For some potential clients, the issue may be whether they can afford the services; others may prefer to do the work internally rather than deal with an outside company.

Sandra MacDonald recently graduated with a degree in marketing after studying part-time for several years at a local university. This fitted well with her plans to be at home to raise her children, and now she was looking for ways to combine her interests in Internet Web site design and marketing. Recently she thought she had come across an ideal opportunity for starting up her own service.

While planning their children's summer activities, Sandra and her husband Tom began poring through the catalogues they had received from children's day and sleep-away camps. This was an annual ritual that involved their two children, David (11) and Nicole (14), as well as Sandra and Tom. Sandra would keep an eye open for pamphlets and newspaper advertising inserts that advertised camps, and she would buy a magazine or two that usually ran articles about camps and how to go about selecting one.

Her kids were experienced campers, having attended sleep-away camps since they were eight. Although they loved camp, their interests were changing and they wanted to consider a new choice for this year that offered more water sports. In particular, Nicole had become quite comfortable with water activities such as kayaking, boating, canoeing, windsurfing, and so forth.

It was while trying to identify and get more information about these sorts of camps that Sandra realized how useful a Web site with this camp information would be. She searched the Internet looking for camp directories, using search engines such as www.google.com or directories such as www.yahoo.com, but found it difficult to get geographically organized information that was useful to her family. She noticed that many of the larger camps had their own Web sites and that some magazine-style Web sites, which wrote about camps and family recreation sold advertising space on each Web page. This obviously provided a source of revenue for the Web managers; in addition to whatever they would charge the individual camps that were listed in their directories.

The cost of maintaining and posting a large Web site space, included $1000 per year for the domain name and hosting of the site with an internet service provider, and $150 per month for software support. Her domain name (the name of her site) would be www.canadian-childrens-camps.com. She also estimated that she would work some 130 to 150 hours per month marketing and managing her business.

All of her design work could be uploaded from her home to the service provider's computer, and users would be able to access the site from anywhere in the world at any time of day by entering the name she chose. However, she soon found out that the challenge was not the design of the site, rather it was generating traffic and building and retaining a customer base.

Now all she had to do was first figure out how to design the Web site so that it would be an attractive and informative site for consumers to visit, and develop an offline and online marketing campaign to build traffic to the site. She considered a magazine approach that would include articles about camping and follow a similar format that printed magazines used, as well as a "database" orientation that would allow users to enter criteria for searching camps they wanted more detailed information about quickly. In either case, revenue could be earned from the camps that would be profiled on the site as well as from advertisers who wanted to reach this particular target audience.

1   Develop an online (Hint: pop-up ads and links on other sites that would attract her target markets) and offline marketing plan that you would recommend to Sandra for launching the camp Web site to both camp advertisers and consumers who would use the service.

2   Create a sketch of the first page that users would find after arriving at Sandra's Web site.

3   What content would you provide about the camps, and how would you price your services?

   a. Online advertising uses two different models of pricing – CPM – which charges based on the number of visitors/readers/watchers, e.g. $15 per 1000 readers. How much does newspaper advertising cost? the Yellow Pages?

   b. The other ad pricing model that is popular on the internet is CPC. This charges a charge per action. E.g. if you click on an ad that appears on a web site, the advertiser will pay anywhere from $0.15 to $0.50 to the web site.

*This case was written by Dr. Brahm Canzer, who at the time of its preparation was associated with John Abbott College and Concordia University.

2   M400 Canada*

Keith Williams and Don Eisner were elated. They had recently returned from Davis, California, where they had acquired the Canadian rights to the M-400 a VTOL (Vertical Take-Off and Landing) craft developed by Paul Moller. The aircraft promised to revolutionize amateur flying in the country. Powered by rotary Wankel engines, the aircraft looked like a car from the "Jetson's" series.

Their preliminary calculations suggested a market potential of 600 units, based on the private airplanes in Canada. This number was increasing at a rate of 8 percent each year. Using these figures, they estimated sales of 20 units per year at $500,000 per unit for an annual volume of $10 million. On this reckoning, they expected to recover the $100,000 that it cost to acquire the Canadian rights to the product within one year. However, as they talked to their consultant they were alarmed to hear him say that it might be some time before the project would take off.

Product Information: The M400

The M-400 is a vertical take-off and landing (VTOL) vehicle designed to combine the most attractive features of a car and a light airplane. Successful flights of earlier test prototypes—together with wind tunnel tests, extensive computer-aided studies, and test bed data—have resulted in the design of a practical VTOL aircraft with low initial cost, ease of operation, inherent operator safety, and economical performance.

M-400 Specifications (source: http://www.moller.com/skycar/m400/)

Passengers:	4
Top speed @ 20,000 ft:	380 mph
Cruise speed @ 29,000 ft (80% Max Range):	300 mph
Cruise speed @ 29,000 ft (Max Range):	210 mph
Cruise speed @ Sea Level (Max Range):	140 mph
Maximum rate of climb:	5500 fpm
Maximum range:	900 miles
Net payload:	750 lbs
Fuel consumption:	28 mpg
Operational ceiling:	29,000 ft
Gross weight:	2400 lbs
Installed engine power:	645 hp
Power boost (emergency):	70%
Dimensions (LxWxH):	19.5' x 8.5' x 7.5'
Takeoff and landing area:	35 ft dia
Noise level at 500 ft:	65 dba (Goal)
Vertical takeoff and landing:	yes
Uses automotive gas:	yes
Emergency parachutes:	yes

The performance data for the M-400 production prototype are derived from design studies and wind tunnel tests. Final performance data will be available only after the flight test program has been completed by mid 2004. FAA flight certification is scheduled for 2006

Cost

Using a principle similar to that of the British Harrier jump jet, the Moller Skycar uses a patented thrust deflection vane system that redirects thrust, enabling it to hover or to takeoff and land vertically from almost any surface. This capability plus the added safety of ducted fans makes it ideal for a wide variety of commercial and military applications. These include private and charter air travel, express delivery, news gathering, border patrol, police and fire work, and search and rescue, to name just a few.

The cost of the M400 is projected to be around $500,000, which is competitive with many twin engine aircraft and helicopters.

Ease of Operation

A Skycar is not piloted like a traditional fixed wing airplane and has only two hand-operated controls, which the pilot uses to inform the redundant computer control system of his or her desired flight maneuvers. Engine starting and operation is nearly identical to that of an automobile.

Safety

There a number of key safety features that makes the M400 one of the safest aircraft to fly:

- Eight Engines
- Redundant Computer Stabilization Systems
- Redundant Fuel Monitoring
- Aerodynamically Stable
- Automated Stabilization
- Inherent Simplicity of the Engines
- Enclosed Fans

Advantages

Low noise is clearly necessary for a Skycar to operate near or within highly populated areas. The Skycar's multiple ducted fan arrangement is designed to generate low fan noise by using modest thrust loading and tip speeds. Hover tests in the earlier M200X demonstrated a noise level of 85 decibels at 50 feet, less than 30% of the noise level produced by a Cessna 150 during take-off. The company's on-going work in mutual noise cancellation is expected to reduce the M400 Skycar noise level sufficiently to eventually allow urban usage.

The Rotapower engine produces little NOx, the most difficult pollutant to eliminate. In addition, using a stratified charge combustion process greatly reduces the unburned hydrocarbons and carbon monoxide emitted.

The absence of unprotected rotating components such as propellers and rotors makes the Skycar friendlier to both users and by-standers.

The Skycar's fuel-efficient engines and ability to run on regular automotive gasoline result in low fuel costs. The Skycar is significantly more fuel efficient in passenger miles per gallon than the tilt-rotor V22 Osprey, helicopters or many commercial jet airplanes.

Vehicle purchase price is a dominant factor in determining overall cost of ownership. For example, the Skycar's purchase price per passenger seat is projected to be 10% of that for the 30 passenger V22 Osprey. Mechanically complex machines like the V22 Osprey and large helicopters are unlikely to undergo significant reduction in manufacturing costs since mass-production of such a large and expensive aircraft is unlikely.

In addition, the Skycar's operating profile is especially attractive given the user's ability to determine his or her own specific departure time and destination, a great advantage over other mass transportation systems.

Company History
In 1981, Discojet Corporation changed its name to the Moller Corporation. The products have evolved as solutions to design problems encountered in a search for a practical VTOL aircraft.

Their mission is to develop and put into use personal transport vehicles that are as safe, efficient, affordable and easy-to-use as automobiles. These would not be constrained by existing transportation networks, and would provide quick and convenient transport to any destination better than any alternative.

These vehicles should have a low environmental impact in terms of noise, emissions, and fuel consumption. Total costs of ownership over the life of a vehicle, including purchase price, operating costs and infrastructure costs should be reasonably low. This would be competing with such alternatives as personal or mass transport vehicles, general aviation, commercial air travel, and rail or motor vehicles.

Facilities
Moller Corporation has a 34,500 square foot of floor space. These facilities include electronics and computer engineering labs, a CAD/CAM lab, a computer controlled machining facility, composite airframe assembly facility, engine assembly and test facility, and sales, marketing, and administrative offices. In addition, there is a 4.5 acre VTOL test facility.

For more information on the company and the product visit http://www.moller.com/. To find out the number of pilots in Canada visit http://www.tc.gc.ca/civilaviation/general/personnel/stats005.htm. For a profile on Canadian pilots visit http://www.copanational.org/non-members/SurveyResults.htm. Finally you can visit this site to discover the number and types of aircraft registered in Canada http://www.tc.gc.ca/aviation/activepages/ccarcs/en/rptbyreg2_e.asp?x_lang=e&year=2003&month=12.

1   Outline the steps that are required in a market opportunity analysis for the M-400 in Canada.

2   What would you suggest in the way of a research design?

3   Environmental factors are important in assessing the value of this opportunity. What are these? Comment on their impact on the venture.

4   What are the estimates for success of the new undertaking?

*This case was written by Dr. Ken Blawatt, who at the time of its preparation was associated with Simon Fraser University as an Adjunct Professor at the University College of the Cariboo.

3   Blue Metropolis Magazine*

After working for Saturday Night in a senior managerial position and for several specialized magazines in the Canadian market, Sarah Kramer felt that she understood the publishing business as well as anyone. However, she was not completely sure that her decision to launch a new Canadian general-interest magazine fashioned after the internationally popular New Yorker was a correct one.

Blue Metropolis would publish articles on the arts, film, entertainment, politics, and business from a Montreal base and target sophisticated, business and professional people in households across Canada. These, she knew, were the consumers that most advertisers of cars, airline tickets, alcoholic beverages, non-alcoholic beverages, financial services, hotels, restaurants, theatres, films, cosmetics, and so on were interested in. Sarah felt that if she could put her creative talents to work along with the network of writers and producers she knew were available, she would be able to produce an attractive magazine of interest to this target audience.

Nonetheless, Sarah was still unclear about many business questions and decided to invest in some marketing research before going any further. This afternoon she was meeting with Matthew Braxton, a market researcher who specialized in media consulting. His general report on the publishing industry, which Sarah had purchased last month as part of the consulting contract, revealed the following:

- There were few competitors for this sort of magazine.
- People got most of their lifestyle news from TV, newspapers, and general magazines such as Time and Maclean's.
- The closest competitor, Saturday Night, had a direct circulation of 60,000 plus another 250,000 through newspaper inserts in selected cities across Canada.
- Advertisers paid $5,000 per full-colour page in Saturday Night, and a 100-page issue generally contained 25 pages of advertising.
- More women than men were interested in this sort of magazine.
- The market was more likely to be made up of people over 35 years of age.
- Economies-of-scale studies showed that printing costs levelled off at $1/unit after 30,000 copies and that mailing costs were also $1/unit.

Sarah knew that many readers would be open to a new magazine, but was not confident that a Montreal-oriented magazine would work for readers in, say, Vancouver. She asked Matthew Braxton to research this point along with a more basic question of what sort of product content readers across Canada would be motivated to buy. Should the magazine contain local listings of cultural events or only do so through advertisements? She even considered the idea of a bilingual magazine that could attract both language markets across Canada, but wondered whether either or both markets might be "turned off" by that sort of presentation.

In addition, she needed to know whether the magazine should be published monthly or quarterly, what the newsstand price should be, and how she should go about building up distribution for subscribers.

Furthermore, she was unsure as to the impact of online magazines and information sites on advertisers and readers. This site will give you some insight http://www.clickz.com/stats/big_picture/traffic_patterns/article.php/3300281.

Matthew Braxton anticipated Sarah's concerns and presented her with a list of content items he intended to use during focus group interviews with potential consumers. If Sarah approved, he would be able to report back to her on just what sort of magazine she should produce. Sarah was impressed with the detail of the survey and approved the plan.

1   What kinds of secondary sources should be investigated? What type of information could be collected from those sources?

2   Assume the role of Matthew Braxton and prepare a full marketing report for Sarah that addresses all of the questions discussed in the case. Conduct your own student focus-group research answering the questions presented in the case. You may also choose to ask other people outside your university.

4   Prepare a plan showing what you expect revenues and expenses to be as Blue Metropolis attempts to reach its targets for subscriptions and retail purchases for its first operating year. Present your plan in quarterly (three-month) segments and explain what marketing activities will be undertaken in each period. Remember, publishers generally try to cover production and distribution costs through subscription and retail sales, and to earn their profit from advertising revenue. Use this information as a guide for estimating reasonable targets.

*This case was written by Dr. Brahm Canzer, who at the time of its preparation was associated with John Abbott College and Concordia University.

| 4 | **Starbucks Pouring Hot in Canada*** |

The battle in the Canadian specialty coffee market is heating up. The strength of this industry can be seen in the proliferation of coffee shops in recent years. Although only 4 percent of adult Canadians drank specialty coffees in 1994, this percentage doubled within a year, and the popularity of these premium-priced beverages remains quite strong.

Seattle-based Starbucks with 7,569 locations around the world, entered Canada in 1987, Starbucks has aggressively sought to increase its market share in large urban centres. Initially, Starbucks confined its operations to Vancouver; its success there motivated entry into other Canadian cities. In 1996, when the company planned its entry into the Toronto market, it stirred up considerable controversy when it attempted to acquire prime locations for its corporate-owned stores adjacent to existing Second Cup franchises. The casualties in this confrontation were neighbourhood cafes, and this resulted in considerable negative press for Starbucks. Nevertheless, the company has continued its penetration of the Canadian market by opening stores in Edmonton and Calgary. Observers are questioning whether this success will continue.

Currently Starbucks operates 53 retail outlets across Canada in major urban centres. (source: Starbucks 2003 Annual Report). Their mission is to become the premier purveyor of the finest coffee in the world, while maintaining uncompromising principles as we grow." For more information on Starbucks visit http://www.starbucks.com/.

What is it that sets Starbucks apart from the competition? Are such differences sustainable, or are they merely part of some fad? How is it that Starbucks has been able to penetrate a market served by such well-known brands as Tim Hortons, Second Cup, A.L. Van Houtte, and Timothy's Coffees of the World? The specialty coffee shops in Canada differentiate themselves according to various aspects of coffee drinking.

Tim Hortons' (http://www.timhortons.com/) president, Paul House, identifies his company as being in the "snack occasion" business and adds that the growth segments are lunches and bagels. The focus of Second Cup (http://www.2ndcup.com/) is on street-level stores—takeout coffee bars in commuter stations, hospitals, and shopping malls.

Van Houtte (http://www.vanhoutte.com/index.html), primarily a wholesale distributor to supermarkets and a supplier of coffee machines in offices and institutions, operates a number of retail outlets. Paul-Andre Guillotte, president of A.L. Van Houtte, says that his establishment caters to 18–25 year-olds who are increasingly using coffee shops as meeting places. Van Houtte's customers view its coffee shops as young, hip places serving high-quality coffee.

The focus for Timothy's Coffees of the World (http://www.timothys.com/) is on the standard cup of fresh-brewed coffee. While Starbucks offers espresso-based products such as caffe latte, caffe mocha, and cappuccino, some would argue that Starbucks' success is attributable to its ability to offer customers a total brand experience that extends beyond the consumption of a beverage. This process has involved a positioning of the company—its ideals and image—with various stakeholder groups: the community, its employees, and its customers.

Starbucks' ability to transform coffee into a lifestyle choice flows from its mission statement, which directs the company to a role of environmental leadership in all facets of its business. These words have been transformed into a variety of socially responsible actions, including sale of a reusable coffee tumbler designed to commemorate the 100th anniversary in 1997 of the YWCA in Vancouver. In 1996, Starbucks and the Hospital for Sick Children in Toronto forged a long-term partnership that resulted in Starbucks making an annual contribution to the hospital foundation and opening a Starbucks location in the hospital's lobby. Starbucks actively supports organizations that benefit children's welfare, AIDS outreach, and environmental awareness; is involved in a variety of community cultural events; and supports a variety of programs in Guatemala, Indonesia, Kenya, and Ethiopia—all coffee-growing countries. This protection of the environment can be seen within the individual stores, where "everything" that can be recycled is: from the cardboard butter patties to the used coffee grounds. Stale-dated coffee is donated to charitable organizations such as women's shelters.

The positive press that the company receives from such community involvement extends to its internal marketing efforts. Despite the recent unionization of workers at some Canadian locations, Starbucks is known for its progressive personnel policies and generous compensation packages. In a proactive move, Starbucks offered all employees, or "partners," the same wages regardless of whether they were unionized. The company's claim that it is in the "people development" business as much as the coffee business is evidenced by its training programs, in which partners are encouraged to share their feelings about selling, about coffee, and about working for Starbucks. They are also encouraged to take personal responsibility for all aspects of their work, including the production of beverages to exact specifications and the encouragement of recycling and conservation wherever possible. Partners devote special attention to educating consumers about the explanations for Starbucks' Italian drink names, the necessity to buy new beans weekly, and the requirement to never let coffee stand for more than twenty minutes. The relationship marketing efforts between Starbucks and its partners have translated into annual staff, or "barista," turnover of 60 percent, compared with 140 percent for hourly workers in the fast-food business.

This affinity toward Starbucks is also felt by customers, 10 percent of whom visit the store twice a day; the average customer visits 18 times a month. The strength of such customer loyalty has provided the company with the luxury of using very little traditional advertising. Instead, the company has concentrated on creating an experience that customers are happy to promote. Starbucks devotees feel that the brand is defined as much by attitude as by products. It is Starbucks' treatment of its employees, the community, and the environment that has earned it respect with customers.

This positive image is backed by premium products, including traditional specialty coffees and the new Frappuccino, a frozen coffee drink that is tremendously popular during the summer. Customers can buy Starbucks ice cream and bottled drinks in the supermarket. Some argue that the proliferation of brand extensions could serve to dilute the core concept.

What have other coffee companies been doing in the wake of Starbucks' aggressive marketing campaigns? Distribution is critical and has been extended beyond traditional retail outlets. There are Second Cup kiosks in all Borders bookstores in Canada, while Starbucks has opened outlets in Chapters bookshops. Second Cup coffee is served on all Air Canada flights, an alliance that accounts for 10 percent of the company's coffee sales in Canada. Second Cup and Tim Hortons operate franchises in hospitals. Tim Hortons coffee is available at over 2,200 company and franchise restaurants, many in rural locations, and through some Esso gas stations, and is promoted with the theme of "You've always got time for Tim Hortons." This is supplemented by the use of an emotional appeal in a "True Stories" advertising campaigns in which the focus is on the unique role of Tim Hortons stores in the community. Lillian, age 86, is shown walking through Lunenburg, Nova Scotia, on her way to enjoying her daily cup of Tim Hortons coffee. Customers have found Lillian to be warm and charming—just the image that the advertising creators were looking for. Another advertisement includes a spot on Sammi, a dog from Saint John, New Brunswick, who picks up her master's coffee from the local drive-through window. The use of such true stories is quite popular with customers in Atlantic Canada.

There are those who question whether the specialty coffee market will continue to grow or whether it is just a fad. Supporters maintain that the proliferation of coffee houses reflects changes in social views, particularly with young adults. Both Starbucks and Second Cup hope to capitalize on the profitability associated with catering to the time-strapped boomer by producing, selling, and playing CDs designed to attract people to the stores. Starbucks even maintains designers and architects in-house who adapt the mellow urban look to a given site and customer demographics.

The creation of such a comfortable environment to complement the eclectic product offerings and corporate image is proving to be quite popular with Canadians in urban centres. Will this success continue in other parts of the country? Is it sustainable over the long run in existing centres? What changes will be necessary over the next few years?

1   Who are the target markets for Starbucks? How do they differ from those of other coffee shops?
2   What is Starbucks' competitive advantage? Is it sustainable?
3   How is the company positioned? Illustrate this with a positioning map that reflects the major players in the coffee market.
4   Does the proliferation of Starbucks' brand extension dilute the core concept and negatively affect the company's positioning and competitive advantage?

*This case was prepared by Judith A. Cumby, Assistant Professor, Faculty of Business Administration, Memorial University of Newfoundland, as a basis for class discussion and is not intended to reflect either an effective or an ineffective handling of management problems.

Philip Parker is the proprietor of Parker's Classics, a men's wear store with three branches in Vancouver. During the last few years Parker's Classics had been experiencing a slight decline in sales. Philip felt that this was attributable to a high level of competition in the Vancouver market. In addition, Holt Renfrew and other upscale stores in the suburbs of Vancouver, together with Eaton's and the upscale Bay in downtown Vancouver, presented a major challenge.

Philip had over 20 years of experience in the men's wear market, having worked in some of Canada's leading department stores for several years. He had also had a two-year stint with a French designer of men's wear. In 1985, at the age of 46, he decided to be his own boss and opened the first of the Parker's Classics stores in the west end of Vancouver. Within four years he had three more stores: one in Vancouver, one in West Vancouver, and one in Coquitlam, a Vancouver suburb.

Parker's Classics quickly established a name for itself in upscale men's wear. Philip prided himself on being able to completely dress an upscale man. Parker's carried a wide range of clothing from casual to semi-formal and formal wear. In addition, the stores had a large selection of male accessories and colognes. Parker's carried such well-known names as Hugo Boss and Armani, as well as its own Parker's Classic suits, specially designed by a New York-based designer.

Growing competition and a slowing economy in the early 1990s had put a stop to the frenzied growth that Parker's experienced in the late 1980s. Sales and profits continued to show a steady decline in 1994 and 1995. Philip knew that he had to do something to reverse this trend. In mid-July 1995 Philip, together with his 27-year-old son Jonathon, who has an MBA degree, and Christine Delaney, the manager of the downtown Vancouver store for the last eight years, met to review the second quarter and devise a strategy for the firm's future.

During the course of the meeting, Christine remarked that she had come to know some of the regular clients well, and that she was surprised to find out that many of them were gay. Philip knew that many of his clients were leading lawyers, bankers, businessmen, and doctors. He too was surprised by this revelation and found it somewhat disconcerting. He expressed his discomfort and asked Jonathon and Christine how this might affect the firm.

Jonathon had some gay friends and immediately saw a business opportunity. His view was that Parker's Classics, in specific locations such as the west end of Vancouver, should openly target gay consumers. Jonathon felt that such a market niching strategy would ensure continued growth for the company. The major competitors, he felt, would be unwilling to go after this market segment. Jonathon asked Christine if she knew what percentage of the customers in her store were gay. Christine did not have a definite answer, but she thought it would be less than 20 percent.

Philip was uncomfortable with his son's idea. He felt that as more gay customers came into his stores he was, perhaps, losing many of his heterosexual clientele and maybe this was the reason for declining performance in the stores. Philip was of the view that openly targeting gay consumers would antagonize other customers. Furthermore, he wasn't comfortable with the idea of associating Parker's Classics' image with gay consumers.

Jonathon felt that "upscale" was not a homogenous market and that there were several subsegments. Christine agreed that going after one smaller segment, the gay market, would give Parker's the edge over its more traditional rivals. Jonathon and Christine felt that the stores that currently attracted gay consumers could specifically target gays without antagonizing other customers. The other stores in the suburbs would not have any specific promotions targeted to the gay market and would continue to go after a broader clientele. Philip disagreed. After a heated exchange of views, all three agreed that further market research was required to determine the percentage of gay customers, as well as social attitudes and possible competitive reaction which might affect such a market niching strategy.

That same evening, Jonathon arranged a meeting with David Gower, a management consultant with considerable experience in lifestyle-based market segmentation. The next day Philip, Jonathon, and Christine had a lunch meeting with David Gower. First, Gower asked Philip if he had considered opening stores in smaller markets in the east as a growth strategy. Philip replied that he wanted to be based on the west coast and did not want to be national at this stage. Philip then voiced his concern over his son's proposal and asked Gower what he knew about the gay market.

Gower then gave a lengthy discourse on how marketers were dealing with the gay market. He pointed out that members of the gay community were often young, well-educated, in high paying jobs, and had a taste for fine living. Gower talked about how consumer product giants like Procter & Gamble and Toyota were seeking detailed demographic information on the gay community. Gower thought that it was only a matter of time before such companies had specific brands and promotions targeted to the gay market. In fact, Toyota had recently placed an ad in an Australian gay magazine.

Philip, still not convinced, asked Gower if there were any companies specifically targeting the gay market, and if so, how they were performing. Gower readily provided some examples. For instance, the Nordstrom department store chain had placed ads in Washington Blade, a gay newspaper, and Calvin Klein had run several ads with nude or partially clothed men. Other clothing stores like Banana Republic and The Gap had run ads featuring well-known gay people. In Canada, Gower said, IKEA, the Swedish furniture manufacturer, had run television ads featuring gay consumers. Gower also mentioned that more information was now available on the gay market, through market research firms such as the Chicago-based Overlooked Opinions, who were specializing in this market.

Philip, as well as Jonathon and Christine, were surprised that some of the leading clothing stores were openly targeting gay consumers. Based on in-store customer surveys, Philip had determined that his clientele was mostly in the 24 to 45 age group and he felt that the older of these consumers might be more conservative in their views. He was still worried about a possible backlash from these people. He probed Gower further about problems and failures associated with targeting the gay market.

Gower narrated the experiences of California-based Levi Strauss, which is considered to be a gay-friendly company. Levi Strauss had to face a boycott, as well as a lot of unwanted publicity, when the Family Research Council, a Washington-based conservative advocacy group, joined boycotts of gay-supportive companies. Other companies, like Kmart, pulled an ad featuring two men after only a few airings, because some people believed it portrayed a gay couple and protested. Gower then said, "I'm not sure if such protests have any long-term implicat ions. I don't think the average heterosexual consumer cares if a company sells its products to gay people. There seems to be a growing tolerance and acceptance."

After mulling over this comment for a few minutes, Philip asked how big the gay market was in Vancouver and the rest of Canada. Philip pointed out that from what Gower had indicated, it appeared that it was only large companies who were taking the risk of going after that particular market. He wanted to know if a small company like his could withstand any negative publicity or protest as a result of targeting the gay market.

Gower said that he would have to do some secondary research and conduct some focus groups to be able to provide answers to such questions. Gower went on to say that the gay market was a growing segment, to which not many companies had paid any attention, and that it was a segment with few dependents. Consequently, this segment had more disposable income to spend on items such as expensive clothes.

As the meeting concluded, Jonathon and Christine were convinced that there was tremendous potential in the gay market. Philip still had lingering doubts, but he agreed to commission a market research study.

1   Do you think that Parker's Classics should target the gay market? Alternatively, should they pursue other growth opportunities? Elaborate.

2   Is the purchase behaviour of the gay consumer different from that of other consumers? Substantiate your answer.

3   Identify promotional themes/messages for the gay market that Parker's Classics might use. What are the potential problems in designing promotional messages for this market?

4   Can Parker's Classics target the gay market without alienating other consumers?

5   In general, what opportunities and problems do you see arising from marketers paying greater attention to the gay market?

*This case was prepared by Dr. Ramesh Venkat of Saint Mary's University as a basis for classroom discussion and is not meant to illustrate either effective or ineffective marketing techniques. Copyright 1995. Used with permission.

6   The Hand Guard*

Alice Dicks was pondering the success of the hand guard that she had developed a number of years ago. As a nurse working for the Canadian Red Cross, she realized there was a need for a device to protect the hands of health care workers responsible for transferring blood between syringes. Alice experimented with several prototypes of a hand guard before progressing to field trials. She hired patent lawyers in Ottawa to ensure that her trademark was legal. With assistance from the National Research Council, an injection mould was developed to produce a hand shield, which was imprinted with the product and corporate names. In response to an invitation, Alice displayed her hand shields at the Medi-Tech trade show in London, Ontario, and lined up a Canadian distributor. So far, Alice had "done everything by the book" and was quite encouraged by the headway she was making in Canada. She decided to attend another medical trade show, this time in Florida. That was when all the trouble started.

In the 1980s, Alice Dicks, RN, had been working at the Canadian Red Cross blood donor clinic in Grand Falls–Windsor, Newfoundland. In order to collect blood from donors, a 16-gauge needle is used. After collection, three samples must be transferred from the thick needle into 7-millilitre test tubes, each of which has rubber on the top. This process requires the health care professional to hold the three test tubes in one hand and the 16-gauge needle in the other. The reason for the transfer to the test tubes is to allow the testing of donated blood for viruses and infections. The transfer to the three test tubes must be made relatively quickly and consecutively. This requires considerable precision and caution by the health care worker so as not to jab oneself in the process. With no protective guard between the 16-gauge needle and the tops of the three test tubes, workers tended to prick themselves with the needle on occasion. Alice did this three times; the most recent stab was caused when she turned suddenly as she heard a donor yell out just before fainting!

Although the opportunity for infection associated with transferring blood had existed for many years, the consequences had suddenly become quite extreme. The prevalence of the HIV virus in the 1980s meant that such accidents could become a death sentence for those who had jabbed themselves with a donor's blood. Now that Alice had stabbed herself with a needle carrying someone else's blood, she had to undergo twelve months of testing to ensure that she had not been infected. In order to be considered safe, three months of negative HIV readings were required, and eventually they were received. During the testing process, Alice was quite worried about her health. She also kept thinking about the fact that there had to be some product out there that would prevent a reoccurrence.

Alice knew that in the blood bank setting in North America, there were thousands of needle pricks happening each year. She searched extensively and found only one apparatus designed to guard against such injuries. It was a very expensive intravenous (IV) line, which would necessitate a change to the clinic's entire blood collection system. Each IV line would have to be discarded after use, thus increasing the operating costs of the blood donor clinics and contributing to the problem of medical waste.

Alice was interested in a lightweight, economical device that she and other workers could carry in their pockets. Such a device should be simple to use, relatively inexpensive, and capable of being reused. That the protective unit should not be disposable was important to Alice, who felt that there is far too much damage being done to the environment through disposal of many items used in the health care sector. She felt it was important that the hand shield be made of a material that could be sterilized after use. Other factors that influenced the product design included the fact that the guard needed to be transparent so that the person transferring the blood could see the test tubes below the protective shield. The material used in the guard needed to be impervious to needle scratches and cuts.

In the beginning, the hand shield was made from solid, opaque plastic. However, Alice soon realized that the guard had to be transparent and somewhat flexible. Initially, she worked with a local company that had designed a shield made from Plexiglas that did not have any rolled edges. However, it was quickly discovered that if you score Plexiglas with a needle, it can slip and puncture your wrist or crack the Plexiglas. Alice knew that there was a definite need for a hand guard, but was at a loss as to how to design a functional and safe product. She called the National Research Council and talked with a petroleum engineer and a specialist in Autocad design. Together, they developed a prototype for the hand guard, which Alice decided to call a Hema-Shield (the word hema means blood).

Field trials of the new product were conducted. Alice felt that this was a critical step to the development of any viable product because the actual users will offer suggestions for improvement. Through information obtained from the field trials and consultation with medical specialists, the Hema-Shield was altered again. The plastic was melted in order to provide rolled edges for the product. These edges would prevent the needle from sliding off the shield during use.

Supported by funding from the Industrial Research Assistance Program of the National Research Council, Alice had a firm in Ontario develop an injection mould that would be used to manufacture the hand guards. The manufacturers suggested a more pliable resin, which was ultimately used in the manufacture of the Hema-Shields. It took six months working with the manufacturers to finalize the design. The mould was imprinted with the product and corporate names, Hema-Shield: Med Search Corp, and these names then appeared on 10,000 hand shields. Alice said that she did not have to do any marketing research. She knew that the demand was there; there was an unfilled niche in the market. What was needed was a suitable product and a means by which to get it to the customers.

Alice hired patent lawyers in Ottawa to register her trademark, Hema-Shield, so that she would be protected from patent infringement. Her lawyers told her that there was no other product registered with the Patent Office of the federal government in Ottawa. She accepted an invitation to display her product at the Medi-Tech show in London, Ontario. Dicks also had brochures developed and displayed at the trade show. There she was approached by a lot of people who wanted to distribute the Hema-Shield. Eventually, she reached an agreement with a distributor in Etobicoke that would receive a commission based on the selling price of between $5.00 and $5.50 per shield.

Alice proceeded to Florida for a medical trade show, where her display generated considerable interest. Shortly after returning to Newfoundland, Alice received a letter from a company in New Jersey that said that she was being sued for patent infringement. The people in New Jersey had developed a silicon patch or graft that was used internally to repair aneurysms and veins. Many years ago, the company had applied to the Canadian government for a patent, but it was not registered in the patent database. As such, the Hema-Shield developed in the United States did not show when an initial patent search was done. Alice explained to the people in New Jersey that her Hema-Shield did not infringe on their product because the two shields served totally different functions. Alice hired new lawyers and was eventually convinced that she would have to change the name of her product. She feels that this infringement of the name was done through no fault of her own; it was the fault of the patent office and the lawyers. Still, Alice was the one incurring more costs and inconvenience.

Alice renamed her product the Med Search Hand Guard. However, with many of the original 10,000 products still in inventory and with the original Hema-Shield name imprinted in the manufacturing mould, Alice had to manually score through the original name before the products could be shipped.

Those who use the product find it quite convenient, almost too convenient from a business perspective. The reorders for the product have been slow because the health care professionals are getting over a year's use from one hand guard. All health care workers at the Canadian Red Cross have to use Alice's product; it is now part of the standard operating procedure in the organization's manual. Her hand guard is also being used by all of the American Red Cross clinics that do not use the expensive and disposable IV line systems. Alice feels that she benefits from word-of-mouth promotion among health care workers. However, she feels that the distributors are not even scratching the market for her hand guard. She says that there are many other markets where blood work is done and the hand guard should be used, such as veterinary clinics and police laboratories.

She realizes that the durable design of her product is not conducive to making a lot of money through repeat orders. However, Alice, a talented artist, is adamant that the environmental damage associated with more medical waste should be stopped. In retrospect, she feels that patents are a waste of money; there is nothing that cannot be copied. There are many examples of copycat products that sell quite well: CDs, Rolex watches, and Fendi bags. What is important, Alice feels, is developing a product that can serve a niche and sell for an attractive price. It is important to get one's trademark known. She feels that advertising is a waste of money in this regard; what is important is direct selling and making contacts through relationship marketing. There are still orders coming in for Alice's hand guard. As well, she is in the process of developing a digitized machine to be used for mixing red blood cells with anticoagulants. Still, Alice wonders what, if anything, she should be doing to increase sales of her hand guard.

For more information visit
http://www.inventivewomen.com/library/library_alice_dicks_nfld.shtml.

1   Would formalized market research prior to the development of the hand guard have helped Alice in any way?

2   Evaluate Alice's decision to use distributors in Ontario in light of her feeling that there are many markets that have not yet been reached.

3   What could Alice have done differently to increase sales?

4   How have Alice's personal values and ethics influenced her business decisions?

*This case was written by Judith A. Cumby, Assistant Professor, Faculty of Business Administration, Memorial University of Newfoundland, as a basis for class discussion and is not intended to reflect either an effective or an ineffective handling of a management problem. The author wishes to thank Alice Dicks for her support and assistance in the preparation of this case.

7   Naturally Yours*

For the past decade, Naturally Yours has been the only company specializing in the distribution of organic produce in western Canada. By 1996, annual sales were over $5 million annually, profits were steady, dividends to members were significant and growing, and the Naturally Yours name was well known and respected in the food business in western Canada.

Naturally Yours has developed its market based on the production of organically grown (chemical-free) produce that appeals to health-conscious and environmentally conscious consumers. The organization is structured as a co-operative. The co-op buys produce from organic farmers, distributes it, and ploughs the profits back into the business. As a result, all members are committed to making the co-operative successful and realize the importance of producing good-quality produce. Naturally Yours has excellent relations with its suppliers, a good client list, and considerable credibility.

The organic food industry in Canada has grown substantially over the past decade. The 2001Census of Agriculture collected data on organic farms in Canada. 2,230 producers, on about 340,000 hectares of land, reported producing certified organic products. This represents just under 1% of the total number of farms in Canada. There are 46 certifying bodies, and 150 processors and distributors in Canada. The Organic food sector experienced an average 20% annual growth in retail sales over the past ten years. (Source: Agriculture Canada)

Organic food imports have also grown dramatically over the past decade. Although the US remains the largest single source of imported organic foods, many other countries have entered the Canadian market. Canadian companies have also been entering foreign markets. In fact, organic grain production is the fastest growing sector and also represents by far the largest export commodity.

Marketing of organic foods has also grown more intense and sophisticated. "Eco-labelling" has grown in popularity as a means of identifying organic foods. Supermarket chains have developed special organic product areas.

Organically grown produce does not always have the "eye-appeal" that conventionally grown produce does. Some segments of the produce market see this difference as cosmetic only and are willing to pay more for produce that is healthier than the conventionally grown equivalent.

A 2000 survey shows that about seven in 10 Canadians have tried organic food, while about 40 per cent purchase organic food "often," which is defined as more than once or twice a year. (For organic producers, the once or twice a year folks are an important target; more on this later.) Market surveys of greater Vancouver area grocery shoppers indicated that 25 percent would be very or somewhat likely to buy organic produce. Ninety percent of those surveyed indicated that they were unhappy about the current pesticide and chemical practices of traditional producers.

Oregon Organics was a well established distributor of organically grown fruits and vegetables in Oregon, Washington, and northern California. When Oregon Organics started producing organic apple juice, the members of Naturally Yours considered doing the same. Oregon Organics was generous in providing Naturally Yours with market information because the two organizations were not direct competitors.

Oregon Organics had tried both high prices and low prices, as well as high and low levels of advertising and promotion. They found that market shares varied, depending on the combination of price and advertising and promotion (see the table below).

Market Shares(%)

	Low Price	**High Price**
Low advertising and promotion	1.2	0.8
High advertising and promotion	2.0	1.0

Given the similarities of the produce markets in western Canada and the western United States, it is thought that these market shares would probably be about the same in Canada. Based on Statistics Canada data, Naturally Yours estimated the size of the apple juice market in western Canada to be 520,000 cases annually. The contribution per case would be $3.50 at the low price and $5.10 at the high price.

Oregon Organics had used only point-of-purchase materials in some areas; in others, it had supplemented point-of-purchase materials with personalized direct mail to a mailing list of known purchasers of organic produce. If "Naturally Yours" were to use similar advertising and promotion materials, point-of-purchase alone would cost approximately $5,000, while the mailing would cost $8,000.

In addition, Naturally Yours would have to hire a part-time sales person to support the new apple juice. The sales person's compensation and expenses would amount to $15,000 annually. Product development costs would be minimal, mostly related to package design. They would total $5,000 in the first year only.

Finally, if "Naturally Yours" wanted to penetrate the food chains, they would have to pay a stocking fee, that could range between $2000 and $3000 per chain.

Some of the co-op members were hesitant to go ahead with the manufacture and distribution of apple juice. They thought it was too risky to get into manufacturing. In a meeting, the members of the co-op decided that they would only go ahead if there was a reasonable chance that the new product would produce a profit by the end of its first year. Additional information can be found at http://www.cog.ca/ and http://atn-riae.agr.ca/info/byproduct-e.htm. A market report on organic foods can be found at http://www.certifiedorganic.bc.ca/WhatsNew/IMPACS_Organic_Mktg_anlysis_for_COABC.doc

1   Provide a financial analysis to support a decision regarding whether
2   Naturally Yours should enter the apple juice market. Indicate clearly whether the numbers support entering the market and, if so, at what price and what level of promotion/ advertising.
3   State your recommendation about whether Naturally Yours should introduce organic apple juice. What factors other than the quantitative ones in question 1 influenced your decision? Support your recommendation.
4   Suggest an advertising campaign for Naturally Yours. As part of your answer, identify the target audience, the advertising goals, and an advertising message and execution approach you would use.

*This case was prepared by Judith A. Cumby, Assistant Professor, Faculty of Business Administration, Memorial University of Newfoundland. The facts of this case are based on the Wild West Organic Harvest Co-operative case, written by Dr. Katherine Gallagher of Memorial University.

8   Diego's*

Dr. Albert Collins, a Montreal physician, faced a difficult decision as to whether or not to invest in a new fast-food franchise concept specializing in Mexican food. Dr. Collins had made several good business investments, and while he thought this was a great opportunity, he recognized that there was a chance it wouldn't succeed. He decided to discuss the concept with his friend Jack Timlin, a marketing consultant, who had advised him on a number of earlier ventures. Dr. Collins arranged a meeting and presented the following information to Timlin.

The Concept

About six months ago, Dr. Collins had read an article in a major U.S. magazine about a relatively new but already successful fast-food franchiser based in Phoenix, Arizona. In operation for less than five years, this franchiser had opened 55 locations (some franchised, some corporately owned) in Arizona and several other southwest states, had sold (to one firm) the franchise rights for 80 locations in Florida, and had sold many other, soon to be built, franchises in the midwestern states.

Although Mexican food is very popular in the southern United States, this firm, in all of its advertising and store signs, always uses the phrase "We serve marinated charbroiled chicken and Mexican food" to indicate that it offers a choice of items so that people who don't like Mexican food can also patronize the chain.

On the door of each location is a sticker stating that this restaurant is approved by the American Heart Association as a healthy place to eat away from home. Dr. Collins believed that this endorsement was obtained because of the manner in which the chicken is prepared. First it is marinated in a secret recipe of natural fruit juices and herbs and then it is charbroiled so that the fat drips out of the meat. Chicken prepared this way is lower in cholesterol than fried chicken and is juicier than barbeque (BBQ) chicken. To further enhance its healthy image, the chain does not serve french fries but does offer baked potatoes and an assortment of salads. The menu strategy is attractive to low carb eaters.

A quote from the article provided a very strong endorsement from at least one customer: "I do not have a great deal of experience in eating Mexican food, but the dishes were different than what I expected. The chicken was tender and juicy and had a subtle flavour—for my taste it was better than BBQ chicken. The other dishes were very tasty and definitely not spicy. If this is what Mexican food is like, I am a convert."

Dr. Collins investigated further and found out that the recipes could not be protected by patent or copyright. In fact, he learned that the Arizona chain found out how a California chain of chicken restaurants marinated their chicken and then they used the recipe themselves. Dr. Collins then purchased some of the American marinated chicken, had it analyzed by a laboratory, and then had a food technologist develop and test the formula and the correct procedures to cook the chicken.

He gathered a group of investors (primarily friends and acquaintances) who liked the concept and were willing to put up most of the money required to open up one or two locations to show that the concept would be successful in Canada. The plan was to sell franchises across the country.

For each location, franchisees would be charged an initial fee plus an ongoing 5 percent royalty on the gross sales of the franchises. In return for these fees, the franchisee would have the right to use the trade name, which the investors decided would be Diego's. The franchisee's staff would be trained to prepare the food as per set procedures and the franchisee would purchase the chicken marinade from the franchiser. The franchisee would be assisted in site selection, construction of the restaurant, and purchasing of the required equipment, and would receive ongoing managerial assistance. In addition, the franchisee would benefit from a co-op advertising program to be funded by a charge of 4 percent of gross sales levied on each location—franchised or corporately owned.

Preliminary Research

Dr. Collins met with the investment group several times, and although nothing was formalized, a considerable amount of preliminary research had been conducted. A location was found for the first Diego's restaurant in a relatively new suburban residential area where most of the homes have been built in the last 10 years. New homes were still being built in the area, and there was enough vacant land to more than double the population of the area. Most of the homes sold for $250,000 to $325,000 (compared to the current Montreal average price of $155,500 per home - 2002). Census data suggested that the typical home owner in this area was raising a young family and had a managerial job or was a professional with a practice that had not yet developed fully.

Studies have shown that most people will travel about 2.5 to 3.5 km (5 minutes) to go to a fast-food restaurant. Since Diego's would be very distinctive, the first few locations probably would draw customers from a slightly larger trading area. Information was obtained from recent census data for the census tracts that would likely constitute the trading area (Exhibit 1).

Investor Group Meeting

After the information was collected, the investors held a meeting where a lively debate took place about the proposed image of Diego's, the target market, and other matters.

The investment group couldn't agree on what image Diego's should have and what types of customers they should concentrate on satisfying. Some of the members wanted to concentrate their efforts on attracting and satisfying families with young children (e.g., offering free magic shows on selected evenings and on weekends, offering children free balloons, and perhaps offering a special children's menu of items that will appeal to children).

One investor argued that this market segment appeared to be important. A recent newspaper article reported the results of an American study that, in 85 percent of the cases when parents go out to eat with their young children, the children make the final decision on which restaurant the family will go to.

Some of the group argued that children are known as very finicky eaters and maybe they wouldn't like Diego's food. They suggested that Diego's should go after the teenage market or possibly should concentrate on the adult fast-food market.

One member of the investment group had conducted an analysis of the competition in the trading area. He noted that at least two competitors in the trading area, McDonald's and Chi Chi's, had special strategies for attracting children. Two other successful restaurants, St. Hubert B.B.Q. and Swiss Chalet (both specialize in BBQ chicken), have outlets in the area. Another group member provided some data prepared by Statistics Canada that dealt with food purchased from restaurants (Exhibit 2).

One of the members of the investor group was a practicing accountant. He estimated that if the average bill at a restaurant of this type was $6.50 (excluding tax) and the actual cost of the food and the packaging was 30 percent of the selling price, the restaurant would need to serve 225,000 meals a year to break even.

Information on traffic flows was also collected. One Thursday, Dr. Collins went to the proposed site and between 12:00 noon and 1:00 pm counted 2,000 cars moving in the four directions at the intersection. Between 5:00 pm and 6:30 pm, the street heading north in front of the site became a "parking lot" as people headed home. He felt that this was a positive sign in that people could stop on the same side of the street as they were already travelling (and not have to cut across traffic), pick up food for supper, and then continue home.

Related to the decision as to which target market(s) to appeal to, some members wondered if people would be confused if the restaurant was simultaneously promoted as a chicken restaurant and as a Mexican food restaurant. That is, would potential customers perceive the chicken as a Mexican dish or would they consider the chicken to be a suitable alternative to BBQ chicken or fried chicken?

Various members of the investment group then raised the following questions and issues:

•   Will consumers recognize the fact that Diego's is really two different restaurants in one, and even if a person does not like Mexican food (or is afraid to try it), he or she can order a very tasty chicken? Or will some stay away because they view Diego's as a Mexican restaurant? Perhaps Diego's is too strong a Mexican name for what we would like to achieve?

Exhibit 1: Trading Area Demographic Data

Age Characteristics of the Population			
Total - All persons	17,705	8,500	9,210
Age 0-4	825	430	395
Age 5-14	1,915	985	935
Age 15-19	1,020	515	505
Age 20-24	1,105	560	545
Age 25-44	4,935	2,490	2,445
Age 45-54	2,765	1,355	1,410
Age 55-64	1,995	935	1,060
Age 65-74	1,570	665	910
Age 75-84	1,230	465	755
Age 85 and over	345	95	250
Median age of the population	41.7	40.0	43.5
% of the population ages 15 and over	84.5	83.4	85.5

Source: Statistics Canada Statistical Reference Centre 2001 Census—Montreal CMA

Exhibit 2: Weekly Food Purchases from Average weekly Quebec household expenditure on restaurants - $33.76

Earnings			
All persons with earnings (counts)	9,635	5,045	4,590
Average earnings (all persons with earnings ($))	34,796	41,480	27,452
Worked full year, full time (counts)	5,380	3,050	2,330
Average earnings (worked full year, full time ($))	47,479	54,485	38,297

Source: Statistics Canada, Family Food Expenditures in Canada

- Both images should be positive. Diego's proposed first location is not far from Chi Chi's, which exposed the consumer to and expanded the market for Mexican food. According to comparisons made by some of the group, Diego's Mexican dishes taste better and will cost less than the same items at Chi Chi's.
- On the other hand, for many years chicken has been more popular in Quebec than in other parts of the country. It may be due to cultural differences or may be the result of the success of the St. Hubert B.B.Q. chain, which started in Quebec (Exhibit 3).
- In addition, over the last three or four years the consumption of chicken across Canada has increased significantly as people switched away from red meats, which are higher in cholesterol than chicken. This ties in very nicely with the emphasis that the American chain places on the health aspect of its chicken meals.
- The growing popularity of low-carb diets may affect consumer perceptions of Mexican restaurants, which may have a preponderance of flour based offerings.

Some of the investors debated whether legally they could use an approach similar to the one Americans use and were not convinced that the "healthy" image will be a unique selling proposition that will cause people to pick their restaurant over the competition. They argued that the Canadian laws concerning food advertising were different and more restrictive than the U.S. laws. In Canada, the advertising of the cholesterol content of food (with the exception of vegetable oils such as Mazola) is prohibited. In addition, it appears that, even if it wanted to, the Canadian Heart Association would be unable, given the present legal environment, to endorse the restaurant. As well, they argued that many Quebecers are not especially health conscious when it comes to food.

One person had obtained a copy of a research study conducted in Montreal about bakery products. This study concluded that French-speaking respondents were less concerned with food additives than the English-speaking segment of the population. It was also found that older people were less concerned with this issue than the younger generation. Quebecers consumed large amounts of especially greasy french fries and poutine (French fries, sauce, and melted cheese). In other parts of Canada, the preference was for crispier, less oily french fries.

Some research conducted in the Montreal area by one of the group indicated that more than half of the respondents want french fries with their BBQ chicken. Consumers like and expect the combination, and that is what the chicken restaurants offer with their meals.

In spite of this information, other investors would like to follow the lead of the American firm and not serve french fries but instead offer a choice of baked potatoes or Mexican rice.

Exhibit 3: Estimated per Capita Regional Differences in Food Consumption National Average 5

100 percent	Chicken	Italian	Chinese	Greek
National	100%	100%	100%	100%
Quebec	125	120	145	130
Ontario	90	75	85	80
Prairies	90	165	35	25
B.C.	90	120	100	85
Atlantic provinces	175	80	55	45

One person pointed out that Quebecers love fine food and are receptive to ethnic foods. However, for some reason, Mexican food has not caught on in Quebec. Taco Bell, a large U.S. Mexican fast-food chain that has opened in Ontario, does not, at this time, have any Quebec locations. In Montreal proper, several small Mexican restaurants have opened. None of them appears to be especially successful.

In addition, one of the investment team visited about a dozen supermarkets (some in the area of the proposed location, others in various parts of Montreal and other suburbs). Each store has a small section of packaged Mexican foods. The managers of these stores described the sales of Mexican foods as "slow but steady."

Because there is a lot of money at stake, the investors paid for some basic research. They conducted focus groups in a restaurant setting similar to what is being considered and the respondents had the chance to taste the food. (Exhibit 4 provides a summary of the comments.) The results of the research were interesting in that in two cases, the findings went against what the investors thought the consumer might want or accept.

First, it was planned to prepare the food out in the front of the restaurant where it could be seen by people inside and outside. This was intended to show that Diego's had nothing to hide and that the food was prepared under hygienic conditions. In addition, it was hoped that seeing the golden brown chicken on the grill and the aroma of cooking chicken would encourage people to order. According to the focus groups, some people viewed this as a strong negative.

Secondly, while travelling through New England, Dr. Collins came across a very successful chain of seafood restaurants that, in order to keep prices low, serves on paper plates and provides plastic cutlery. This makes sense because Harvey's and other fast-food chains also use disposables. Again, based on the results of the focus groups, there seems to be resistance in Montreal to eating chicken in this way.

Exhibit 4: Focus Group Comments

Positive Comments
- The food is delicious.
- Great food.
- I never tasted Mexican food before; it is really good and not at all spicy.
- I am happy that you don't serve french fries. My seven-year-old son just ate nutritious food, not the junk food that he prefers.
- I enjoyed the food. The chicken was moist but not greasy.
- I liked it. I would come back again.
- I hope it opens soon. I am bored and fed up with the traditional fast foods.

Negative Comments
- The chicken looks yellow. What's wrong with it? Is it cheaper quality chicken?
- I don't think French Canadians are ready to eat BBQ chicken on paper plates using plastic cutlery.
- I don't want to see the chicken being cooked. I don't want to know that it was once a living thing.
- The chickens were brought to the grill in a pail. Do they use the same pail to wash the floors?
- For me BBQ chicken and french fries go together. Something is missing and the meal is not enjoyable without french fries.

Another research finding was of special interest and requires more study. When respondents were offered a choice between traditional BBQ sauce and salsa, a Mexican sauce, the vast majority opted for the BBQ sauce. Was it because it was something unknown? Was it the fear of something spicy? Or, perhaps, it was just a habit.

The Decision

Dr. Collins concluded the presentation to Timlin with the following comments: "As you can see, there is a lot of information to consider. In fact, I am confused as to what I should do. I know that the concept is successful in Arizona but I have also obtained a great deal of information, some of which is not positive, about duplicating this concept in Canada and particularly in Quebec.

"I don't know if I should invest in this project or not. If it succeeds, it will be the chance of a lifetime to make a lot of money. Should I go into it, or not? What, if anything, can be done to improve the concept so that the risk of failure will be reduced?"

1. What would you recommend that Dr. Collins do? Why?

*This case was written by Maurice Borts, who at the time of its preparation was associated with McGill University. Copyright 1998 by Marketec Business Consultants Ltd. All rights reserved. No portion of this case may be reproduced by any means without the prior written permission of Marketec, 20 Blue Heron Court, Ottawa, Ontario, K1L 8J7. The author acknowledges the assistance of David Roy and Michel Seguin of Statistics Canada in providing the relevant data.

9   Doug Hanson Buys a Car*

Shortly after Doug Hanson started his new job at The Family Health Club in the spring of 2003, he realized that his 1994 Honda Civic, which he had bought from the original owner in 1997, was no longer the sporty new car it once was. Each day that Doug drove to work, his need for a new car became more and more apparent. Every morning before starting his car, he said a quick prayer before turning the key in the ignition. When he actually made it into the parking lot at work, he let out a sigh of relief. He was thankful that his Civic, which had almost 330,000 kilometres on it, had survived another ten kilometre journey.

Doug, who was born and raised in Pembroke, Ontario, had recently obtained his BA degree from the University of Ottawa. He selected this university because it offered good academics and was close to home. On graduating, Doug decided to move to Vancouver, British Columbia. Vancouver not only offered him an alternative to the harsh weather of the East, but also provided him an affordable graduate education. Doug planned to go to Simon Fraser University for an MBA degree.

Doug's trek to the West Coast was an adventure, to say the least. The Civic broke down once while passing through Saskatchewan and had a tough time making it through the Rockies. When Doug finally arrived in Vancouver, he knew he had pushed the Celica to its limit. He realized that before long he would have to retire the nine-year-old car.

In the spring of 2003, Doug also began to work part time on his MBA. This meant driving more kilometres each week to get to the SFU campus. Clearly, his need for a new car was becoming more obvious. Unfortunately, he was not making enough money to afford a new car.

In the spring of 2004, Doug was promoted to manager of his department, and his salary increased significantly. He was now in a position to seriously consider replacing his car. Coincidentally, Doug's 73-year-old landlady, Edna Johnson, informed him that she was getting ready to trade in her 2001 Buick LaSabre. A friend of hers at the bridge club had just purchased a 2004 Toyota Camry. Mrs. Johnson was so impressed with the manoeuvrability and ease of handling of the Camry that she made up her mind to buy one of her own.

Mrs. Johnson's Buick was in mint condition. She always kept the car in the garage, so the car never saw dust, let alone a scratch. In addition, the car had only been driven 48,000 kilometres, and all parts appeared to be in perfect shape. The Toyota dealership offered to give her $8,000 for the Buick as a trade-in. Her car was in such good condition that she felt as though she would be giving it away at this price. However, she did not want the hassle of trying to sell it on the open market, so she was left with no other alternative.

As she saw Doug out in the street tinkering with his car once again, the thought crossed her mind to offer it to him before she traded it in. She told Doug that he could have the car for the same price that the dealer had offered her. In addition, because Doug was such a reliable tenant, she would allow him to pay it off over six months.

Clearly this was a golden opportunity for Doug to solve his transportation problems. He knew the Buick was in excellent shape, and he could get at least $500 for his car! On top of that, she was willing to take payments! Doug told her that he would think it over. He had two days to make his decision before Mrs. Johnson would go for her new Toyota.

Doug knew that he could not pass up such a good deal, yet he felt he would not be entirely happy with the Buick. The idea of driving a Buick was not particularly appealing to him. Every day, when Doug pulled into the parking lot at work, he admired the latest sports cars driven by his co-workers and clientele. Additionally, his girlfriend had recently bought a 2003 Acura Integra. Doug had hoped to purchase a car similar to hers.

The next morning, while paging through the Vancouver Sun, Doug noticed an ad offering a "lease special" for 2000 Acura Integras. The ad stated that one could lease this vehicle for only $250 a month. Doug's first impression was how affordable driving a brand new Acura could be. He called the telephone number listed in an effort to get more information. He knew that his girlfriend had purchased her car for approximately $26,000. She had made a $9,000 down payment and was paying $300 a month on a $17,000 loan. Doug knew that he could not afford a $9,000 down payment, but $250 a month was no problem.

Leasing a car is certainly different from owning one. After the lease term, you have to give the car back. In addition, the dealership usually limits the number of kilometres that can be driven each year. Doug considered these factors but felt that if he could drive an Acura for $250 a month without having to come up with a down payment, he would be satisfied. He planned to visit the dealership the following weekend to inquire about the lease.

When he arrived home from work one day, he saw his neighbor, Jay Smith, polishing his 1969 Corvette. The Corvette was one of three high-performance vehicles that Jay, an avid race enthusiast, owned. Jay would often help Doug when he was having trouble with the Celica. He had known Jay for a couple of years, and always enjoyed talking to him about the latest sports cars on the market. He decided to run the idea of purchasing Mrs. Johnson's car by Jay for some feedback. "Buick does make a decent car, but I have never been too impressed by their styling or performance," Jay responded. "I have always classified them as family cars. What you need is a sports car. There are a lot of new models out this year. For someone your age, shopping for a sports car should be like taking a kid into a candy store!"

"I only wish that I could afford something sporty," returned Doug. "What do you mean," Jay replied. "In my latest issue of Car and Driver, I saw a handful of new sporty models available for under $20,000. You just got a nice raise, and I'm sure you could afford the payments! Why don't you wait here and I'll go inside and get the magazine for you." "Maybe Jay is right," Doug thought to himself as Jay ran inside. "Perhaps I need something sporty."

With all the ideas about cars floating around in his head, he decided to get some additional information. Later that evening he decided to give his Uncle Barry a call. Barry, who lived back in Ontario, had been a mechanic for many years. He had helped Doug fix his car a few times, and even helped him put in a new clutch before he left for B.C. Doug respected his opinion very much.

After telling Barry his problem, his uncle suggested that he look into the Chevy Cavalier. "Yeah, if I were in your shoes, I might consider the Cavalier. It has a good four cylinder and antilock brakes all around. It even has a decent stereo in it." "Sounds interesting, do you know what they're going for?" asked Doug. "I think they're somewhere in the $14,000 range." "That's cheap," said Doug. "Oh, and I read somewhere that they come standard with a five-year 100,000 kilometre warranty," added Barry. Doug's uncle also reminded him that he should "Buy Canadian." "Speaking of Canadian cars," said Doug, "Let me tell you about the deal my landlady offered me on her 2001 Buick." Doug told his uncle about Mrs. Johnson's offer. "Gee, that sounds like a great deal," said Barry. "I wish I lived in Vancouver. I'd snap that one up in a second."

Doug woke up early the following Saturday morning excited to begin his search for a car. He figured he would spend the entire day test-driving new cars. His first stop was the Acura dealership. He soon learned that since he had never had a previous car loan, he was not qualified for the lease program. This was not mentioned in the newspaper ad or during the course of his telephone conversation with the dealership. Regardless, the salesman tried to encourage Doug to buy an Acura, but they started at the high end of his price range. It became apparent to Doug that the ad was just a "come on." He was annoyed with the misleading sales tactics and decided to look elsewhere.

His next stop was the Honda dealership where he had always taken his Civic for servicing. Doug had a great deal of confidence in Honda, considering his Civic had served him well the past ten years.

As he was browsing through the lot, he was approached by a salesman. He soon discovered that the only Honda besides the Civic that potentially suited him was the S2000. Doug did not want to buy another Civic because he was not impressed with the new body design. The S2000 was Honda's four-cylinder sports model. He had seen one on the freeway and admired its sleek design. A major drawback with the S2000 was the fact that it was a small two-seater. Furthermore, it started at over $25,000.

His next stop was the Dodge dealer. He had seen the new Lancer model pictured in the Car and Driver magazine was impressed with its looks. It came in three versions. The base model had a four-cylinder engine that had very little horsepower. The midrange version also had four cylinders, but its multivalve engine design gave it 50 percent more horsepower than the base model. As for the top of the line version, this car had the most powerful engine due to its turbo design. The base model started at around $24,000, the midrange sold for approximately $29,000, and the highest priced model sold for close to $34,000. Despite the different engines, all three models had the same body design.

Doug test-drove the base model first. It drove smoothly; however, it had very little pickup. The midrange version was priced at the upper limits of his range, but he decided to test-drive it anyway. He was extremely pleased with the overall performance of this car. The turbo model was priced beyond his range, not to mention the fact that the insurance would be almost double that of the other two models.

Doug really liked the midrange S2000 and decided to negotiate a deal. The asking price for the car he was interested in was $28,300. It had all of the extras Doug wanted. Furthermore, it was the only one on the lot that came in the colour he wanted. After haggling with the sales manager, the two agreed on a selling price of $27,300. In addition, the dealership gave Doug $1,000 for his Civic as a trade-in. He even qualified for the special first-time-buyer interest rate for his car loan. Doug went with his gut feeling and decided to buy the car.

After signing the necessary papers, Doug was given the keys to his first brand-new car. He felt somewhat numb at this point. Doug was about to drive his car off the lot when the salesman ran after him yelling, "Stop, wait just a minute!" "What's the matter?!" asked Doug. The salesman replied, "Just give me a minute—you look so good next to that car I want to take a picture." The salesman pulled out his camera and snapped the picture. Doug was flabbergasted, but managed to crack a big smile anyway.

As he pulled his new car into the driveway, Doug was greeted by Mrs. Johnson and his neighbour Jay. They both admired his S2000. Doug couldn't help but feel proud. He gave them both a spin and told them all about the great deal he got.

In the following weeks, Doug continued to enjoy his new car. He especially liked knowing that it would get him to work on time without fail. One day, while going through his mail, he noticed a large envelope from the dealership. "I wonder what this is," he thought to himself. He opened it and found a calendar with a picture of him standing beside his new car. There were also valuable coupons inside for discounts on an oil change, a tune-up, and other services. Doug set the items aside and reminisced about the day he purchased his car, knowing that he made the right choice.

1   Show how Doug Hanson's behaviour relates to the consumer problem-solving process outlined in Chapter 6 of this text.
2   Summarize Doug's evaluation process as it relates to each of the cars he considered.

*This case was written by Barbara Schneider and Doug Henkel under the supervision of David S. Litvack. Copyright 1993. Faculty of Administration, University of Ottawa.

10   Crankcase Transmission*

Bill Hartley was worried. He and his family were travelling on vacation to Western Canada when his recreational vehicle, a Ford truck camper, began acting up. Thinking a transmission adjustment might be necessary, he dropped the camper off that morning at a franchised transmission centre in Sault Ste. Marie, Ontario, for diagnosis and took his family to a nearby shopping mall. Now, some four hours later, he was told that he would require a rebuilt transmission, a new torque converter, an external cooler, and other items that would cost twice the few hundred dollars he had expected to pay out. He was running short on time and had to decide within the next hour what he should do.

The Company
Crankcase Transmission is a Canadian franchise organization. It began operations in the 1960s. Based on a business strategy that simply states we only do transmissions, the organization grew to its present size as a major servicer of automotive transmissions in the country. Part of its success has been due to an excellent selection of reputable franchisees who are supported by the franchiser in terms of national advertising, operations support, financing, and even real estate development. Its network of over 200 centres permits a nationwide warranty program, and its fleet account program provides franchisee access to over 250,000 motor vehicles.

The company actively promotes its franchise network through radio and television ads. As a result of its promotional campaign and recognized service, most people trust and accept the merits of Crankcase Transmission.

A Consumer Problem
In July, Bill Hartley and his wife and young daughter loaded up their truck camper and began a four-week holiday that would take them from Toronto to the Canadian Rockies and beyond. Bill sensed that the transmission should be looked at since the odometer on the ten-year-old Ford XLT F250 was approaching the 100,000 kilometre mark. The motor, a powerful 460 (only a few months old), was in perfect working order, but he felt a bit of slippage from time to time when reversing the vehicle. He also noted a bit of transmission oil leakage and found that he had to add a pint of fluid every few weeks.

On the third day, while travelling between Sudbury and Sault Ste. Marie, Bill noticed that the vehicle was beginning to generate a low growl from what he perceived to be the transmission area whenever he attempted to exceed 100 kilometres an hour. Worried about the noise and concerned about the transmission, he decided to stop in Sault Ste. Marie early the next day to have the unit checked out. A fellow camper who happened to be a mechanic recommended Crankcase Transmission in the city.

The Initial Examination
The initial contact with Crankcase Transmission personnel was reassuring. The manager was very helpful, and Randy, the serviceman assigned to check out Hartley's truck, was friendly and confident. He drove the camper a few blocks in the city, revving the engine and using the vehicle's low gears to check for slippage. As they returned to the centre, Randy

told Hartley that there appeared to be some slippage, and that they should remove the bottom pan and inspect the transmission.

He stated that at worst the repair would cost $700. The good news was that they could do it that day by 5 p.m. and that Bill and his family could then continue on their way.

Bill considered the situation with his wife. Since they were a bit pressed for time, they decided to allow Randy to proceed, at least with the inspection. They barely had $700 in reserve, and his wife was worried about being caught short on the trip.

They returned to the centre's office, where Hartley was asked whether he could take the camper off the truck or if he would prefer to leave it on. If he were to leave it on the truck, it would have to be worked on at a second franchise centre in another part of town, apparently owned by the same operator. At 9:30 a.m., the manager of the second centre cheerfully drove the Hartley family to a nearby large shopping mall so that they could browse and keep themselves entertained while the inspection and possible reconditioning took place.

"What we normally do," said Leonard Pissey, "is remove the pan, inspect the seals, ports, and gaskets, and replace whatever is worn out. It's really quite simple. Give me a call in an hour and I'll tell you how we're doing." At 10:30 a.m., Bill called Pissey, who was unable to take the call. At 11:30 Bill called again. This time Pissey said they were just removing the pan and asked Hartley to call back. After lunch, at 12:30, Bill called Pissey again.

The Problem

Pissey: Well, we've checked over your unit. I'm afraid it's going to cost a bit more than we thought.

Hartley: (becoming concerned): How much?

Pissey: You need a new torque converter, a C6 unit and . . .

Hartley: Wait a minute, Leonard. Aren't those things all a part of the transmission?

Pissey: Yes they are, but you see yours is . . .

Hartley: Leonard, your people quoted me $700 at the worse possible condition. Now what is this all about?

Pissey: Mr. Hartley, if you want your unit repaired the best possible way, you need this work done!

Bill pauses, becoming angry now. He doesn't understand mechanical things but he feels there is something amiss. Nevertheless, he knows his anger will not gain anything at this point.

Hartley: How much, Leonard?

Pissey: Counting the new external cooler you need for your transmission, it'll be about 1,500 dollars.

Hartley: Hold on! Why an external cooler? I've driven that truck and camper for 100,000 kilometres over a period of thirteen years in weather hot and cold and never had a problem! Without an external cooler!

Pissey: Well, Mr. Hartley, if you want the company to give you a twelve-month warranty, you have to have the cooler! Now if you lived in town here we would guarantee our work, but if you want another centre in Toronto or Winnipeg to honour the job, you need the cooler. That's company policy!

Hartley: I'll call you back in half an hour!

Bill goes to discuss the problem with his family.

1. How does the company's reputation assist or hinder in Bill Hartley's deliberations?
2. Are all franchisees the same, and are they consistent with the company's image of service, and so on?
3. What should Hartley do?
4. What are the marketing implications from the case?

*This case was written by Dr. Ken Blawatt, who at the time of its preparation was associated with Simon Fraser University as an Adjunct Professor at the University College of the Cariboo.

11   Ralph the Optician*

"The new glasses that you selected yesterday are ready. Try them on and I will make the final adjustments. Now look at yourself in the mirror—these new glasses help convey your image of success and good taste.

"Maurice, now that I looked after you as my customer, I want to become your client. I need some advice about a threat that my business is facing. If you have some time we could have a coffee in my office and I will tell you about my dilemma."

I agreed. Ralph poured two cups of freshly brewed Blue Mountain coffee and closed the door to his office so that we would not be disturbed.

"Maurice, I have been an optician for almost 30 years and over time, with hard work, I built a successful business and I now earn a good income. I take pride in the fact that over the years I was able to successfully adjust to the major changes in my business. For example, there have been technical changes such as the introduction of contact lenses, shatterproof lenses, and graduated bifocals. My staff and I periodically attend seminars and courses so that we are knowledgeable about the latest innovations.

"Other kinds of changes have been more difficult for me. Over time, major optical firms such as Lens Crafters and Sears started to operate in Canada. These chains tend to place great emphasis on heavy promotion and low price. In addition, Lens Crafters offers the convenience that your new lenses will be ready in about an hour.

"In fact, the share of the market held by independent opticians such as me is declining as the price-sensitive segment of the market grows. In spite of reduced market share, my sales are growing because the market is now growing quickly thanks to aging baby boomers. As people age, usually starting in their 40s they tend to need reading glasses or glasses for distance. Even people who wear contact lens often require reading glasses for close work. There is also evidence that as some people age, they are less likely to wear contacts for long periods of time.

"What did I do to protect my business against my large, price-oriented competitors?

"First, I upgraded the type of frames that I carry. Instead of carrying a large selection of low and medium price frames by unknown manufacturers, we have upgraded and place the emphasis on well-known, quality designs such as Fendi, Gucci, Hugo Boss, Alfred Sung, and Givenchy. It is not uncommon for a person to pay between 300 and 450 dollars for a new pair of glasses at my store. This is very different from the chains, where I think the average price would probably be between 100 and 150 a pair.

"Secondly, my staff and I are very careful to give the customer as much time as needed for choosing the proper frames, to fully answer questions, and to explain any technical differences between the options. We never rush a decision. In fact, many of our customers have been dealing with us for years, and if possible we try to greet them by name and acknowledge the fact that we recognize and appreciate their ongoing business. Based on statistics, the average pair of glasses lasts two years. However, some of my customers are fashion conscious and buy new frames more often.

"Third, I implemented a print and radio advertising program. Although my budget is modest compared to the major chains, I make an impact by concentrating my promotion in periodic short bursts when I feature a special item or a sale.

"Although all opticians sell products which enhance sight, my product is different in that I help clients not only see better but also look better and convey the image that they want. A frame makes a statement on your face, and the statement changes from style to style. To support the fashion orientation of my business, I purchased a camera and TV device that allows a person to more objectively see how he or she looks in the frame. In addition, I subscribe to magazines such as Vogue and Elle to see what frames are being shown to the fashion leaders.

"Everybody who sells glasses is basically in competition with everybody else. However, some of us are licensed as opticians and others are optometrists. Opticians specialize in selling glasses; optometrists are permitted to sell glasses but they are also trained to diagnose eye disease and to prescribe corrective lenses. Ophthalmologists, on the other hand, are medical doctors who specialize in eye diseases. They prescribe corrective lenses, but most do not sell glasses or contact lenses.

"Because I don't prescribe lenses, it is important to me to be located close to ophthalmologists' offices and to hospitals with eye clinics, so that it is convenient for clients to enter my store after they receive a new vision prescription. As you know, the location of my store is excellent in that I am close to a large number of busy ophthalmologists and two major hospitals.

"The aggressive chains sell their products on different variations of price. For example, Costco charges substantially less than you might expect to pay for contact lenses and bifocals. Their prices on frames also tend to be good value. However, because Costco does volume business, their customer service is not as good as mine. In addition, their selection of frames is oriented toward more popular price points, and although the frames tend to be reasonably fashionable, they are designed for the mass market. They do not sell the same frames that I do. Costco does not advertise or run promotions. Their promotion is mainly through word-of-mouth advertising and a large membership who appreciate the Costco philosophy of low markup, low or no-frills service.

"Another pricing technique used by some competitors is the famous two-for-one sale. Some of these two-for-one sales offer really good value to the shopper. Because of the high markup on frames and glasses, the retailer can actually make some money on a true two-for-one sale. However, some two-for-one sales are designed to offer you a deal on part of the purchase, but you must pay full price on the rest. For example, the sale may be two-for-one for the lenses, but you pay full price for the frames (or vice versa). Sometimes, any additional features that you select, such as scratchproof or UV coating, are charged at full price for both pairs.

"Because of the multitude of brand names and styles, it is very difficult for most of us to know what is a fair price for a pair of frames and lenses. Because we lack the expertise, we have to take the seller's word for quality and price. The sale boils down to which seller(s) does the buyer trust.

"Maurice, I apologize for being so long-winded to get to my problem. I read in yesterday's newspaper that Costco is planning to open a new outlet about eight kilometres from my store. I need to know what kinds of changes I should make to my operation (I think you call it a marketing mix), so that I will not lose a lot of business to my new competitor.

"About three months ago, I participated in an omnibus marketing research study and asked people why they prefer to do business with a specific source of eyewear. This is a sample of the type of responses given [see appendix]."

Appendix: Respondent Quotations—Omnibus Study

RALPH'S

> - I spend thousands of dollars each season on designer clothes. Why should I risk hurting my appearance by wearing inexpensive glasses or glasses that are not in fashion?
> - I want distinctive frames. I do not want to see many people wearing the same style of frames.
> - The first thing that people notice is your face. If I have to wear glasses, they should help to convey a very positive first impression of who I am.
> - I trust Ralph and his staff. The frames and the lenses that they have recommended have always been excellent.
> - I like their service, never rushed, always helpful. One thing that I especially like in today's impersonal world—they greet me by name.
> - A friend told me how satisfied she was with Ralph's selection of frames and his service. She was right. In the last six years, I bought five pairs of glasses from Ralph's.

COSTCO

> - My insurance company allows me to spend up to $150 for a pair of glasses. I try to find a deal so that I do not have to pay anything out of my pocket.
> - I usually wear contacts. I need an inexpensive pair of glasses for the occasional time when I can't wear my contact lenses.
> - I am on a tight budget. If I can save money and still get a quality product, I am especially happy.
> - I have been shopping at Costco for many years. I trust their pricing. In addition, I like being able to shop for eyewear at the same time I shop for other things.
> - When I go to another optician, a member of the staff wants to help me select my frames and gives me an opinion of how he or she thinks I look in the frames. I

prefer to browse and make up my own mind as to how I look. At Costco, there is no pressure to buy.
➢ Glasses are glasses.

Some other sources http://www.opticians.ca/ and Online opticians stores across Canada, which includes prices and models.
http://www.shopincanada.com/Health___Medical/Opticians_Dispensing/.

    1.   What changes to the marketing mix would you recommend?

*This case was written by Maurice Borts, who at the time of its preparation was associated with McGill University. The author acknowledges the cooperation and assistance of Denise Villeneuve and Greta Auerbach. Copyright 1995 by Marketec Business Consultants Ltd. All rights reserved. No portion of the case may be reproduced by any means without the prior written permission of Marketec, 20 Blue Heron Ct., Ottawa, Ontario K1L 8J7.

12   Sleepy-Inn Motel

Jack Roth is trying to decide whether he should make some minor changes in the way he operates his Sleepy-Inn Motel or if he should join either the Days Inn (http://www.daysinn.com/) or Holiday Inn motel chains (http://www.holiday-inn.com/). Some decision must be made soon because his present operation is losing money. But joining either of the chains will require fairly substantial changes, including new capital investment if he goes with Holiday Inn.

Jack bought the recently completed 60-room motel two years ago after leaving a successful career as a production manager for a large producer of industrial machinery. He was looking for an interesting opportunity that would be less demanding than the production manager job. The Sleepy-Inn is located at the edge of a very small town near a rapidly expanding resort area and about one-half mile off a major highway. It is 10 miles from the tourist area, with several nationally franchised full-service resort motels suitable for "destination" vacations. There are a Best Western, a Ramada Inn, and a Hilton Inn, as well as many "mom and pop" and limited service–lower price motels in the tourist area. The highway near the Sleepy-Inn carries a great deal of traffic since the resort area is between several major metropolitan areas. No development has taken place around the turnoff from the interstate highway. The only promotion for the tourist area along the interstate highway are two large signs near the turnoffs. They show the popular name for the area and that the area is only 10 kilometres to the west. These signs are maintained by the tourist area's Tourist Bureau. In addition, the state transportation department maintains several small signs showing (by symbols) that near this turnoff one can find gas, food, and lodging. Jack does not have any signs advertising Sleepy-Inn except the two on his property. He has been relying on people finding his motel as they go toward the resort area.

Initially, Jack was very pleased with his purchase. He had travelled a lot himself and stayed in many different hotels and motels, so he had some definite ideas about what travellers wanted. He felt that a relatively plain but modern room with a comfortable bed, standard bath facilities, and free cable TV would appeal to most customers. Furthermore, Jack thought a swimming pool or any other non-revenue-producing additions were not necessary. He also felt a restaurant would be a greater management problem than the benefits it would offer. However, after many customers commented about the lack of convenient breakfast facilities, Jack served a free continental breakfast of coffee, juice, and rolls in a room next to the registration desk.

Day-to-day operations went fairly smoothly in the first two years, in part because Jack and his wife handled registration and office duties—as well as general management. During the first year of operation, occupancy began to stabilize around 55 percent of capacity. But according to industry figures, this was far below the average of 68 percent for his classification—motels without restaurants.

After two years of operation, Jack was concerned because his occupancy rates continued to be below average. He decided to look for ways to increase both occupancy rate and profitability and still maintain his independence.

Jack wanted to avoid direct competition with the full-service resort motels. He stressed a price appeal in his signs and brochures—and was quite proud of the fact that he had been able to avoid all the "unnecessary expenses" of the full-service resort motels. As a result, Jack was able to offer lodging at a very modest price—about 40 percent below the full-service hotels and comparable to the lowest-priced resort area motels. The customers who stayed at Sleepy-Inn said they found it quite acceptable. But he was troubled by what seemed to be a large number of people driving into his parking lot, looking around, and not coming in to register.

Jack was particularly interested in the results of a recent study by the regional tourist bureau. This study revealed the following information about area vacationers:

1. 68 percent of the visitors to the area are young couples and older couples without children.
2. 40 percent of the visitors plan their vacations and reserve rooms more than 60 days in advance.
3. 66 percent of the visitors stay more than three days in the area and at the same location.
4. 78 percent of the visitors indicated that recreational facilities were important in their choice of accommodations.
5. 13 percent of the visitors had family incomes of less than $20,000 per year.
6. 38 percent of the visitors indicated that it was their first visit to the area.

After much thought, Jack began to seriously consider affiliating with a national motel chain in hopes of attracting more customers and maybe protecting his motel from the increasing competition. There were constant rumours that more motels were being planned for the area. After some investigating, he focused on two national chain possibilities: Days Inn and Holiday Inn. Neither had affiliates in the area.

Days Inn of America, Inc., is an Atlanta-based chain of economy lodgings. It has been growing rapidly and is willing to take on new franchisees. A major advantage of Days Inn is that it would not require a major capital investment by Jack. The firm is targeting people interested in lower-priced motels—in particular, senior citizens, the military, school sports teams, educators, and business travellers. In contrast, Holiday Inn would probably require Jack to upgrade some of his facilities, including adding a swimming pool. The total new capital investment would be between $300,000 and $500,000, depending on how fancy he got. However, Jack would be able to charge higher prices—perhaps $85 per day on the average, rather than the $55 per day per room he's charging now.

The major advantages of going with either of these national chains would be their central reservation systems—and their national names. Both companies offer toll-free reservation lines nationwide, which produce about 40 percent of all bookings in affiliated motels.

A major difference between the two national chains is their method of promotion. Days Inn uses little TV advertising and less print advertising than Holiday Inn. Instead, Days Inn emphasizes sales promotions. In a recent campaign, for example, Blue Bonnet margarine users could exchange proof-of-purchase seals for a free night at a Days Inn. This tie-in led to the Days Inn system selling an additional 10,000 rooms. Further, Days Inn operates a September Days Club for over 300,000 senior citizens who receive such benefits as discount rates and a quarterly travel magazine. This club accounts for about 10 percent of the chain's room revenues.

Both firms charge 8 percent of gross room revenues for belonging to their chain—to cover the costs of the reservation service and national promotion. This amount is payable monthly. In addition, franchise members must agree to maintain their facilities—and make repairs and improvements as required. Failure to maintain facilities can result in losing the franchise. Periodic inspections are conducted as part of supervising the whole chain and helping the members operate more effectively.

1   Evaluate Jack Roth's present strategy.
2   What should he do? Explain.

13 New North Media*

Late one afternoon in 2003, Chris Keevill burst into the cubicle of David Alston. He announced that a new business concept had been given the first green light by their employer, NBTel. He had two days to produce promotional material for a trade show he would be attending. With David's pc, some copy writing, and a photograph of a child's building blocks and a toy telephone, Chris and David produced the first brochure for what would become New North Media.

New North Media's initial business partners were the New Brunswick Telephone Company Limited (NBTel) and Nortel (Northern Telecom), a major hardware and software provider for communications networks. Nortel had been a longtime partner with the small, innovative New Brunswick telco. The two companies had made a highly advanced telecommunications network available to the province's 750,600 residents, which helped New Brunswick earn a reputation for being the industry's LivingLAB™ (LivingLAB is a trademark of NBTel.). (for more information on NBTel and Nortel visit: http://www.nortelnetworks.com/products/01/contivity/nbtel.html.)

NBTel was than merged into Aliant Inc.(www.aliant.ca)., which includes all of the maritime telco's and In May of 2000 New North Media in turn was merged into Innovatia Inc. (http://www.innovatia.net/) Innovatia focuses on the development and sale of Internet-based applications for marketing and delivery through Aliant's operating companies, and abroad through other service providers.

The original services that New North Media offered to consumers have been built around a specific telephone technology. New North's first mandate was to create services that require the use of the Vista 350, a Nortel telephone that has a small liquid crystal display screen and several programming buttons in addition to the usual buttons available on touch-tone phones.

In the late 1990's two factors contributed to changing New North Media's focus. The first was the decline of technology stocks and the collapse of the dot com bubble. The second was the erosion of Nortel's business. In response New North Media was merged into Innovatia and its business model was changed.

When New North Media was merged into Innovatia, the company's focus was much different. It was to create and deliver quality knowledge services through a comprehensive suite of products that included eLearning, Technical Documentation, TeleWeb Sales and TeleWeb Service. They formed collaborative partnerships to drive improved employee performance, increased sales and operational efficiencies for Original Equipment Manufacturers (OEMs) and Network Service Providers (NSPs) in telecommunications, IT, and global enterprise. There was no longer a direct connection to specific product lines or even specific proprietary technologies.

Product Descriptions

eLearning: eLearning blends both web-based and traditional learning techniques to provide custom eLearning solutions. They have a proven development process and a robust technology infrastructure which allows them to manage content and delivery in a user-friendly format that costs less, takes less time to complete, and can be immediately applied to the work site. There is a combination of live online classrooms, self-paced online learning, facilitated online learning, and physical classroom training.

Technical Documentation: Documentation (manuals, technical product information) based on engineering and design feature specifications for hardware and software is developed. Products include installation manuals, software configuration guides, user guides, technical reference guides, release notes, on-line "help", etc

TeleWeb Sales: Innovatia performs early-stage account work, qualifies leads, and leverage existing customer relationships. It helps grow revenues, reduce sales and marketing costs, and improve customer satisfaction and loyalty. Innovatia inside sales professionals can also expand sales pipelines and help reach prospects and customers with greater frequency and timeliness.

TeleWeb Service: Customers receive information and advice on enterprise product features, specifications, interoperability, configuration, and protocols. This multi-lingual and multi-channel service extends beyond the capabilities of a conventional contact center.

1   Why was there a change from the original New North Media business model to the Innovatia model? What market factors had an impact on this process.

2   How are is Innovatia's market segmentation different from that of New North Media?

3   Is the new approach niche marketing or segmentation?

*This case was written by Mark Henderson, who at the time of its preparation was associated with the Electronic Commerce Centre of the University of New Brunswick at Saint John. Based on interviews with David Alston, New North Media conducted 16 and 29 July 1997.

14   Dalton Olds, Inc.

Bob Dalton owns Dalton Olds, Inc., an Oldsmobile-Nissan dealership in Richmond, British Columbia. Bob is seriously considering moving into a proposed auto mall—a large display and selling area for 10 to 15 auto dealers, none handling the same car brands. This mall will be a few miles away from his current location but easily available to his present customers and quite convenient to many more potential customers. He can consider moving now because the lease on his current location will be up in one year. He is sure he can renew the lease for another five years, but he feels the building owner is likely to want to raise the lease terms, so his total fixed costs will be about $100,000 more per year than his current fixed costs of $650,000 per year. Moving to the new mall will probably increase his total fixed costs to about $1.1 million per year. Further, fixed costs—wherever he is—will probably continue to rise with inflation. But he doesn't see this as a major problem. Car prices tend to rise at about the same rate as inflation, so these rising revenues and costs tend to offset each other.

Bob Dalton is considering moving to an auto mall because he feels this is the future trend. Malls do seem to increase sales per dealership. Some dealers in auto malls have reported sales increases of as much as 30 percent over what they were doing in their former locations outside the mall. The auto mall concept seems to be a continuing evolution from isolated car dealerships to car dealer strips along major traffic arteries to more customer-oriented clusters of dealerships that make it easier for customers to shop.

Bob is considering moving to a mall because of the growing number of competing brands and the desire of some consumers to shop more conveniently. Instead of just the Big Three, now over 30 different brands of cars and 15 brands of trucks compete in the North American market—not including specialty cars such as Lamborghini and Rolls-Royce. Increasing competition is already taking its toll on some domestic and foreign car dealers as they have to take less profit on each sale. For example, even owners of luxury car franchises such as Porsche, Audi, and Acura are having troubles, and some have moved into malls. Dealer ranks have thinned considerably, too. Failures are reported all the time. Recently, some dealers tried to become "megadealers" operating in several markets, but this did not work too well because they could not achieve economies of scale. Now owners of multiple dealerships seem to be going to malls to reduce their overhead and promotion costs. And if customers begin to go to these malls, then this may be the place to be—even for a dealer with only one or two auto franchises. That's the position that Bob Dalton is in with his Oldsmobile and Nissan franchises. And he wonders if he should become well positioned in a mall before it is too late.

Bob Dalton's dealership is now selling between 550 and 700 new and used cars per year, at an average price of about $21,000. With careful management, he is grossing about $1,000 per car. This $1,000 is not all net profit, however. It must go toward covering his fixed costs of about $650,000 per year. So if he sells more than 650 cars he will more than cover his fixed costs and make a profit. Obviously, the more cars he sells beyond 650, the bigger the profit—assuming he controls his costs. So he is thinking that moving to a mall might increase his sales and therefore lead to a larger profit. A major question is whether he is likely to sell enough extra cars in a mall to help pay for the increase in fixed costs. He is also concerned about how his Oldsmobile products will stand up against all of the other cars when consumers can more easily shop around and compare. Right now, Bob has some loyal customers who regularly buy from him because of his seasoned, helpful sales force and his dependable repair shop. But he worries that making it easy for these customers to compare other cars might lead to brand switching or put greater pressure on price to keep some of his "loyal" customers.

Another of Bob's concerns is whether the Big Three car manufacturers will discourage dealers from going into auto malls. Now these auto manufacturers do not encourage dealers to go into a supermarket setting. Instead, they prefer their dealers to devote their full energies to one brand in a freestanding location. But as real estate prices rise, it becomes more and more difficult to insist on freestanding dealerships in all markets and still have profitable dealerships. The rising number of bankruptcies of dealerships in financial difficulties has caused the manufacturers to be more relaxed about insisting on freestanding locations.

For more information on the Canadian Automotive industry visit http://strategis.ic.gc.ca/epic/internet/inauto-auto.nsf/en/HomE.

1 Evaluate Bob Dalton's present and possible new strategy.
2 What should Bob Dalton do? Why?

15   Lucas Foods*

Harold Riley was marketing manager of Lucas Foods, a diversified food manufacturing and wholesaling company based in Calgary. The company had recently had some success with a new product, Gold Medal Crumpettes. Jerry Lucas, the president of Lucas Foods, asked his marketing manager to recommend an appropriate strategy for the new product that would best capture the available opportunity and support the mission of the company.

The Industry
Lucas Foods was in the food manufacturing and wholesaling business, marketing a broad product line that included frozen egg products, shortening, flour, baking mixes, spices, and bulk ingredients. Its primary customers were the five major national food wholesalers, with smaller regional wholesalers and independent grocery stores accounting for a smaller portion of its sales.

Gold Medal Crumpettes was a recent entry in Lucas Foods' bakery products group. It fell into the class commonly known as biscuits. Competitive products in this class included crumpets, scones, English muffins, and tea biscuits. Competition also came from a variety of substitute items such as toast, doughnuts, and muffins. Biscuit producers included such prominent names as Weston Bakeries (http://www.weston.ca/) and McGavin Foods Ltd. domestically, as well as the American firm of S.B. Thomas, which concentrated on English muffins and dominated that market.

Lucas Foods estimated that the product life cycle for specialty bakery goods was from five to seven years. Generally, if a new product was going to be successful, it enjoyed quick acceptance in the marketplace. Introduced in 2003, Gold Medal Crumpettes had had limited distribution. They had been sold in Alberta and Saskatchewan and had been recently introduced in Manitoba, Montana, and Minnesota. Safeway was the only major chain to carry the item in Canada, but sales growth had been steady to date.

History of Lucas Foods
The company was originally formed under another name over 50 years ago. It specialized in frozen egg products and later diversified into cabbage rolls and frozen meat products. The company was purchased by a major brewery in 1972, but the frozen egg portion of the business was sold back to the original owners six years later. They sold the business to Jerry Lucas in 1979. Since then, sales have doubled to their present annual level of $12 million.

The company followed a "portfolio approach" to its product line, regularly adding or deleting items according to established criteria with respect to the marketing cycle. With the single exception of frozen egg products, no specific product or product family dominated its overall product offering. (An exception was made for frozen egg products because of their unique life cycle and recession-proof qualities.)

In its statement of business mission, Lucas Foods indicated a desire to grow to an annual sales level of $50 million and to become a major national food manufacturer and wholesaler, as well as an exporter. Its major competitive weapons were believed to be its excellent reputation, product knowledge, marketing expertise, and level of customer service.

Marketing Gold Medal Crumpettes

Lucas Foods believed that the consumption of biscuit items was uniform across age groups, seasons, and geographic locations. It is a mature market. The merchandise itself was targeted toward the "upscale buyer." Package design, pricing policy, and product ingredients positioned Gold Medal as high priced and high quality relative to the competition. Therefore, the primary variables for segmenting the market were socioeconomic: Gold Medal Crumpettes were a luxury item.

The Crumpettes were designed to incorporate the taste and texture of scones, English muffins, and biscuits, and could be eaten with or without butter, either toasted or untoasted. They were available in four flavours—plain, raisin, cheese, and onion—and the company had plans to add three more flavours, including pizza. The product could be stored frozen. The name Gold Medal Crumpettes was specifically selected to imply quality.

Since wholesale food distribution in Canada was dominated by relatively few firms, management felt that it had little choice in the distribution of its products. Lucas Foods did not own a large warehouse to store its finished baked goods but manufactured Gold Medal Crumpettes to order. The merchandise was then transported by common carrier to various customers under net-30-days credit terms.

The goal of the company's promotional efforts was to stimulate and encourage consumer trial of the product. There was some radio advertising when the item was first introduced. Although Lucas suggested the retail price, the distributor, especially in the case of Safeway, did most of the promotion. Typical promotions included:

- Representatives distributing free samples in supermarkets to shoppers.
- Crossover coupon promotions with jam companies.
- Mailout coupons to consumers.
- Free products to stores.
- Temporary price reductions for distributors.

Exhibit 1: Total Potential Market for Gold Medal Crumpettes (Yearly sales)

	Cases	Volume
Alberta	43,000	$ 602,000
Canada	960,000	$ 13,440,000
United States	9,600,000	$134,400,000

So far, $50,000 had been spent on the promotion of Gold Medal Crumpettes. To complement these promotional efforts, Lucas Foods had three salespeople who, along with the marketing manager, regularly called on all major accounts.

Gold Medal's high price was consistent with its positioning and was arrived at after evaluating consumer surveys and the company's production costs. The expected price sensitivity of the market was also considered. A package of eight biscuits retailed for $2.89.

The product was sold to supermarket chains in cases of 12 packages, with a factory price of $14 per case. Manufacturing costs, including allocated overhead, were $9.40 per case. This provided a contribution margin of $4.60 per case, or 30 percent. Production capacity was available for up to 16,000 cases per month.

Capturing the Opportunity

For an estimate of the potential market for Gold Medal Crumpettes, see Exhibit 1.

Harold Riley judged that Lucas Foods held a 16 percent share of the Alberta market. The Alberta consumer had been very receptive to the product, but outside Alberta the company had only a limited reputation and was not well known as a wholesale food supplier. This lack of awareness made it more difficult for the item to obtain the acceptance of retailers. Also, the company faced an almost total lack of consumer awareness outside the province.

If Gold Medal succeeded in obtaining quick acceptance in new markets, competitors might view the development of a similar product as an attractive proposition. This could be particularly distressing if the competitor taking such an action was a major producer with an existing broad distribution system. Therefore, the speed with which Gold Medal Crumpettes could be introduced and developed into a dominant market position was very important to the long-term survival and profitability of the item. There was also the question of whether or not the degree of consumer acceptance the product had achieved in Alberta could be repeated in other areas.

Pricing research conducted by the company indicated that consumers were not prepared to cross the $3 price level at retail. If production costs were to rise and force an increase in selling price, sales might decline. Also while the earlier exchange rate allowed Lucas to be quite competitive in the American market, the stronger Canadian dollar could damage the company's export position.

Selecting a Strategy

Harold Riley had to propose a marketing strategy to Jerry Lucas that he considered would best take advantage of the opportunity available to Gold Medal Crumpettes. He was considering three alternatives:

1. Maintenance of the product's existing market coverage and strategy. This implied limiting distribution and focusing the company's efforts on the Prairie provinces and the states of Montana and Minnesota.

2. Phased expansion. This would involve expanding across Canada, region by region, to become a major force in the Canadian biscuit market and begin selective entry into the American market.

3. Rapid expansion. This approach would involve an attempt to expand rapidly in both countries, to precede and preferably preempt competitive products in all markets, and to seek a dominant position in the North American biscuit market.

During their early discussions, Jerry had pointed out that the company had the financial capacity to undertake any of these options. It was a question of how to best focus the available resources.

Before evaluating his alternatives, Harold drew up the following criteria to guide him in coming to an appropriate decision:
- The alternative should be feasible.
- The alternative should be profitable.
- The market opportunity should be exploited as far as possible while still meeting the first two criteria.
- The alternative should fit into the activities of the company.
- The alternative should be consistent with the mission of the company.
- The alternative should be consistent with Lucas Foods' portfolio management approach concerning return, risk, and diversity.
- There should be early evidence to support the alternative.

1   Which of the three possible strategies should Lucas Foods follow?

2   Why is the strategy chosen a better choice than the other two possibilities?

*This case was written by John Fallows under the supervision of Dr. Walter S. Good, who at the time of this case's preparation was associated with the University of Manitoba.

16   Runners World

Tamara Lang, owner of the Runners World, is trying to decide what she should do with her retail store and how committed she should be to her current target market.

Tamara is 36 years old, and she started her Runners World retail store in 1994 when she was only 24 years old. She was a nationally ranked runner herself, and felt that the growing interest in jogging offered real potential for a store that provided serious runners with the shoes and advice they needed. The jogging boom helped to quickly turn Runners World into a profitable business, and Tamara made a very good return on her investment for the first five or six years. However, sales flattened out as more and more people found that jogging was hard work—and hard on the body, especially the knees. For the past three years, sales have slowly declined and Tamara has dabbled in various changes to try to recover her lost profitability.

From 1994 until 2000, Tamara emphasized Nike shoes, which were well accepted and seen as top quality. At that time, Nike's aggressive promotion and quality shoes resulted in a positive image that made it possible to get a $5 to $7 per pair premium for Nike shoes. Good volume and good margins resulted in attractive profits for Tamara Lang.

Committing so heavily to Nike seemed like a good idea when its quality was up and the name was good. But in the late 1990s Nike quality began to slip. It hurt not only Nike but retailers such as Tamara who were heavily committed to the Nike line. Now Nike has gotten its house in order again, and it has worked hard at developing other kinds of athletic shoes, including walking shoes, shoes for aerobic exercise, basketball shoes, tennis shoes, and cross-trainers.

While Nike was making these changes and emphasizing engineering function, a number of other firms started to focus on fashion and style in their shoe lines. In addition, with this shift more and more consumers—including many who don't really do any serious exercise—were just buying running shoes as their day-to-day casual shoes. As a result, many department stores, discount stores, and regular shoe stores put more emphasis on athletic shoes in their product assortment.

All of this change has forced Tamara to reconsider the emphasis in her store and to question what she should do. As growth in sales of running shoes started to flatten out, Tamara was initially able to keep profits up by adding a line of running accessories for both men and women. Her current customers seemed to be a ready market for a carefully selected line of ankle weights, warm-up suits, athletic bras, T-shirts, and water bottles. These items offered good margins and helped with profits. However, as the number of serious runners declined, sales of these items dropped off as well, and Tamara and her salespeople found that they were "pushing" products that other customers didn't want. Further, many of the sporting goods stores in the Runners World market area started to offer similar items—often at lower prices.

Tamara also tried adding specialized shoes for other types of athletic activities—such as shoes for serious walkers and for aerobic exercise. She was hopeful that some of the past runners would be interested in high-quality shoes designed specifically for walking or other types of exercise. However, demand for these shoes hasn't been strong, and keeping a varied line in stock—without fast turnover—is an expensive proposition.

For the past few years traffic in the store has continued to drop. In addition, an increasing number of the customers who come in the store to browse do only that—and leave without buying anything. From discussions with many of these shoppers, Tamara is pretty certain that they're more interested in style, fashion, and economy than in the high-quality shoes designed for specific athletic activities that she carries. For example, a number of customers who came in looking for "walking shoes" left quickly when they realized that Tamara's walking shoes were in the $120 and up range.

Part of the problem is that a number of retail chains offer lower-cost and lower-quality versions of similar shoes as well as related fashion apparel. Even Wal-Mart has expanded its assortment of athletic shoes—and it offers rock-bottom prices. Other chains, like Lady Foot Locker, have focused their promotion and product lines on specific target markets.

Tamara is not certain what to do. Although sales have dropped, she is still making a reasonable profit and has a relatively good base of repeat customers—primarily serious runners. She worries that she'll lose their loyalty if she shifts the store further away from her running "niche" toward fashion and casual wear. Even a change in the name of the store—to pull in more customers who are not runners—might have a serious impact on her current customers.

An important question that Tamara is debating is whether there really is a big enough market in her area for serious athletic shoes. Furthermore, is there a market for the Nike version of these shoes that tends to emphasize function over fashion? She has already added shoes from other companies to provide customers with more choices, including some lower-priced ones. She is trying to decide if there is anything else she can do to better promote her current store and product line, or if she should think about changing her strategy in a more dramatic way. At a minimum, that would involve retraining her current salespeople and perhaps hiring more fashion-oriented salespeople.

She thinks that a small shift in emphasis probably won't make much of a difference. Actually, that's what she's tried already. But a real shift in emphasis would require that Tamara make some hard decisions about her target market and her whole marketing mix. She's got some flexibility—it's not like she's a manufacturer of shoes with a big investment in a factory that can't be changed. On the other hand, she's not certain she's ready for a big change—especially a change that would mean starting over again from scratch. She started Runners World because she was interested in running and felt that she had something special to offer. Now, she worries that she's just clutching at straws without a real sense of purpose—or any obvious competitive advantage. She also knows that she is already much more successful than she ever dreamed when she started her business—and in her heart she wonders if she wasn't just spoiled by growth that came fast and easy at the start.

1   Evaluate Tamara Lang's present strategy. Evaluate the alternative strategies she is considering.
2   What should she do? Why?

17   Huntoon & Balbiera

The partners of Huntoon & Balbiera are having a serious discussion about what the firm should do in the near future.

Huntoon & Balbiera is a large regional chartered accounting firm based in Calgary, Alberta, with branch offices in Edmonton and Saskatoon. Huntoon & Balbiera has nine partners and a professional staff of approximately 105 accountants. Gross service billings for the fiscal year ending June 30, 2003, were $6.9 million. Financial data for 2001, 2002, and 2003 are presented in Exhibit 1.

H&B's professional services include auditing, tax preparation, and bookkeeping. Its client base includes municipal governments (cities, villages, and townships), manufacturing companies, professional organizations (lawyers, doctors, and dentists), and various other small businesses. A good share of revenue comes from the firm's municipal practice. Exhibit 1 gives H&B's gross revenue by service area and client industry for 2001, 2002, and 2003.

Exhibit 1 Fiscal Year Ending June 30

	2001	2002	2003
Gross billings	$6,900,000	$6,400,000	$5,800,000
Gross billings by service area:			
Auditing	3,100,000	3,200,000	2,750,000
Tax preparation	1,990,000	1,830,000	1,780,000
Bookkeeping	1,090,000	745,000	660,000
Other	720,000	625,000	610,000
Gross billings by client industry:			
Municipal	3,214,000	3,300,000	2,908,000
Manufacturing	2,089,000	1,880,000	1,706,000
Professional	1,355,000	1,140,000	1,108,000
Other	242,000	80,000	78,000

At the monthly partners' meeting held in July, Pat Hogan, the firm's managing partner (CEO), expressed concern about the future of the firm's municipal practice. Hogan's presentation to his partners appears below:

Although our firm is considered to be a leader in municipal auditing in our geographic area, I am concerned that as municipals attempt to cut their operating costs, they will solicit competitive bids from other accounting firms to perform their annual audits. Due to the fact that the local offices of most of the Big Six firms* in our area concentrate their practice in the manufacturing industry—which typically has December 31 fiscal year-ends—they have "available" staff during the summer months.

Therefore, they can afford to low-ball competitive bids to keep their staffs busy and benefit from on-the-job training provided by municipal clientele. I am concerned that we may begin to lose clients in our most established and profitable practice area.†

Ann Yost, a senior partner in the firm and the partner in charge of the firm's municipal practice, was the first to respond to Pat Hogan's concern.

Pat, we all recognize the potential threat of being underbid for our municipal work by our Big Six competitors. However, H&B is a recognized leader in municipal auditing in Alberta, and we have much more local experience than our competitors. Furthermore, it is a fact that we offer a superior level of service to our clients—which goes beyond the services normally expected during an audit to include consulting on financial and other operating issues. Many of our less sophisticated clients depend on our nonaudit consulting assistance. Therefore, I believe, we have been successful in differentiating our services from our competitors'. In many recent situations, H&B was selected over a field of as many as 10 competitors even though our proposed prices were much higher than those of our competitors.

Pat Hogan responded that as a result of the accounting scandals and the bankruptcy of Arthur Andersen, many companies are careful about hiring the same company to do an audit and provide consulting services.

*The "Big Five" firms are a group of the five largest chartered accounting firms in Canada. They maintain offices in almost every major Canadian city. Until recently, these firms were known as the "Big Eight," but after several mergers they have come to be known as the "Big Six." After the bankruptcy, they will become known as the "Big Four."

†Organizations with December fiscal year ends require audit work to be performed during the fall and in January and February. Those with June 30 fiscal year ends require auditing during the summer months.

The partners at the meeting agreed with Ann Yost's comments. However, even though H&B had many success stories regarding its ability to retain its municipal clients—despite being underbid—it had lost three large municipal clients during the past year. Ann Yost was asked to comment on the loss of those clients. She explained that the lost clients were larger municipalities with a lot of in-house financial expertise—and therefore less dependent on H&B's consulting assistance. As a result, H&B's service differentiation went largely unnoticed. Ann explained that the larger, more sophisticated municipals regard audits as a necessary evil and usually select the low-cost reputable bidder.

Pat Hogan then requested ideas and discussion from the other partners at the meeting. One partner, Joe Reid, suggested that H&B should protect itself by diversifying. Specifically, he felt that a substantial practice development effort should be directed toward manufacturing. He reasoned that since manufacturing work would occur during H&B's off-season, H&B could afford to price very low to gain new manufacturing clients. This strategy would also help to counter (and possibly discourage) Big Six competitors' low-ball pricing for municipals.

Another partner, Bob LaMott, suggested that "if we have consulting skills, we ought to promote them more, instead of hoping that the clients will notice and come to appreciate us. Furthermore, maybe we ought to be more aggressive in calling on smaller potential clients."

Another partner, John Smith, agreed with LaMott but wanted to go further. He suggested that they recognize that there are at least two types of municipal customers and that two (at least) different strategies be implemented, including lower prices for auditing only for larger municipal customers and/or higher prices for smaller customers who are buying consulting, too. This caused a big uproar from some who said this would lead to price-cutting of professional services and that H&B didn't want to be price cutters: "One price for all is the professional way."

However, another partner, Megan Cullen, agreed with John Smith and suggested they go even further—pricing consulting services separately. In fact, she suggested that the partners consider setting up a separate department or even a separate company to address governance issues for consulting—like the Big Four have done. This can be very profitable business. However, it is a different kind of business and eventually may require different kinds of people and a different organization. For now, however, it may be desirable to appoint a manager for consulting services—with a budget—to be sure it gets proper attention. This suggestion too caused serious disagreement. Some of the partners knew that having a separate consulting arm had led to major conflicts in some firms. The main problem seemed to be that the consultants brought in more profit than the auditors, but the auditors controlled the partnership and did not properly reward the successful consultants—at least as they saw it!

Pat Hogan thanked everyone for their comments and charged them with thinking hard about the firm's future before coming to a one-day retreat (in two weeks) to continue this discussion and come to some conclusions.

1   Evaluate Huntoon & Balbiera's situation.
2   What strategy(ies) should the partners select? Why?

18   Blackburn Company

Frank Blackburn, owner of Blackburn Company, feels his business is threatened by a tough new competitor. And now Frank must decide quickly about an offer that may save his business.

Frank Blackburn has been a sales rep for lumber mills for about 20 years. He started selling in a clothing store but gave it up after two years to work in a lumberyard because the future looked much better in the building materials industry. After drifting from one job to another, Frank finally settled down and worked his way up to manager of a large wholesale building materials distribution warehouse in Hamilton, Ontario. In 2002, he formed Blackburn Company and went into business for himself, selling carload lots of lumber to lumberyards in the Niagara Peninsula area.

Frank works with five large lumber mills on the West Coast. They notify him when a carload of lumber is available to be shipped, specifying the grade, condition, and number of each size board in the shipment. Frank isn't the only person selling for these mills—but he is the only one in his area. He isn't required to take any particular number of carloads per month—but once he tells a mill he wants a particular shipment, title passes to him and he has to sell it to someone. Frank's main function is to find a buyer, buy the lumber from the mill as it's being shipped, and have the railway divert the car to the buyer.

Having been in this business for 20 years, Frank knows all of the lumberyard buyers in his area very well, and is on good working terms with them. He does most of his business over the telephone from his small office, but he tries to see each of the buyers about once a month. He has been marking up the lumber between 4 and 6 percent—the standard markup, depending on the grades and mix in each car—and has been able to make a good living for himself and his family. The going prices are widely publicized in trade publications, so the buyers can easily check to be sure Frank's prices are competitive.

In the last few years, a number of Frank's lumberyard customers have gone out of business, and others have lost sales. The problem is competition from several national home-improvement chains that have moved into Frank's market area. These chains buy lumber in large quantities direct from a mill, and their low prices are taking some customers away from the traditional lumberyards. Some customers think the quality of the lumber is not quite as good at the big chains, and some stick with the lumberyards out of loyalty. However, if it weren't for a boom in the construction market—helping to make up for lost market share—Frank's profits would have taken an even bigger hit.

Six months ago, things got worse. An aggressive young salesman set up in the same business, covering about the same area but representing different lumber mills. This new salesman charges about the same prices as Frank but undersells him once or twice a week in order to get the sale. Many lumber buyers—feeling the price competition from the big chains and realizing that they are dealing with a homogeneous product—seem to be willing to buy from the lowest-cost source. This has hurt Frank financially and personally—because even some of his old friends are willing to buy from the new competitor if the price is lower.

The near-term outlook seems dark, since Frank doubts that there is enough business to support two firms like his, especially if the markup gets shaved any closer. Now they seem to be splitting the shrinking business about equally, as the newcomer keeps shaving his markup.

A week ago, Frank was called on by Mr. Talbott of Bear Mfg. Co., a large manufacturer of windows and accessories. Bear doesn't sell to the big chains; instead, it distributes its line only through independent lumberyards. Talbott knows that Frank is well acquainted with the local lumberyards and wants him to become Bear's exclusive distributor (sales rep) of residential windows and accessories in his area. Talbott gave Frank several brochures on the Bear product lines. He also explained Bear's new support program, which will help train and support Frank and interested lumberyards on how to sell the higher-markup accessories. Talbott explained that this program will help Frank and interested lumberyards differentiate themselves in this very competitive market.

Most residential windows of specified grades are basically "commodities" that are sold on the basis of price and availability, although some premium and very low-end windows are sold also. The national home-improvement chains usually stock and sell only the standard sizes. Most independent lumberyards do not stock windows because there are so many possible sizes. Instead, the lumberyards custom order from the stock sizes each factory offers. Stock sizes are not set by industry standards; they vary from factory to factory, and some offer more sizes. Most factories can deliver these custom orders in two to six weeks, which is usually adequate to satisfy contractors, who buy and install them according to architectural plans. This part of the residential window business is well established, and most lumberyards buy from several different window manufacturers in order to ensure sources of supply in case of strikes, plant fires, and so on. How the business is split depends on price and the personality and persuasiveness of the sales reps. And given that prices are usually similar, the sales rep–customer relationship can be quite important.

Bear Mfg. Co. gives more choice than just about any supplier. It offers many variations in 1/8-inch increments, to cater to remodellers who must adjust to many situations. Talbott has approached Frank Blackburn in part because of Frank's many years in the business. Another reason is that Bear is aggressively trying to expand, relying on its made-to-order windows, a full line of accessories, and a newly developed factory support system to help differentiate it from the many other window manufacturers.

To give Frank a quick big picture of the opportunity he is offering, Talbott explained the window market as follows:
1 For commercial construction, the usual building code ventilation requirements are satisfied with mechanical ventilation. So the windows do not have to operate to permit natural ventilation. They are usually made with heavy-grade aluminum framing. Typically, a distributor furnishes and installs the windows. As part of its service, the distributor provides considerable technical support, including engineered drawings and diagrams, to the owners, architects, and/or contractors.

2   For residential construction, on the other hand, windows must be operable to provide ventilation. Residential windows are usually made of wood, frequently with light-gauge aluminum or vinyl on the exterior. The national chains get some volume with standard size windows, but lumberyards are the most common source of supply for contractors in Frank's area. These lumberyards do not provide any technical support or engineered drawings. A few residential window manufacturers do have their own sales centres in selected geographic areas, which provide a full range of support and engineering services, but none are anywhere near Frank's area.

Bear Mfg. Co. feels that a big opportunity exists in the commercial building repair and rehabilitation market—sometimes called the retrofit market—for a crossover of residential windows to commercial applications, and it has designed some accessories and a factory support program to help lumberyards get this "commercial" business. For applications such as nursing homes and dormitories (which must meet commercial codes), the wood interior of a residential window is desired, but the owners and architects are accustomed to commercial grades and building systems. And in some older facilities, the windows may have to provide supplemental ventilation for a deficient mechanical system. So what is needed is a combination of the residential operable window with a heavy-gauge commercial exterior "frame" that is easy to specify and install. And this is what Bear Mfg. Co. is offering with a combination of its basic windows and easily adjustable accessory frames. Two other residential window manufacturers offer a similar solution, but neither has pushed its products aggressively and neither offers technical support to lumberyards or trains sales reps like Frank to do the necessary job. Talbott feels this could be a unique opportunity for Frank.

The sales commission on residential windows would be about 5 percent of sales. Bear Mfg. Co. would do the billing and collecting. By getting just 20 to 30 percent of his lumberyards' residential window business, Frank could earn about half of his current income. But the real upside would come from increasing his residential window share. To do this, Frank would have to help the lumberyards get a lot more (and more profitable) business by invading the commercial market with residential windows and the bigger-markup accessories needed for this market. Frank would also earn a 20 percent commission on the accessories—adding to his profit potential.

Frank is somewhat excited about the opportunity because the retrofit market is growing. And owners and architects are seeking ways to reduce costs (which Bear's approach does—over usual commercial approaches). But he is also concerned that a lot of sales effort will be needed to introduce this new idea. He is not afraid of work, but he is concerned about his financial survival.

Frank thinks he has three choices:
1   Take Talbott's offer and sell both products.
2   Take the offer and drop lumber sales.

3   Stay strictly with lumber and forget the offer.

Talbott is expecting an answer within one week, so Frank has to decide soon.
1   Evaluate Frank Blackburn's current strategy and how the present offer fits in.
2   What should he do now? Why?

19   KASTORS, Inc.

Rick Moore, marketing manager for KASTORS, Inc., is trying to figure out how to explain to his boss why a proposed new product line doesn't make sense for them. Rick is sure it's wrong for KASTORS, Inc., but isn't able to explain why.

KASTORS, Inc., is a producer of malleable iron castings for automobile and aircraft manufacturers, as well as a variety of other users of castings. Last year's sales of castings amounted to over $70 million.

KASTORS also produces about 30 percent of all the original equipment bumper jacks installed in new American-made automobiles each year. This is a very price-competitive business, but KASTORS has been able to obtain its large market share through frequent personal contact between the company's executives and its customers—supported by very close cooperation between the company's engineering department and its customers' buyers. This has been extremely important because the wide variety of models and model changes often requires alterations in the specifications of the bumper jacks. All of KASTORS's bumper jacks are sold directly to the automobile manufacturers. No attempt has been made to sell bumper jacks to final consumers through hardware and automotive channels, although they are available through the manufacturers' automobile dealers.

Tim Owen, KASTORS's production manager, now wants to begin producing hydraulic garage jacks for sale through automobile-parts wholesalers to retail auto parts stores. Owen saw a variety of hydraulic garage jacks at a recent automotive show and knew immediately that his plant could produce these products. This especially interested him, because of the possibility of using excess capacity, now that auto sales are down. Furthermore, he says, "jacks are jacks," and the company would merely be broadening its product line by introducing hydraulic garage jacks. (Note: Hydraulic garage jacks are larger than bumper jacks and are intended for use in or around a garage. They are too big to carry in a car's trunk.)

As Tim Owen became more enthusiastic about the idea, he found that KASTORS's engineering department already had a design that appeared to be at least comparable to the products now offered on the market. None of these products have any patent protection. Furthermore, Owen says that the company would be able to produce a product that is better made than the competitive products (i.e., smoother castings, and so forth)—although he agrees that most customers probably wouldn't notice the difference. The production department estimates that the cost of producing a hydraulic garage jack comparable to those currently offered by competitors would be about $48 per unit.

Rick Moore, the marketing manager, has just received a memo from Bill Borne, the company president, explaining the production department's enthusiasm for broadening KASTORS's present jack line into hydraulic jacks. Bill Borne seems enthusiastic about the idea, too, noting that it would be a way to make fuller use of the company's resources and increase its sales. Borne's memo asks for Rick's reaction, but Bill Borne already seems sold on the idea.

Given Borne's enthusiasm, Rick Moore isn't sure how to respond. He's trying to develop a good explanation of why he isn't excited about the proposal. He knows he's already overworked and couldn't possibly promote this new line himself—and he's the only sales rep the company has. So it would be necessary to hire someone to promote the line. And this sales manager would probably have to recruit manufacturers' agents (who probably will want 10 to 15 percent commission on sales) to sell to automotive wholesalers who would stock the jack and sell to the auto parts retailers. The wholesalers will probably expect trade discounts of about 20 percent, trade show exhibits, some national advertising, and sales promotion help (catalogue sheets, mailers, and point-of-purchase displays). Furthermore, Rick Moore sees that KASTORS's billing and collection system will have to be expanded because many more customers will be involved. It will also be necessary to keep track of agent commissions and accounts receivable.

Auto parts retailers are currently selling similar hydraulic garage jacks for about $99. Rick Moore has learned that such retailers typically expect a trade discount of about 35 percent off the suggested list price for their auto parts.

All things considered, Rick Moore feels that the proposed hydraulic jack line is not very closely related to the company's present emphasis. He has already indicated his lack of enthusiasm to Tim Owen, but this made little difference in Tim's thinking. Now it's clear that Rick will have to convince the president or he will soon be responsible for selling hydraulic jacks.

1   Contrast KASTORS, Inc.'s current strategy with the proposed strategy.
2   What should Rick Moore say to Bill Borne to persuade him to change his mind? Or should he just plan to sell hydraulic jacks? Explain.

20   Bemis Cable, Inc.

Jack Meister, vice president of marketing for Bemis Cable, Inc., is deciding how to organize and train his sales force—and what to do about Tom Brogs.

At its Pittsburgh and Montreal plants, Bemis Cable, Inc., produces wire cable ranging from .5 inch to 4 inches in diameter. Bemis sells across the United States and Canada. Customers include firms that use cranes and various other overhead lifts in their own operations—ski resorts and amusement parks, for example. The company's main customers, however, are cement plants, railway and boat yards, heavy-equipment manufacturers, mining operations, construction companies, and steel manufacturers.

Bemis employs its own sales specialists to call on and try to sell the buyers of potential users. All of Bemis's sales reps are engineers who go through an extensive training program covering the different applications, product strengths, and other technical details concerning wire rope and cable. Then they are assigned their own district—the size depending on the number of potential customers. They are paid a good salary plus generous travel expenses, with small bonuses and prizes to reward special efforts.

Tom Brogs went to work for Bemis in 1998, immediately after receiving a civil engineering degree from McGill University. After going through the training program, he took over as the only company rep in the Quebec district. His job was to call on and give technical help to present customers of wire cable. He was also expected to call on new customers, especially when inquiries came in. But his main activities were to (1) service present customers and supply the technical assistance needed to use cable in the most efficient and safe manner, (2) handle complaints, and (3) provide evaluation reports to customers' management regarding their use of cabling.

Tom Brogs soon became Bemis's outstanding representative. His exceptional ability to handle customer complaints and provide technical assistance was noted by many of the firm's customers. This helped Tom bring in more sales dollars per customer and more in total from present customers than any other rep. He also brought in many new customers—mostly heavy equipment manufacturers in Quebec. Over the years, his sales have been about twice the sales rep average, and always at least 20 percent higher than the next best rep—even though each district is supposed to have about the same sales potential.

Tom's success established Quebec as Bemis's largest-volume district. Although the company's sales in Quebec have not continued to grow as fast in the last few years because Tom seems to have found most of the possible applications and won a good share for Bemis, the replacement market has been steady and profitable. This fact is mainly due to Tom Brogs. As one of the purchasing agents for a large machinery manufacturer mentioned, "When Tom makes a recommendation regarding use of our equipment and cabling, even if it is a competitor's cable we are using, we are sure it's for the best for our company. Last week, for example, a cable of one of his competitors broke, and we were going to give him a contract. He told us it was not a defective cable that caused the break but rather the way we were using it. He told us how it should be used and what we needed to do to correct our operation. We took his advice and gave him the contract as well!"

Four years ago, Bemis introduced a unique and newly patented wire sling device for holding cable groupings together. The sling makes operations around the cable much safer, and its use could reduce hospital and lost-time costs due to accidents. The slings are expensive, and the profit margin is high. Bemis urged all its representatives to push the sling, but the only sales rep to sell the sling with any success was Tom Brogs. Eighty percent of his customers are currently using the wire sling. In other areas, sling sales are disappointing.

As a result of Tom's success, Jack Meister is now considering forming a separate department for sling sales and putting Tom Brogs in charge. His duties would include travelling to the various sales districts and training other representatives to sell the sling. The Quebec district would be handled by a new rep.

1   Evaluate Jack Meister's strategy(ies).
2   What should he do about Tom Brogs—and his sales force? Explain.

21   Honda Hit•Run•Throw*

Greg and Todd were a little nervous just before the Year-end Honda Hit•Run•Throw (HHRT) Meeting with Honda Canada. They felt that they had done a good job in staging the national final at SkyDome the week before, particularly in light of the fact that both men had been newly hired by Baseball Canada (http://www.baseball.ca/). However, this was a new domain.

Greg White, a graduate student in human kinetics at the University of Ottawa, had started with the organization as a student intern some four months earlier. But at that time he had done PR work with the national junior team and was not really acquainted with the HHRT program. When Lee Ann Lalonde resigned her HHRT national coordinator position for another job less than a month before the national final, Greg was appointed to the position on an interim basis. He knew that this was a great career opportunity, but also felt that it would be a tremendous challenge.

Todd Wallin's tenure with Baseball Canada was even more abbreviated. He had been hired as manager of events and marketing for the organization just a few weeks prior. Although he had accumulated a significant amount of sport marketing experience through previous positions with the Ottawa Rough Riders and Synchro Canada, he was still familiarizing himself with his new surroundings.

As if staging the national final of HHRT within such a short period had not been enough, the two were then required to quickly gather the annual data (in concert with the ten provincial coordinators) in order to piece together a final summary report, which was presented to Honda Canada. It had truly been a "baptism by fire" for the new recruits!

"I want to congratulate you both on an excellent event last week," said Richard Pendrill, marketing manager for Honda Canada, as he took his seat at the far end of the board room in the Toronto Blue Jays front office at SkyDome. "I also think that you've done a fine job with the Final Report."

The kind words were quite comforting to the two Baseball Canada representatives. However, just as they began to feel that the pressure was lifting, Mr. Pendrill turned the heat up once more. "I'm going to cut to the chase . . . what happened to our numbers in Ontario this year?"

Mr. Pendrill was referring to the low number of participants in Ontario—the largest market in Canada, and the most highly targeted province for the title sponsor. Despite attracting more than 36,000 children between the ages of 7 and 13 to the program Canada-wide, Ontario had only managed to register 4,500 participants—a failure by any yardstick.

Following a somewhat passionate debate between the various partners, the meeting was adjourned. The participants agreed that Baseball Canada would conduct market research among local baseball coordinators across the province to get their feedback pertaining to the program. The following factors, among others, would be surveyed: awareness level, strengths, weaknesses, why they did or did not participate, whether they would again in the following year, and suggestions. This information was to be used to produce a brief marketing strategy to be implemented for HHRT in the province of Ontario in the following year. Just when the two thought they could relax, it was back to the drawing board.

It was an onerous task attempting to contact these individuals on such short notice. Often the contact names that were available to them were presidents of the organizations, not the minor baseball coordinators themselves. In other cases, there were no contact names or numbers at all, just the address of the organization (which was of little use given the time constraints). In the end, about 40 coordinators were contacted—a response rate of 15 to 20 percent. (Some of the key points of the survey are summarized in Exhibit 2.)

A few days after completing the survey, Todd and Greg met to discuss the program results over the past year, the recent Ontario survey, and the marketing strategy that they would create and implement in response to this data.

An Overview of HHRT in 1997

In 1997 Honda Canada, the Toronto Blue Jays, Major League Baseball Canada, and Baseball Canada joined forces for the third consecutive year to present Honda Hit•Run•Throw on a national basis. The program also received generous support from Easton Sports Canada, Irvin Sports (Cooper), All Sport Insurance Marketing, Gatorade, and Heritage/Sport Canada. The program was delivered in Ontario by Baseball Canada, the Ontario Baseball Association, and the Toronto Blue Jays, with the first-named organization taking the leadership role.

Exhibit 1: Some Key Statistics

	1996 Level	1997 Estimate	1997 Actual	% of '97 Estimate	% Change from '96
Participation	34,101	33,350	36,856	110.5	18.1
Sites	305	305	330	108.2	18.2
Media Coverage	5,374,521	—	6,082,009	—	113.2

Honda Hit•Run•Throw is a grass roots baseball skills competition for kids aged 7 to 13. There are currently four categories, which are based on age and gender. The first three age groups—Pre-Rookie, Rookie, and Mosquito—are co-ed; the last, Pee Wee, is gender exclusive (i.e., there are separate categories for boys and girls). Events are held at the local level, with winners advancing to regional, provincial, and, finally, national competitions. It is very easy to implement—all that is required is a limited amount of equipment and any open field. It is volunteer driven, which keeps costs down, but also creates some problems.

Overall, Honda Hit•Run•Throw was a success in 1997. Despite disappointments in individual provinces, it achieved 110.5 percent of the estimated participation for the year, surpassing the previous year's participation (18.1 percent) and site (18.2 percent) numbers by a healthy margin. The media coverage allotted to the program also expanded, realizing a 13.2 percent increase in newsprint coverage over 1996 (see Exhibit 1).

Honda Hit•Run•Throw was not, however, free of setbacks in 1997. Poor weather, staff turnover, problematic supplier deals, and declining registration in baseball nationwide were obstacles for the program (sports such as soccer and softball are cutting into baseball registration). Despite such difficulties, the program continued to grow and expand, entrenching itself as a rite of spring in communities across Canada. The most glaring exception was Ontario.

Baseball Canada's provincial affiliates had varying financial results in 1997. About half of the provinces announced a small profit from the program; others suffered losses, which sometimes reached $5,000. Despite some adverse results, the provinces are steadfast in their support of the program.

In contrast to 1996, Baseball Canada was unable to administer the program at a break-even level. Over the past year, Baseball Canada invested some $40,000 into HHRT. The problems associated with new suppliers and excess shipping costs accounted for some of the loss. Nevertheless, it was agreed that in order to continue administering the program at the current level, the bottom line would have to be improved through the introduction of new revenues and/or cost-cutting measures.

The Task Ahead

"Given that Honda's goal for Ontario in 1997 was 8,000 participants, I think that we really need to knock their socks off in 1998," said Todd. "To do that we need to enrol 9,000 to 10,000 kids. That won't be easy, given the political situation."

"You know, I don't understand why there has been such a problem with participation," said Greg, scratching his head. "The OBA alone has approximately 100,000 kids enrolled who are eligible to participate in HHRT." Greg was referring to the Ontario Baseball Association, the dominant body for baseball in the province, and Baseball Canada's affiliate in Ontario. "Why wouldn't baseball people be interested in a program that is fun and exciting, and is an excellent way to introduce newcomers to the sport?" he continued rhetorically.

"I agree, it is hard to understand," remarked Todd. "I think it's a lack of communication through the volunteer hierarchy, coupled with an already busy summer schedule. Even if local organizers want to run an HHRT event, they don't know who to contact, or they don't have time to do it by the time they do find out about it. Events simply have to be decided earlier. We can't tell people in the spring and expect a positive response in that short a time frame."

Greg nodded in agreement. "Then there's the matter of Little League. Many of the eligible participants for HHRT are Little League members." Little League, an American-based organization that rivals the OBA, boasted an estimated 20,000 members in Ontario, most of them in the Ottawa and Windsor areas. "It is frustrating when you have two groups that basically have the same wants and needs but are separated by politics. It sure would be great if we could secure their support, but if we want to bring them on board, they will surely want a slice of the pie. I think we could give their organization some publicity through the program but we certainly don't have the resources to give them any monetary compensation."

"From what I understand, the OBA has invited some Little League organizers to their upcoming convention," Todd suddenly remembered. "That would be a great chance to promote the program among both OBA and Little League, and kill two birds with one stone!"

"With the Baseball Canada and OBA conventions coming up in a few weeks, it would be great if we could announce that the program will be full speed ahead for 1998," said Greg. "That would give our people plenty of notice to execute the proper planning for the year ahead."

"But it's not just Little League that makes things tricky," replied Todd with a sigh. "The situation isn't made any easier by the rift between some members of the OBA and the Blue Jays. These problems will make it difficult to increase our numbers. If we can't get beyond the politicking and lack of communication, we may have to move beyond the traditional market of baseball associations, and target other organizations with kids in those age groups."

"It would also be good to encourage more female participation," said Greg. "The competition is open to both genders, but only the Pee Wee category is gender exclusive—the rest are co-ed. Adding an extra category would cost us more, but it could really spark female participation."

"You're absolutely right," said Todd enthusiastically. "Girls' participation is on the rise, and we need to capitalize on that. If we could, it might open the door for more sponsorship opportunities."

"The survey also indicated that there are other areas we could exploit, like tournaments," said Greg. "We need to go to where the kids already are, and tournaments offer that opportunity. Also, the volunteer structure is already in place, so it wouldn't be difficult to stage. I think it would add value to the tournament . . . it could be used like an all-star competition. And what about summer camps and schools? We've had some camps involved in the past. If we could penetrate these two markets, the possibilities would be staggering."

"I agree, but we have to be careful not to bite off more than we can chew," said Todd. "The financial and human resources that are currently available to the HHRT program are very limited. It might be best to solidify our position in our more traditional markets before we jump into foreign territory. That said, I don't think we should rule out the idea altogether. Maybe we could do some test marketing in these areas."

"I guess you're right, it is difficult to manoeuvre when you're operating with such limited resources," said Greg. "One thing is for sure—it's great to work with first-class organizations like the Blue Jays and Major League Baseball. They believe the program is very important for developing baseball awareness in the community. They also give us a lot of marketing support, not to mention that potential sponsors are attracted by the opportunity to affiliate themselves not just with amateur but also with big-league baseball."

"You know, there was some talk that we could promote the program through the Blue Jays Caravan," said Todd, referring to the promotional event that visits major Canadian cities each winter in anticipation of the new baseball season. "It would be an excellent way to highlight our relationship with the Blue Jays and Major League Baseball, and would give HHRT a promotional shot in the arm!"

"We should also exploit our connections at TSN [The Sports Network]," added Greg. "The CRTC [Canadian Radio-television and Telecommunications Commission] has made it clear that an important part of TSN's operational mandate is to help promote amateur sport in Canada. They [TSN] have said they are willing to give us some public service spots to help promote our programs."

After talking things over, they agreed that the program still had much potential. They also felt that despite shortcomings in Ontario in 1997, the program was a success. After a mere three years of operation on a national basis, HHRT boasted more than 36,000 competitors at more than 300 sites across Canada. The work would be hard for the two newcomers, but both felt assured about the value of the program and their ability to move it to the next level.

1   What were the alternatives open to Baseball Canada?

2   Which of these alternatives should be chosen? Explain.

Exhibit 2 Some Key Points from Ontario Survey

Awareness

- Most organizations are aware of program. Many of the contacted had hosted in past.
- It was difficult getting contacts' numbers for organizations that have not hosted.
- Politics between rival organizations was a factor. Little League, for instance, is a separate entity and will not share its contacts with Baseball Canada.
- There is no clear channel by which local organizations become aware of HHRT.

> Ontario Baseball Association (OBA: provincial)
> Honda
> Little League (rival)
> Baseball Canada (national)

Strengths

- Most organizations felt that HHRT was a competitive yet fun day for kids and parents and that it was a valuable program.
- Good value in kits; lots of goodies for kids.

> Autographed Blue Jays Baseball
> Sizzler (baseball) cards
> Scorecards

                    Hot dogs/Gatorade
                    Poster

Suggested Improvements
- Place, time, and date of regionals should be established early (it would help improve coordination of dates for local events).
- Timely delivery of site kits is critical.
- Some events run long.
- Need national hot dog sponsor for picnic.
- Additional promotional support would be welcomed.
- New, gender-exclusive categories would encourage girls' participation.

Honda Dealer Involvement
- Mostly supportive. In some situations, however, the support was little more than verbal.
- Often, local coordinators expected more support.
- Need to reinforce perception that Honda is primary backer of program.

Why Organizations Didn't Host
- Some local organizations didn't have volunteer capacity.
- Short season and many other baseball events.
- Lack of awareness in Metro Toronto.

Registration
- Most registration begins early in year with mail-out; this is often followed by sit-down registration in March/April.
- Most organizations were positive about including HHRT literature at registration.
- HHRT Regional Meetings
- Most coordinators indicated that they would attend a regional coordinator meeting.
- Little League presidents' meetings are held on a monthly basis.

Support for 1998
- Most organizations said they would host again.
- Of those who have not previously hosted, most were interested in doing so.

Comments
- Organizations have to book their fields early.
- Improve promotional vehicles.
- Set regional events early.

Recommendations
- Need to solidify sponsorship deal early in order to move ahead with certainty.
- Kiosk and presentation at Baseball Canada and OBA conventions only one of several promotional opportunities with target market.

- Little League officials in Ottawa districts will attend OBA convention; this will be a good opportunity to get more associations on board.
- Make presentations at Little League presidents' meetings.
- Continuous communication is key.
- Use a mail-out as an initial approach to organizations in December or before.
- Host regional HHRT meetings with local coordinators (January/February).
- Make some promotional literature available for organizations at registration time (early in year, in some cases as early as December of the current year).
- Add incentives for local coordinators to host (Blue Jay tickets, etc.).
- For associations that are reluctant to host due to small volunteer base (or whatever), offer support in the first year. After that they may become more accommodating.
- Must get Sudbury to host local and regional event for Northern Ontario. This is a key for maintaining a presence in that region.
- Must raise awareness nationally.
- Build the event around a larger event (tournament) or Photo Day.
- Must keep value in kits; this is particularly salient in generating excitement at new sites.

*This case was written by Gregory B. White under the supervision of David S. Litvack, Faculty of Administration, University of Ottawa, Ottawa.

22   Kelman Mfg., Inc.

Al Kelman, the marketing manager of Kelman Mfg., Inc., wants to increase sales by adding sales reps rather than playing with price, which is how Al describes what Henry Kelman, his father and Kelman's president, is suggesting. Henry is not sure what to do, either. However, he does want to increase sales, so something new is needed.

Kelman Mfg., Inc., is a leading producer in the plastic forming machinery industry. It has patents covering over 200 variations, but Kelman's customers seldom buy more than 30 different types in a year. The machines are sold to plastic forming manufacturers to increase production capacity or replace old equipment.

Established in 1952, the company has enjoyed a steady growth to its present position, with annual sales of $50 million.

Some six firms compete in the Canadian plastic forming machinery market. For more information on the Canadian plastics industry visit http://strategis.ic.gc.ca/epic/internet/inplastics-plastiques.nsf/en/home. Several Japanese, German, and Swedish firms compete in the global market, but the Kelmans have not seen them in western Canada. Apparently, the foreign firms rely on manufacturers' agents who have not provided an ongoing presence. They don't follow up on inquiries, and their record for service on the few sales they have made is not good. So the Kelmans are not worried about them right now.

Each of the Canadian competitors is about the same size and manufactures basically similar machinery. Each has tended to specialize in its own geographic area. None has exported much because of high labour costs in Canada. Four of the competitors are located in the east, and two—including Kelman—are in the west. The other western Canadian firm is in Calgary, Alberta. All of the competitors offer similar prices and sell F.O.B. their factories. Demand has been fairly strong in recent years. As a result, all of the competitors have been satisfied to sell in their geographic areas and avoid price-cutting. In fact, price-cutting is not a popular idea in this industry. About 20 years ago, one firm tried to win more business and found that others immediately met the price cut—but industry sales (in units) did not increase at all. Within a few years, prices returned to their earlier level, and since then competition has tended to focus on promotion, avoiding price.

Kelman's promotion depends mainly on six company sales reps, who cover British Columbia and the Prairies. In total, these reps cost about $660,000 per year, including salary, bonuses, supervision, travel, and entertaining. When the sales reps are close to making a sale, they are supported by two sales engineers, at a cost of about $120,000 per year per engineer. Kelman does some advertising in trade journals—less than $50,000—and occasionally uses direct mailings. But the main promotion emphasis is on personal selling. Any personal contact outside the western market is handled by manufacturers' agents, who are paid 4 percent on sales—but sales are very infrequent. Henry Kelman is not satisfied with the present situation. Industry sales have levelled off and so have Kelman's sales, although the firm continues to hold its share of the market. Henry would like to find a way to compete more effectively in the other regions because he sees great potential outside of western Canada.

Competitors and buyers agree that Kelman is the top-quality producer in the industry. Its machines have generally been somewhat superior to others in terms of reliability, durability, and productive capacity. The difference, however, usually has not been great enough to justify a higher price (because the others are able to do the necessary job) unless a Kelman sales rep convinces the customer that the extra quality will improve the customer's product and lead to fewer production line breakdowns. The sales rep also tries to sell Kelman's better sales engineers and technical service people—and sometimes is successful. But if a buyer is only interested in comparing delivered prices for basic machines—the usual situation—Kelman's price must be competitive in order for it to get the business. In short, if such a buyer has a choice between Kelman's and another machine at the same price, Kelman will usually win the business in its part of the western market. But it's clear that Kelman's price has to be at least competitive in such situations.

The average plastic forming machine sells for about $220,000, F.O.B. shipping point. Shipping costs within each major region average about $4,000—but another $3,000 to $6,000 must be added on shipments from western Canada to Ontario or Quebec (and vice versa).

Henry Kelman is thinking about expanding sales by absorbing the extra $3,000 to $6,000 in freight cost that arises if a customer in eastern Canada buys from his western Canadian location. By doing this, he would not be cutting price in those markets but rather reducing his net return. He thinks that his competitors would not see this as price competition—and therefore would not resort to cutting prices themselves.

Al Kelman, the marketing manager, disagrees. Al thinks that the proposed freight absorption plan would stimulate price competition in the eastern markets and perhaps in western Canada as well. He proposes instead that Kelman hire some sales reps to work the eastern markets, selling quality rather than relying on the manufacturers' agents. He argues that two additional sales reps in each of these regions would not increase costs too much, and might greatly increase the sales from these markets over those brought in by the agents. With this plan, there would be no need to absorb the freight and risk disrupting the status quo. Adding more of Kelman's own sales reps is especially important, he argues, because competition in the east is somewhat hotter than in the west, due to the number of competitors (including foreign competitors) in the region. A lot of expensive entertaining, for example, seems to be required just to be considered as a potential supplier. In contrast, the situation has been rather quiet in the west because only two firms are sharing this market and each is working harder near its home base. The eastern competitors don't send any sales reps to western Canada, and if they have any manufacturers' agents, they haven't gotten any business in recent years.

Henry Kelman agrees that his son has a point, but industry sales are levelling off and Henry wants to increase sales. Furthermore, he thinks the competitive situation may change drastically in the near future anyway, as global competitors get more aggressive and some possible new production methods and machines become more competitive with existing ones. He would rather be a leader in anything that is likely to happen rather than a follower. But he is impressed with Al's comments about the greater competitiveness in the other markets and therefore is unsure about what to do.

1 Evaluate Kelman's current strategies.

2 Given Henry Kelman's sales objective, what should Kelman Mfg. do? Explain.

23   Ontario Rutabaga Council*

In June 2003, Smithfield Communications was retained by the Ontario Rutabaga Council (ORC) to develop a new promotional campaign for Ontario rutabagas. This was a fairly unusual account for the medium-sized agency, which specialized in agriculture. The average Smithfield client had a promotional budget of $4 million. The firm's clients included a number of organizations in the fertilizer, chemical, feed, and seed industries. They also handled a few industrial accounts, the largest of which was the $6 million Warren ("Windows to the World") Window account.

The agency was established in 1986 by Simon Smithfield, a former sales representative for John Deere. Smithfield had started by working with equipment accounts, but as the business prospered and the staff expanded, the firm moved into other areas of agribusiness and industrial products. The agency remained fairly conservative in its approach. Smithfield's own specialty was slogans, but the agency's real emphasis was on "quality" promotion designed to inform customers. Though Smithfield himself had no formal marketing training, he was a great believer in hiring account executives with a marketing background because he recognized that ad executives couldn't work in a vacuum.

"We have to work on behalf of the client! We have to look at their strategy or help them develop one. Otherwise they may as well toss their money down a rat hole for all the good a flashy ad campaign will do! What's more, we gotta have the guts to tell them their ideas stink! We owe them that honesty!"

This philosophy was still at work at Smithfield, though Simon had retired. Every junior account man was thoroughly versed in the philosophy and history of the company.

Though the agency dealt mainly with agribusiness accounts, Smithfield had never been in favour of hiring only those with an agricultural background. As Simon often said, "Too narrow-minded! If he grew up on a hog farm in Simcoe, then basically he thinks he has the last word on hogs! In this business you need a wide range of experience and a quick, open mind."

Most of Smithfield's junior ad people came right out of university. One of the latest additions was Ted Banner, a graduate of the Ontario Agricultural College. Ted had been with Smithfield for two years. He learned fast and was quite ambitious. To date, his greatest success had been the brochure for Farnum Feed. On the basis of his past performance, Smithfield executives felt that he was ready to take on the ORC account.

Ted realized that this was his big chance. The ORC account was expected to increase to around $300,000 for 2004-2005, and he planned to make the campaign a real landmark. However, he knew he must do his homework first, so he began studying all the background material he had collected on the ORC.

Rutabaga Industry in Canada

Canadian rutabagas were originally used as feed for sheep that were bound for New England markets in the mid-1800s. In those days, rutabagas were called turnips. The sheep buyers themselves tried the vegetable and ordered more for their own consumption. These early turnips were a far cry from the sweeter-tasting turnip developed in the 1930s and known as the Laurentian. This variety became known officially as rutabaga in 1967. The rutabaga is large and globular in shape, with yellow flesh and a purple top. Usually it is waxed to preserve it during shipping and storage. Rutabagas vary in size from one to three pounds and the wholesale price ranges anywhere from 20 to 22 cents a pound.

Ontario is the centre for Canadian rutabaga production, though some Canadian competition comes from Quebec and P.E.I. The Ontario industry supports 130 growers and a number of shippers and packers. In 2003, the farm value of rutabagas in Ontario was $7.2 million, making it the eighth-highest for vegetables grown in Ontario. Rutabagas reach the consumer by way of the following channel: Farmer to Packer to Shipper to Wholesaler to Supermarkets and Fruit and Vegetable Stores.

A large percentage of the Ontario rutabaga crop is shipped to the United States; in fact, rutabagas account for approximately 15 to 20 percent of the value of all fresh and processed vegetables exported to the United States from Canada. Rutabagas are also grown in the United States, but Ontario rutabagas are considered superior. Since there is no tariff on rutabagas, Canadian rutabagas compete effectively in price with American-grown ones.

Past Promotional Efforts
Although the ORC had coordinated promotional programs on behalf of rutabaga producers for many years, its efforts were hampered by small budgets, which often varied significantly from year to year. For example, last year the ORC had a $60,000 promotional budget, while the year before it was over $100,000. This budget was used, mainly in the United States, to promote rutabagas to housewives as a unique and different vegetable. In the United States, most rutabagas are consumed south of the Mason Dixon Line and east of the Mississippi River, and the ORC felt that the main competition in this area was white turnips and turnip greens; hence, their program of differentiating the rutabaga.

To formulate their promotional program, the ORC hired the advertising agency J.B. Cruikshank Ltd. This agency prepared a promotion mix consisting of magazine ads, press releases for radio, a TV video, and a video for high school family science teachers. All of this was developed around the persona of "June Conway," the fictional resident home economist for the ORC.

The magazine ads appeared in Woman's Day and Family Circle magazines during the months of November (the beginning of the holiday season in the United States, which is the peak period of rutabaga consumption) and April (the end of the turnip season in the United States). These full-page ads stressed new uses and recipe ideas, and featured a sample recipe and picture. They mentioned but did not stress nutrition, and they included a free write-in offer of a rutabaga recipe book. The agency reported that this phase of the program received "a reasonable response" of 1,000 requests per month.

Other aspects of this promotional program included press releases for radio and a short TV video. The agency hoped the radio releases would be aired in the late morning or early afternoon on women's shows. The television video, produced at a cost of $28,000 and titled "Everything You Wanted to Know About Rutabagas—But Didn't Know Who to Ask," was distributed upon request to cable TV channels for use at their convenience. The agency felt that "this scheduling gave the video excellent exposure without requiring the ORC to pay for air time." The film highlighted the growing of rutabagas and their nutritional value, and included attractive recipe ideas. In addition to this, a new video, "The Ontario Rutabaga in the Kitchen," was distributed to high school family science teachers.

The TV video, like the magazine ads, included a write-in address for recipes, but response here was not as high as for the magazines. Mr. Cruikshank explained, "This doesn't indicate less interest, but rather that TV viewers are less likely to copy an address down and mail for more information than those who see advertisements in a magazine or newspaper." Mr. Cruikshank further reported that "by use, the video appears successful. All ten prints are booked well in advance." He encouraged the ORC to increase the number of video copies and increase the number of high school videos available. Board member Fred Hunsberger supported this idea—especially increasing the number of high school videos available. He felt that "we have to let those kids know what a good value tur—uh, rutabagas are. If we get them early on, we've got them for life."

Current Situation
The ORC's president, Clyde Carson, was not as excited as Fred about Cruikshank's suggestion. He had recently seen a publication titled "Report on the New England Market for Canadian Rutabagas," which documented a decline in rutabaga consumption in that area. Further research revealed that per capita, rutabaga consumption had been declining for the past twenty years, and that growers were reducing their acreage or leaving the industry altogether. Clyde presented these depressing statistics to the ORC and suggested a new "marketing strategy" such as that discussed at a seminar he had recently attended. As expected, Clyde ran into heavy opposition from other board members, who did not understand what a marketing strategy was and who were more interested in increasing their production levels. Fred Hunsberger had been particularly adamant about keeping their current promotional program:

"Clyde, we're already telling 'em about all the vitamins and offering free recipes. Now what woman wouldn't jump at a free recipe? And that June Conway is a mighty fine woman! The way she talks about those rutabagas just makes my mouth water. And the kids are sure to like the video. I sure would have been pleased to see videos when I was in school! That TV cable film is doing the job too. Booked solid all last year. It looks real classy to have our own TV film. Just a fluke that consumption is down. People don't know when they're well off these days. You wait! The old values will come back soon and people will see that turnips—uh, rutabagas—are good solid food!"

Clyde persevered, and finally got the board to agree to a large-scale study of the North American rutabaga market. This project was funded mainly by the Ontario Ministry of Agriculture and involved two stages. The first stage was to obtain rutabaga awareness and consumption information from 2,000 Canadian and 6,000 American households. More detailed information was obtained in the second stage on consumption, attitudes, and preferences from 300 households in Canada and 800 in the United States. Based on this report, Clyde was able to convince the ORC that a drastic overhaul was needed. The first thing they did was find a replacement for J.B. Cruikshank Ltd., the ad agency responsible for "Everything You Always Wanted to Know About . . ." Fred Hunsberger had insisted that Smithfield Communications be hired as a replacement: "That's a classy outfit! I knew old Sim when he was with Massey and I'll never forget his big 'Keep Pace With Case' campaign. That's what we need. A catchy slogan! It will turn the tide in a few weeks. Look at the milk people. My grandkids won't stop singing 'Drink Milk, Love Life.' Drives me crazy but they say it sells the milk. Why not tur—uh, rutabagas too? Of course, we'll keep June Conway."

Clyde didn't argue with Fred, though he privately felt that perhaps Smithfield Communications was not the best choice and questioned the usefulness of a slogan. Fred, on the other hand, thought that Smithfield Communications' familiarity with agriculture would be an asset. The two men planned a meeting with Ted Banner, the Smithfield Communications manager assigned to the ORC account.

Research Project Results
Ted Banner sat at his desk at the offices of Smithfield Communications. In front of him were various documents and folders containing background and past promotional programs of the ORC. On top of the pile was a manuscript, "Consumer Analysis of the North American Rutabaga Market," the report that presented the results of the large-scale survey done in 2003. Ted knew that this report had to form the basis of his recommendations to the ORC. In preparation for his initial meeting with Clyde Carson and Fred Hunsberger, Ted looked through the report and summarized the main points.

Common product names
The report revealed that the product is called by many different names, including rutabaga, swede, swede turnip, and turnip. In the United States, 78 percent of consumers referred to the product as a rutabaga, compared to only 20 percent in Canada.

Awareness and frequency of use
Consumers were placed in one of six categories depending on their awareness and frequency of rutabaga use. These results are shown in Exhibit 1.

The first category is relatively small and includes people who are not aware of rutabagas. The second category includes people who are aware of rutabagas but have never purchased one. This group is relatively small in Canada but large in the United States. The third group includes people who have not purchased a rutabaga in the last twelve months. These are probably "lapsed users" who have discontinued use of the product. This is a relatively small group.

The last three groups are classified as current rutabaga users and account for 64 percent of Canadian consumers and 31 percent of American consumers. The heavy-user segment accounts for 16 percent of Canadian consumers and only 3 percent of American consumers.

Exhibit 1: Rutabaga Market Segments, United States and Canada

Market Segments	Percent of Canadian Households	Percent of US Households
Non-user, not aware	11	14
Non-user, aware	16	40
Lapsed user (not used in past year)	8	14
Light user (less than 4 times a year)	23	19
Medium user (5 to 12 times a year)	25	9
Heavy user (more than 12 times a year)	16	3

User and non-user profiles

Analysis of the above groups in terms of demographic characteristics revealed some distinct profiles. In Canada, rutabaga usage tends to be highest among older consumers, consumers who live in rural areas and small communities, French-speaking Canadians, families whose female head is either a homemaker or retired, and families whose male and female head have less education. American results are very similar, with rutabaga usage being highest among older consumers, lower-income families, families whose male and female heads have less education, single-person households, and blacks.

Vegetable purchase criteria

Consumers in the study were asked to rank six possible purchase criteria. The highest-ranking criteria were quality, nutritional value, and taste preference. Price and the time needed to prepare the vegetable were of some but lesser importance. Rutabaga users consistently ranked price higher than taste preference. Non-users ranked taste preference ahead of price.

Consumers in both countries responded to a series of statements designed to measure attitudes toward a number of issues related to vegetable and rutabaga usage. The following attitudes emerged:

- Consumers feel they are eating about the right quantity and variety of vegetables, but a sizable group think they should eat more and a greater variety. This is particularly true for the non-user segment.
- Rutabagas are not considered expensive relative to other vegetables, but consumers stated that large price increases could cause some reduction in consumption.
- A large percentage of consumers increased their purchases of rutabagas when they were on special. Most consumers felt that rutabagas were seldom "featured" items at their stores.
- Most consumers felt that rutabagas are neither conveniently located nor attractively displayed at their stores. Also, they often aren't available at all.

- A large percentage of consumers felt that rutabagas are generally too large for the size of their household. They indicated an interest in pre-sliced, ready-to-cook rutabagas or, especially in the United States, ready-to-serve rutabaga casseroles.
- Most consumers judge product quality by external appearance, and many felt that the rough, black or brown spots on the exterior of the rutabaga indicated inferior quality.
- Many consumers commented on the difficulty of preparing a rutabaga.
- Most consumers have little information on the nutritional value of rutabagas and would like more.

Reasons for non and lapsed users

Both non-users and lapsed users listed not liking the taste as the main reason for non-use. The second-most-frequent reply given by non-users was that they didn't know how to cook or prepare them. Lapsed users listed several secondary reasons: too much trouble to prepare, too hard to cut, poor quality, and prefer vegetables that are more nutritious.

Purchase and use

Rutabaga users were asked about their purchase and use of the product. Their responses indicated the following:

- Approximately one-half of all users decide to purchase the product after entering a store.
- Almost all purchases were made in supermarkets.
- The most popular methods of preparation are boiled and mashed.
- Less than 30 percent of all users serve the vegetable raw.
- The vegetables that consumers consider close substitutes for rutabagas are carrots and squash.
- Most consumers consider the rutabaga as an ordinary everyday dish.
- Over 80 percent of all current users indicated that they were using rutabagas just as often or more often than five years ago.
- Most consumers obtain recipe ideas from magazines and newspapers.

Ted's Reaction

After thoroughly studying the background information and the research report, Ted knew that the problem he faced was far more complex than he imagined. His telephone conversations with Clyde Carson indicated that Carson was aware of the severity and complexity of the problem, but Carson hinted that other council members expected a "magic cure-all" along the lines of the famous "Keep Pace With Case" campaign of a few years ago. Ted knew he would need to call on all his tact as well as his past marketing background in order to come up with a promotional campaign for the ORC. His first task, however, would be to develop a set of marketing strategy recommendations based on the research report he had just read.

1   What is the current situation at the Ontario Rutabaga Council? Why is consumption declining?

2   Evaluate the current promotional program. What recommendations should Ted have for the board?

3   Outline a promotional program based on the above recommendations.

*This case was prepared by Thomas Funk and Jane Funk of the Ontario Agricultural College at the University of Guelph, Guelph, Ontario. It is intended as a basis for classroom discussion and is not designed to present either correct or incorrect handling of administrative problems. Some data in the case have been disguised to protect confidentiality.

24   Fraser Company*

Alice Howell, president of the Columbia Plastics Division of the Fraser Co., leaned forward at her desk in her bright, sunlit office and said, "In brief, our two options are either to price at a level that just covers our costs or we face losing market leadership to those upstart Canadians at Vancouver Light. Are there no other options?" Tamara Chu, Columbia's marketing manager, and Sam Carney, the production manager, had no immediate reply.

Columbia Plastics, based in Seattle, Washington, had been the area's leading manufacturer of plastic moulded skylights for use in houses and offices for almost 15 years. However, two years earlier, Vancouver Light, whose main plant was located in Vancouver, British Columbia, Canada, 150 miles to the north of Seattle, had opened a sales office in the city and sought to gain business by pricing aggressively. Vancouver Light began by offering skylights at 20 percent below Columbia's price for large orders. Now, Vancouver Light had just announced a further price cut of 10 percent.

Company Background
The primary business of the Fraser Co., which had recently celebrated the 50th anniversary of its existence, was the supply of metal and plastic fabricated parts for its well-known Seattle neighbour, Boeing Aircraft. Until the 1960s, Boeing had accounted for more than 80 percent of Fraser's volume, but Fraser then decided to diversify in order to protect itself against the boom-and-bust cycle that seemed to characterize the aircraft industry. Even now, Boeing still accounted for nearly half of Fraser's $50 million† in annual sales.

Columbia Plastics had been established to apply Fraser's plastic moulding skills in the construction industry. Its first products, which still accounted for nearly 30 percent of its sales, included plastic garage doors, plastic gutters, and plastic covers for outdoor lights, all of which had proved to be popular among Seattle home builders. In 1968, Columbia began production of what was to be its most successful product, skylights for homes and offices. Skylights now accounted for 70 percent of Columbia's sales.

The Skylight Market
Although skylights varied greatly in size, a typical one measured 3 feet by 3 feet and would be installed in the ceiling of a kitchen, bathroom, or living room. It was made primarily of moulded plastic with an aluminum frame. Skylights were usually installed by homebuilders upon initial construction of a home, or by professional contractors as part of a remodelling job. Because of the need to cut through the roof to install a skylight and to then seal the joint between the roof and skylight so that water would not leak through, only the most talented of "do-it-yourselfers" would tackle this job on their own. At present, 70 percent of the market was in home and office buildings, 25 percent in professional remodelling, and 5 percent in the do-it-yourself market.

Skylights had become very popular. Homeowners found the natural light they brought to a room quite attractive and perceived skylights to be energy conserving. Although opinion was divided on whether the heat loss from a skylight was more important to consumers than the light gained, the general perception was quite favourable. Homebuilders found that featuring a skylight in a kitchen or other room was an important plus in attracting buyers, and they often included at least one skylight as a standard feature in a home. Condominium builders had also found that their customers liked the openness that a skylight seemed to provide. Skylights were also a popular feature of the second homes that many people owned on Washington's lakes or in ski areas throughout the northwest.

In Columbia Plastics' primary market area of Washington, Oregon, Idaho, and Montana, sales of skylights had levelled off in recent years at about 45,000 units per year. Although Columbia would occasionally sell a large order to California homebuilders, such sales were made only to fill slack in the plant and, after including the cost of transportation, were only break-even propositions at best.

Four homebuilders accounted for half the sales of skylights in the Pacific Northwest. Another five bought an average of 1,000 each, and the remaining sales were split among more than 100 independent builders and remodellers. Some repackaged the product under their own brand name; many purchased only a few dozen or less.

Columbia would ship directly only to builders who ordered at least 500 units per year, although it would subdivide the orders into sections of one gross (144) for shipping. Most builders and remodellers bought their skylights from building supply dealers, hardware stores, and lumberyards. Columbia sold and shipped directly to these dealers, who typically marked up the product by 50 percent. Columbia's average factory price was $200 when Vancouver Light first entered the market.

Columbia maintained a sales force of three for making contact with builders, remodellers, and retail outlets. The sales force was responsible for Columbia's complete line of products, which generally went through the same channels of distribution. The cost of maintaining the sales force, including necessary selling support and travel expense, was $90,000 annually.

Until the advent of Vancouver Light, there had been no significant local competition for Columbia. Several California manufacturers had small shares of the market, but Columbia had held a 70 percent market share until two years ago.

Vancouver Light's entry
Vancouver Light was founded in the early 1980s by Jennifer McLaren, an engineer, and Carl Garner, an architect, and several of their business associates, in order to manufacture skylights. They believed that there was a growing demand for skylights, but there was no ready source of supply available in western Canada. Their assessment proved correct, and their business was successful.

Two years ago, the Canadian company had announced the opening of a sales office in Seattle and devoted her attention to selling skylights only to the large-volume builders. Vancouver Light announced a price 20 percent below Columbia's, with a minimum order size of 1,000 units to be shipped all at one time. It quickly gained all the business of one large builder, True Homes, a Canadian-owned company. In the previous year, that builder had ordered 6,000 skylights from Columbia.

A year later, one of Columbia's sales representatives was told by the purchasing manager of Chieftain Homes, a northwest builder who had installed 7,000 skylights the previous year, that Chieftain would switch to Vancouver Light for most of its skylights unless Columbia was prepared to match Vancouver's price. Columbia then matched that price for orders above 2,500 units, guessing that smaller customers would value highly the local service that Columbia could provide. Chieftain then ordered 40 percent of its needs from Vancouver Light. Two small builders had since switched to Vancouver Light as well. Before Vancouver's latest price cut had been reported, Tamara Chu, Columbia's marketing manager, projected that Vancouver Light would sell about 11,000 units this year, compared to the 24,000 that Columbia was now selling. Columbia's volume represented a decline of 1,000 units per year in each of the last two years, following the initial loss of the True Homes account.

Columbia had asked its lawyers to investigate whether Vancouver Light's sales could be halted on charges of export dumping—that is, selling below cost in a foreign market—but a quick investigation revealed that Vancouver Light's specialized production facility provided a 25 percent savings on variable cost, although one-third of that was lost due to the additional costs involved in importing and transporting the skylights across the border.

The Immediate Crisis
Alice Howell and her two colleagues had reviewed the situation carefully. Sam Carney, the production manager, had presented the cost accounting data, which showed a total unit cost of $135 for Columbia's most popular skylight. Vancouver Light, he said, was selling a closely similar model at $144. The cost of $135 included $15 in manufacturing overheads, directly attributable to skylights, but not the cost of the sales force or the salaries, benefits, and overheads associated with the three executives in the room. General overheads, including the sales force and executives, amounted to $390,000 per year at present for Columbia as a whole.

Tamara Chu was becoming quite heated about Vancouver Light by this time. "Let's cut the price a further 10 percent to $130 and drive those Canadians right out of the market! That Jennifer McLaren started with those big builders and now she's after the whole market. We'll show her what competition really is!"

But Carney was shocked: "You mean we'll drive her and us out of business at the same time! We'll both lose money on every unit we sell. What has that sales force of yours, Tamara, been doing all these years if not building customer loyalty for our product?"

"We may lose most of our sales to the big builders," cut in Howell, "but surely most customers wouldn't be willing to rely on shipments from Canada? Maybe we should let Vancouver Light have the customers who want to buy on the basis of price. We can then make a tidy profit from customers who value service, need immediate supply, and have dealt with our company for years."

1   Should the Fraser Company match Vancouver Light's prices, undercut that firm, or continue its current pricing policy?
2   Why is your choice superior to the other two courses of action?

*This case was written by Dr. Charles Weinberg, who at the time of its preparation was associated with the University of British Columbia.
†All prices and costs are in U.S. dollars.

25   Lee Steel Supply and Service*

Lee Steel Supply and Service (LSSS) is a medium-sized processor and distributor of rolled steel and aluminum products. The company was originally established as a dealer in scrap iron products in 1946. The initial facility in Buffalo, New York, has been expanded to include an 80,000-square-foot manufacturing plant, warehouse, and sales office. The total New York market is covered from this location. In 1957, a 30,000-square-foot warehouse and sales office was set up in Mississauga, Ontario, to service the nearby Canadian market. The company's present sales volume is $45 million, with 65 percent in New York and the remainder in Ontario.

The Product Mix

The LSSS product line is classified into three basic categories:

1   Standard finished products: These include such items as cold-rolled slit coil, sheared-to-size blanks (which manufacturers employ directly in their production processes), and standard-size steel sheets.

2   Items preprocessed for inventory: Examples of products in this category are 28-gauge 36-inch by 98-inch galvanized sheets and 60-inch by 120-inch 14-gauge hot-rolled sheet, as used in the manufacture of oil tanks.

3   Custom job processing orders: Recent custom orders have included 100,000 pounds of customer-supplied 43-inch, 22-gauge, cold-rolled coil to be slit into 8 1/2-inch widths, and 50,000 pounds of customer-supplied galvanized satin coat 32-inch, 24-gauge coil to be slit into 1 1/2-inch widths. Although relatively insignificant in dollar volume, the custom operation accounts for almost 30 percent by weight of the metal processed by LSSS.

Technology and Production Methods

The production process consists of three major operations: shearing, slitting, and cutting to length. Each of these job centres consists of a number of machines. This production flow presents scheduling difficulties because of the varied number of products and operations performed. Although machinery obsolescence is very low, monthly maintenance costs are high due to the need to keep equipment in working order. Generally, there is a conscious attempt by LSSS management to purchase unusual, specialized equipment to produce specialized products. In this way, competition can be effectively eliminated for a number of products, which allows LSSS considerable flexibility in price setting.

Customer Profile

No major customers account for a large portion of volume. In fact, LSSS's largest customer represents only 4 percent of total dollar sales. Likewise, no single product contributes significantly to the firm's total revenue.

Most of LSSS's customers are located in the Buffalo and Toronto–Montreal areas. Typically, product requirements for these two major markets differ considerably. Thus, separate sales strategies have been developed.

Present Industry Situation

Early in 2003, Brian Matthews, general manager of LSSS, was somewhat pessimistic about future business prospects. The economy was almost one year into a recessionary period. Government action designed to tone down inflation had resulted in an unprecedented level of unemployment. As a result, 2003 dollar sales were down almost 8 percent below 2002, and 2004 expectations were poor.

At present, inventories and production are high throughout the industry, causing price deterioration in most product lines. The North American Steel industry had been suffering under the impact of cheap steel imports from Brazil, China and Eastern Europe. There may be some easing of market conditions due to the move by Stelco to seek bankruptcy protection, but it would only be short term. Another factor is the increasing demand from China for steel, with the potential for changing it from an exporter to a net importer.

General Pricing Guidelines

Essentially, LSSS uses a cost-plus basis in determining selling prices. A base processing cost is established for each order, consisting of labour-machine costs (electricity, maintenance, and other variable costs). This figure is added to material and scrap freight costs and subtracted from the estimated selling price to set the gross margin for that particular order. The net margin is obtained by subtracting the fixed costs allocated to each order (plant overhead, marketing, paperwork, and administration).

To determine the cost of production for each order, the cost at each phase of production is calculated. Using a two-shift basis, the base processing costs of each machine are calculated per hour. These costs are revised monthly.

The various overhead costs are determined weekly and allocated to each order. To calculate these costs, the total plant production in hours is determined and each order receives a percentage of these costs in relation to its percentage of the total weekly production.

Price lists are accordingly established for the standard items produced. The production cost estimates are checked each month, but in each order-cost determination, changes are made only when long-term trends would justify them.

To facilitate this cost-plus basis of pricing, LSSS has a computerized record keeping system. Administration, sales, delivery, and other such costs are reported weekly. Each cost centre within the plant reports its costs to the administrative department on a daily basis, and monthly production reports are subsequently prepared. The reports produced show breakdowns by customer, total order cost, total order price, and total gross margin.

The ultimate responsibility for pricing rests with Brian Matthews. Three people working in the administrative department report directly to him. In theory, the two people in administration at Mississauga report directly to him as well. In practice, these people nearly always act independently, since the Ontario market is distinct from that of New York.

Actual Pricing

The pricing guidelines referred to above are often modified considerably in actual practice. The major factor affecting final price is the particular demand–supply situation existing at the time of sale.

Gross margins on orders to different customers vary widely—from 5 to 60 percent on standard items and up to 100 percent on custom orders. Generally, as the demand for a product rises, prices are increased for all except the best customers. Irregular or occasional customers are charged the highest price obtainable.

In general, the high-margin products are characterized by low turnover. They include small custom orders and sophisticated products that require specialized equipment. Low-margin products are high-turnover items and are produced in large quantities for two or three customers. Competitive pressure on these quantity products is the major reason for the lower margins. There is very little relationship, however, between gross margin and order regularity, customer size, and so forth.

Other criteria, although infrequently used, influence the pricing process. For example, prices may be lowered to obtain orders that will employ unused capacity, to fill delivery trucks, or to obtain very large orders.

The high dollar value of inventories, combined with handling costs, obsolescence, and spoilage (rust), results in extremely high inventory carrying costs. As a result, "stress pricing," or selling at less than cost, will occasionally be undertaken to get rid of very-slow-moving items. Also, LSSS will sell a product as a "loss leader" to pick up sales of a higher-margin product.

Matthews frequently revises his price lists and sends them to all salespeople as the lower limit on which to base their quotations. One of the key factors by which he evaluates the performance of his salespeople is the price above this "lower limit" that the salespeople can obtain for their products.

Situation 1

LSSS has been requested by the New York State government to submit a quotation on work for a very large construction project. Although he is not certain of the exact figures, Brian Matthews thinks this could represent a sizable revenue, based on his present method of pricing. To his knowledge, four other firms have been asked to bid. Alternatively, Matthews knows that if Stelco is pushed into bankruptcy, LSSS will not have the capacity to handle both the contract and the expected heavy Canadian demand for his firm's products. In this situation, he would prefer to forgo the New York government contract, because the Canadian bankruptcy would generate large profits due to the short supply of metal. However, if LSSS does not win the contract and the Canadian strike does not occur, LSSS will most certainly operate only at a marginal profit level. Furthermore, if he wants to be certain of winning the contract, Matthews will have to submit a very low bid to the state, and this would result in quite low profits.

Situation 2

In an effort to expand market share significantly, Superior Steel, the major competitor of LSSS, has lowered the price of its rolled-steel products to a level below the cost price of similar products carried by LSSS. In pursuing this strategy, Superior Steel hopes to lower its fixed costs per order enough to permit it to undercut LSSS substantially in the long run.

Situation 3

Early in 2002, Brian Matthews was concerned about the discrepancy between LSSS's formal pricing policy and the company's actual pricing practices. He believed that the formal policy should be updated to conform more closely with current market conditions.

In May, Matthews hired a second-year MBA student, Bill Witzel, to work on this problem as a summer project.

1   Evaluate the pros and cons of each alternative in Situation 1. What pricing strategy should Brian Matthews employ in Situation 1?

2   Evaluate the alternatives available to LSSS in Situation 2 and design a suitable strategy in response to the Superior Steel move.

3   Provide a "business school" impression of LSSS's actual pricing practice in Situation 3 and suggest how the company can improve its pricing policy.

26   Cutters, Inc.

Tony Kenny, president and marketing manager of Cutters, Inc., is deciding what strategy—or strategies—to pursue.

Cutters, Inc., is a manufacturer of industrial cutting tools. These tools include such items as lathe blades, drill press bits, and various other cutting edges used in the operation of large metal cutting, boring, or stamping machines. Tony Kenny takes great pride in the fact that his company, whose $5.2 million sales in 2003 is small by industry standards, is recognized as a producer of a top-quality line of cutting tools.

Competition in the cutting-tool industry is intense. Cutters competes not only with the original machine manufacturers but also with many other larger domestic and foreign manufacturers that offer cutting tools as one of their many different product lines. This has had the effect, over the years, of standardizing the price, the specifications, and, in turn, the quality of the competing products of all manufacturers. It has also led to fairly low prices on standard items.

About a year ago, Tony was tiring of the financial pressure of competing with larger companies enjoying economies of scale. At the same time, he noted that more and more potential cutting-tool customers were turning to small tool and die shops because of specialized needs that could not be met by the mass production firms. Tony thought that perhaps he should consider some basic strategy changes. Although he was unwilling to become strictly a custom producer, he thought that the recent trend toward buying customized cutting edges suggested that new markets might be developing—markets too small for the large, multiproduct-line companies to serve profitably but large enough to earn a good profit for a flexible company of Cutters' size.

Tony hired a marketing research company, Holl Associates, to study the feasibility of serving these markets. The initial results were encouraging. It was estimated that Cutters might increase sales by 65 percent and profits by 90 percent by serving the emerging markets. This research showed that there are many large users of standard cutting tools that buy directly from large cutting-tool manufacturers (domestic or foreign) or from wholesalers that represent these manufacturers. This is the bulk of the cutting-tool business (in terms of units sold and sales dollars). But there are also many smaller users all over North America who buy in small but regular quantities. And some of these needs are becoming more specialized. That is, a special cutting tool may make a machine and/or worker much more productive, perhaps eliminating several steps with time-consuming setups. This is the area that the research company sees as potentially attractive.

Next, Tony had the sales manager hire two technically oriented market researchers (at a total cost of $60,000 each per year, including travel expenses) to maintain continuous contact with potential cutting-tool customers. The researchers were supposed to identify any present or future needs that might exist in enough cases to make it possible to profitably produce a specialized product. The researchers were not to take orders or sell Cutters' products to the potential customers. Tony felt that only through this policy could these researchers talk to the right people.

The initial feedback from the market researchers was most encouraging. Many firms (large and small) had special needs—although it often was necessary to talk to the shop supervisor or individual machine operators to find these needs. Most operators were making do with the tools available. Either they didn't know that customizing was possible or they doubted that their supervisors would do anything about it if they suggested that a more specialized tool would increase productivity. But these operators were encouraging because they said that it would be easier to persuade supervisors to order specialized tools if the tools were already produced and in stock than if they had to be custom made. So Tony decided to continually add high-quality products to meet the ever-changing, specialized needs of users of cutting tools and edges.

Cutters' potential customers for specialized tools are located all over North America. The average sale per customer is likely to be less than $500, but the sale will be repeated several times within a year. Because of the widespread market and the small order size, Tony doesn't think that selling direct, as is done by small custom shops, is practical. At the present time, Cutters sells 90 percent of its regular output through a large industrial wholesaler, National Mill Supplies, Inc., which serves the entire area east of the Manitoba–Ontario border and carries a very complete line of industrial supplies (to "meet every industrial need"). Each of National's sales reps sells over 10,000 items from a 910-page catalogue. National Mill Supplies, although very large and well known, is having trouble moving cutting tools. National is losing sales of cutting tools in some cities to newer wholesalers specializing in the cutting-tool industry. The new wholesalers are able to give more technical help to potential customers and therefore better service. National's president is convinced that the newer, less-experienced firms either will realize that they can't maintain a substantial profit margin along with their aggressive strategies, or will eventually go broke trying to overspecialize.

From Tony's standpoint, the present wholesaler has a good reputation and has served Cutters well in the past. National Mill Supplies has been of great help in holding down Tony's inventory costs by increasing the inventory in National's 35 branch locations. Tony has received several complaints about the lack of technical assistance given by National's sales reps, as well as their lack of knowledge about Cutters' new special products, but he feels that the present wholesaler is providing the best service it can. All its sales reps have been told about the new products at a special training session, and a new page has been added to the catalogue they carry with them. Tony dismisses the complaints as "the usual things you hear when you're in business."

Tony thinks there are more urgent problems than a few complaints. Profits are declining, and sales of the new cutting tools are not nearly as high as forecast, even though all research reports indicate that the company's new products meet the intended markets' needs perfectly. The high costs involved in producing small quantities of special products and in adding the market research team, together with lower-than-expected sales, have significantly reduced Cutters' profits. Tony is wondering whether it is wise to continue to try to cater to the needs of many specific target markets when the results are this discouraging. He also is considering increasing advertising expenditures in the hope that customers will pull the new products through the channel.

He is also considering setting up an E-commerce site that could sell directly to the market, bypassing his wholesaler. He could avoid channel conflict by allowing the customer to order online and his wholesaler could then deliver offline.

1   Evaluate Cutters' situation and Tony Kenny's present strategy.

2   What should he do now?

27   Unilever, Ltd.*

Joe Hall is product manager for Lever 2000 Soap. He was just transferred to Unilever, Ltd., a Canadian subsidiary of Unilever Group, Inc., from world headquarters in New York. Joe is anxious to make a good impression because he is hoping to transfer to Unilever's London office. He is working on developing and securing management approval of next year's marketing plan for Lever 2000. His first job is submitting a draft marketing plan to Sarah Long, his recently appointed group product manager, who is responsible for several such plans from product managers like Joe.

Joe's marketing plan is the single most important document he will produce on this assignment. This annual marketing plan does three main things:

1   It reviews the brand's performance in the past year, assesses the competitive situation, and highlights problems and opportunities for the brand.
2   It spells out marketing strategies and the plan for the coming year.
3   Finally, and most importantly, the marketing plan sets out the brand's sales objectives and advertising/promotion budget requirements.

In preparing this marketing plan, Joe gathered the information in Exhibit 1.
Joe was somewhat surprised at the significant regional differences in the bar soap market.

1   The underdevelopment of the deodorant bar segment in Quebec with a corresponding overdevelopment of the beauty bar segment. But some past research suggested that this is due to cultural factors—English-speaking people have been more interested than others in cleaning, deodorizing, and disinfecting. A similar pattern is seen in most European countries, where the adoption of deodorant soaps has been slower than in North America. For similar reasons, the perfumed soap share is highest in French-speaking Quebec.
2   The overdevelopment of synthetic bars in the Prairies. These bars, primarily in the deodorant segment, lather better in the hard water of the Prairies. Nonsynthetic bars lather very poorly in hard-water areas—and leave a soap film.
3   The overdevelopment of the "all other" segment in Quebec. This segment, consisting of smaller brands, fares better in Quebec, where 43 percent of the grocery trade is done by independent stores. Conversely, large chain grocery stores dominate in Ontario and the Prairies.

Joe's brand, Lever 2000, is a naturally based skin care bar that is highly perfumed. His business is relatively weak in the key Ontario market. To confirm this share data, Joe calculated consumption of Lever 2000 per thousand people in each region. See Exhibit 2.

These differences are especially interesting since per capita sales of all bar soap products are roughly equal in all provinces.

A consumer attitude and usage research study was conducted approximately a year ago. This study revealed that consumer "top-of-mind" awareness of the Lever 2000 brand differed greatly across Canada. This was true despite the even expenditure (by population) of advertising funds in past years. Also, trial of Lever 2000 was low in the Maritimes, Ontario, and British Columbia. See Exhibit 3.

The attitude portion of the research revealed that consumers who had heard of Lever 2000 were aware that its natural qualities was joined with a high fragrance level. This was the main selling point in the copy, and it was well communicated by Lever 2000's advertising. The other important finding was that consumers who had tried Lever 2000 were satisfied with the product. About 70 percent of those trying Lever 2000 had repurchased the product at least twice.

Joe has also discovered that bar soap competition is especially intense in Ontario. It is Canada's largest market, and many competitors seem to want a share of it. The chain stores are also quite aggressive in promotion and pricing, offering specials, in-store coupons, and so on. They want to move goods. And because of this, two key Ontario chains have put Lever 2000 on their pending delisting sheets. These chains, which control about half the grocery volume in Ontario, are dissatisfied with how slowly Lever 2000 is moving off the shelves.

Exhibit 1: Past 12-Month Share of Bar Soap Market (percent)

	Maritimes	Que.	Ont.	Man/Sask.	Al.	BC
Deodorant segment						
Zest	21.3%	14.2%	24.5%	31.2%	30.4%	25.5%
Dial	10.4	5.1	12.8	16.1	17.2	14.3
Lifebuoy	4.2	3.1	1.2	6.4	5.8	4.2
Beauty bar segment						
Camay	6.2	12.3	7.0	4.1	4.0	5.1
Lux	6.1	11.2	7.7	5.0	6.9	5.0
Dove	5.5	8.0	6.6	6.3	6.2	4.2
Lever 2000	2.1	5.6	1.0	4.2	4.2	2.1
Lower-priced bars						
Ivory	11.2	6.5	12.4	5.3	5.2	9.0
Sunlight	6.1	3.2	8.2	4.2	4.1	8.0
All others (including stores' own brands)	26.9	30.8	18.6	17.2	16.0	22.6
Total bar soap	100%	100%	100%	100%	100%	100%

Exhibit 2: Standard Cases of 3-Ounce Bars Consumed per 1,000 People in 12 Months

	Maritimes	Que.	Ont.	Man/Sask.	Al.	BC
Lever 2000	2.1	5.6	1.0	4.2	4.2	2.1
	4.1	10.9	1.9	8.1	4.1	6.2
Sales index	66	175	31	131	131	100

Now Joe feels he is ready to set a key part of the brand's marketing plan for next year: how to allocate the advertising/sales promotion budget by region.

Lever 2000's present advertising/sales promotion budget is 20 percent of sales. With forecast sales of $4 million, this would amount to an $800,000 expenditure. Traditionally such funds have been allocated in proportion to population. See Exhibit 4.

Joe feels he should spend more heavily in Ontario, where the grocery chain delisting problem exists. Last year, 36 percent of Lever 2000's budget was allocated to Ontario, which accounted for only 12 percent of Lever 2000's sales. Joe wants to increase Ontario spending to 48 percent of the total budget by taking funds proportionately from all other areas. Joe expects this will increase business in the key Ontario market, which has over one-third of Canada's population, because it is a big increase and will help Lever 2000 "out-shout" the many other companies who are promoting heavily.

Joe presented this idea to Sarah, his newly appointed group product manager. Sarah strongly disagrees. She has also been reviewing Lever 2000's business and feels that promotion funds have historically been misallocated. It is her strong belief that, to use her words, "a brand should spend where its business is." Sarah believes that the first priority in allocating funds regionally is to support the areas of strength. She suggested to Joe that there may be more business to be had in the brand's strong areas, Quebec and the Prairies, than in chasing sales in Ontario. The needs and attitudes toward Lever 2000, as well as competitive pressures, may vary a lot among the provinces. Therefore, Sarah suggested that spending for Lever 2000 in the coming year be proportional to the brand's sales by region rather than to regional population.

Joe is convinced this is wrong, particularly in light of the Ontario situation. He asked Sarah how the Ontario market should be handled. Sarah said that the conservative way to build business in Ontario is to invest incremental promotion funds. However, before these incremental funds are invested, a test of this Ontario investment proposition should be conducted. Sarah recommended that some of the Ontario money should be used to conduct an investment-spending market test in a small area or town in Ontario for 12 months. This will enable Joe to see if the incremental spending results in higher sales and profits—profits large enough to justify higher spending. In other words, an investment payout should be assured before any extra money is spent in Ontario. Similarly, Sarah would do the same kind of test in Quebec, to see if more money should go there.

Exhibit 3: Usage Results (in percent)

	Maritimes	Que.	Ont.	Man/Sask.	Al.	BC
Respondents aware of Lever 2000	20%	58%	28%	30%	32%	16%
Respondents ever trying Lever 2000	3	18	2	8	6	4

Exhibit 4: Allocation of Advertising/Sales Promotion Budget, by Population

	Maritimes	Que.	Ont.	Man/Sask.	Al.	BC	Canada
Percent of population	100%	27%	36%	8%	8%	11%	100%
Possible allocation of budget based on population (in 000s)	$80	$216	$288	$64	$64	$88	$800
Percent of Lever 2000 business at present	7%	51%	12%	11%	11%	8%	100%

Joe feels this approach would be a waste of time and unduly cautious, given the importance of the Ontario market and the likely delistings in two key chains.

1   Evaluate the present strategy for Lever 2000 and Joe's and Sarah's proposed strategies.
2   How should the promotion money be allocated? Should investment-spending market tests be run first? Why? Explain.

*Adapted from a case prepared by Daniel Aronchick, who at the time of its preparation was marketing manager at Thomas J. Lipton, Limited.

28   Imperial Lumber Limited*

Imperial Lumber is a large forest-products company based in Vancouver, British Columbia. Major product divisions include plywood, panelling, pulp, and lumber. The company is fully integrated. Operations include everything from logging camps and manufacturing plants to approximately 25 retail branches located coast-to-coast in Canada.

Susan McKay, central division manager for Imperial, had to make training and remuneration decisions regarding her sales reps (see Exhibit 1). The decisions were complicated by a number of factors:

1   Head office had indicated that due to the downturn in 2003 and the softwood lumber dispute with the US, a maximum of four reps could be recommended for maximum salary increments based on performance.

2   Two of the branches in her division were showing signs of atypical performance. Windsor's sales and gross profits were down substantially because of that district's reliance on the automobile industry, which was no longer a major customer. On the other hand, Ottawa, a new branch, was experiencing rapid growth. One of the central division objectives for 2004 and 2005 was to penetrate this market as rapidly as possible in an attempt to capture a large share of the residential construction contractors' business.

3   McKay knew that sales volume figures for reps could be misleading to the extent that much of Imperial's product mix (approximately 85 lines) generated substantially different gross profits. Just because a representative produced a substantial sales volume did not automatically imply an associated large gross profit. Furthermore, the price a representative might obtain for the company's products was, within limits, a function of how well he or she could negotiate terms with the customer.

Exhibit 1:

TO: S. McKay, Central Division Manager
FROM: L. Meredith, Sales Analyst II
DATE: February 1, 2004

Attached [Exhibit 2] is the sales and gross profit analysis for our representatives in the Central Division. I hope this will be of some use in your efforts to determine:

(a) Which of the employees from Central Division you wish to send to the annual training program in order to improve sales performance.

(b) Those employees you wish to recommend for maximum salary increments due to outstanding performance in the previous year.

The representatives have been ranked according to sales achievement for 2003.

Exhibit 2: Analysis of Sales Staff Ranked According to Average Sales Dollars per Month and Average Gross Profit per Month as at December 31

Basis Month Average	Name	Location	Sales Rank	Average Sales per month	G.P. rank	Average G.P. per month	Other Duties
12	S. Richards	Toronto	1	312,510	2	34,915	
12	R. McCain	Toronto	2	301,950	3	34,134	
7	N. Walker	Hamilton	3	299,420	6	28,560	
10	G. Pedersen	Kingston	4	295,650	1	35,478	
12	L. Nielson	Hamilton	5	287,777	4	29,842	
12	J. Morrison	Thunder Bay	6	284,920	9	25,643	
8	B. Brumec	Ottawa	7	280,000	5	28,840	
12	G. Andrews	Thunder Bay	8	273,255	11	18,581	
12	E. Davis	Kingston	9	268,125	10	17,696	
12	F. Gordon	Hamilton	10	230,122	12	14,958	
12	F. Scott	Thunder Bay	11	228,500	13	14,853	SSR*
6	J. Kyle	Ottawa	12	214,752	8	28,400	
12	M. Fisk	Kingston	13	204,912	14	13,319	SSR
4	R. Blackman	Ottawa	14	193,155	7	28,520	ASR†
12	A. Hobson	Windsor	15	181,122	16	9,056	
12	A. McDonald	Toronto	16	150,110	15	9,757	
12	P. Greenway	Windsor	17	115,055	17	5,753	
12	E. Fleischer	Windsor	18	92,110	18	4,606	

The Ottawa sales force was doing well for relative "newcomers" to the company (see Exhibit 2, "Basis Month Average" column). Their gross profit/sales ratios were above average (Brumec, 10.3; Kyle, 13.2; and Blackman, 14.8). Consideration of their sales volumes (which fell in the middle to lower end of the distribution) had to be tempered by the fact that Ottawa was a new branch and that these salespeople were still developing new accounts. Andrews, Davis, Gordon, and McDonald all had gross profit/sales ratios below average (6.8, 6.6, 6.5, and 6.5, respectively). They all had at least one year's experience with Imperial. They all came from branches where their colleagues were able to substantially "outperform" them. Finally these people all fell in the middle to lower range of the sales volume ranking.

McKay, after careful consideration of the data, recommended:
- Richards, McCain, and Pedersen receive maximum salary increments.
- Andrews, Davis, Gordon, and McDonald receive further training in order to upgrade their sales skills.

1   Given the wide range of possible recommendations, why did Susan McKay select these people?
2   Give your justification for her decision.

*This case was prepared by Professor Lindsay Meredith, who at the time of its preparation was associated with Simon Fraser University.

29   **Parker Instruments Ltd.***

Parker Instruments Ltd. (PI) is a British firm that operates as a manufacturer and an importer/distributor. Its field is electronic instruments, and the imported products account for about 75 percent of sales. One of the companies Parker Instruments represents in the United Kingdom is Electro Industries (EI), a Canadian precision instrument firm. PI and EL have been working together for about 10 years. The relationship between the two companies was good for a number of years. Then things started to go wrong, and this was accentuated by an accident a year ago that robbed EI of its top two executives. George Parker feels strong ties to EI but is increasingly worried by the Canadian company's seeming indifference to its international operations in general and to the relationship with PI in particular.

George Parker locked the door of his car and walked across the parking lot toward the station entrance. Although it was a sunny spring morning and the daffodils and tulips provided welcome colour after the grayness of winter, Parker hardly noticed. Within a few minutes, the train from London would be arriving with Bruce MacDonald, the export sales manager for Electro Industries. Parker would be spending the day with MacDonald, and he wondered what the outcome of their discussions would be.

Parker Instruments Ltd.

George Parker was managing director of Parker Instruments Ltd., part of a small, family-owned U.K. group of companies. The company gained its first sales agency in 1923 (from an American manufacturer), which made it one of the most well-established international trading firms in electronic instruments. PI sales were the equivalent of about $1 million, with 75 percent coming from imported distributed items and 25 percent from sales of its own manufactured items. The company had a total of 15 employees.

PI was the British distributor for 15 manufacturers located in the United States, Canada, Switzerland, and Japan. Like many firms, it found that the 80/20 rule held true: About 80 percent of its import sales of $750,000 were generated by 20 percent of the distributorships it held. With current sales of $165,000, the Electro Industries distributorship was an important one.

Electro Industries

Electro Industries was a younger and larger organization than its U.K. distributor. Located in southern Ontario, it was founded in the mid-1950s and had current sales of $4 million and a workforce of 90 employees. EI had developed a strong reputation over the years for its high-precision instrumentation and testing equipment, and this led to considerable market expansion. The company had moved in a number of new product directions. The original products were very precise devices for use in standards laboratories. From this base it had more recently established a presence in the oceanographic and electric power fields.

As a result of this expansion, 80 percent of its sales were now made outside Canada, split evenly between the United States and offshore markets. In the United States, the company had its own direct-sales organization, whereas indirect methods were used elsewhere. In the "best" 15 offshore markets, EI had exclusive distributors; in 30 other markets, it relied on commission agents.

Working Together

EI and PI first made contact in New York City, and the two companies agreed to work together. George Parker was on a business trip in the United States when he received a cable from his brother saying that a representative of EI wanted to get in touch with him. Parker and his wife met the senior executive in their hotel room and, after initial introductions, settled down to exchange information. At some point, Parker, who had had a hectic day, fell asleep. He awoke to find that PI was now more or less EI's U.K. distributor, his wife having kept the discussion rolling while he slept.

The two firms soon began to prosper together. The distributorship gave PI a product line to complement those it already carried. Furthermore, the EI instruments were regarded as the "Cadillacs" of the industry. This ensured entry to the customer's premises and an interest in the rest of the PI product line. As far as EI was concerned, it could hardly have chosen a more suitable partner: PI's staff was technically competent, facilities existed for product servicing, and customer contacts were good. Moreover, as time passed, George Parker's long experience and international connections proved invaluable to EI. He was often asked for an opinion prior to some new move by the Canadian producer. Parker preferred to have a close working relationship with the firms he represented, so he was happy to provide advice. In this way, PI did an effective job of representing EI in the United Kingdom and helped with market expansion elsewhere.

As might be expected, the senior executives of the companies got along well together. The president and vice president of marketing—EI's "international ambassadors"—and George Parker progressed from being business partners to becoming close personal friends. Then, after nine successful years, a tragedy occurred: the two EI executives were killed in an airplane crash on their way home from a sales trip.

The tragic accident created a management succession crisis within EI. During this period, international operations were left dangling while other priorities were attended to. Nobody was able to take charge of the exporting activities that had generated such good sales for the company. Although there was an export sales manager, Bruce MacDonald, he was a relative newcomer, having been in training at the time of the accident. He was also a middle-level executive, whereas his international predecessors were the company's most senior personnel.

From Parker's point of view, things were still not right a year later. The void in EI's international operations had not been properly filled. Bruce MacDonald had proved to be a competent manager, but he lacked support because a new vice president of marketing had yet to be appointed. A new president headed the company, but he was the previous vice president of engineering and preferred to deal with technical rather than business issues. So despite the fact that MacDonald had a lot of ideas about what should be done internationally (most of which were similar to George Parker's ideas), he lacked both the position and the support of a superior to bring about the necessary changes.

While the airplane accident precipitated the current problems in the two companies' relationship, Parker realized that things had been going sour for a couple of years. At the outset of the relationship, EI executives had welcomed the close association with PI. Over time, however, as the manufacturer grew in size and new personnel came along, it seemed to Parker that his input was increasingly resented. This was unfortunate, because Parker believed that EI could become a more sophisticated international competitor if it considered advice given by informed distributors. In the past, EI had been open to advice and had benefited considerably from it. Yet, there were still areas where EI could effect improvements. For example, its product literature was of poor quality and was often inaccurate or outdated. Prices were also worrisome. EI seemed unable to hold its costs, and its competitors now offered better value-for-money alternatives. Other marketing practices needed attention, also.

The Oceanographic Market
One area where EI and PI were in disagreement was the move into the oceanographic field. George Parker was pleased to see EI moving into new fields, but wondered if EI truly appreciated how "new" the field was. In a way, he believed the company had been led by the technology into the new field rather than having considered the fit between its capabilities and success criteria for the new field. For example, the customer fit did not seem even close. The traditional buyers of EI products for use in standards laboratories were scientists, some of whom were employed by government, some by industry, and some by universities. By and large, they were academic types, used to getting their equipment when the budget permitted. As a result, selling was "gentlemanly," and follow-up visits were required to maintain contacts. Patience was often required, since purchasing cycles could be relatively long. Service needs were not extensive, for the instruments were used very carefully.

In contrast, the oceanographic products were used in the very demanding sea environment. Service needs were acute, due not just to the harsh operating environment but also to the cost associated with having inoperable equipment. For example, ocean research costs were already high but became even higher if faults in shipboard equipment prevented taking sea measurements. In such a situation, the customer demanded service today or tomorrow, wherever the faulty equipment was located. The oceanographic customer was also a difficult type—still technically trained but concerned about getting the job done as quickly as possible. Purchasing budgets were much less of a worry; if the equipment was good, reliable, and with proven back-up, chances were it could be sold. But selling required more of a push than the laboratory equipment.

When EI entered the oceanographic field, a separate distributor was appointed in the United Kingdom. However, the arrangement did not work out. EI then asked George Parker to carry the line, and with great reluctance he agreed. The lack of enthusiasm was due to Parker's perception that his company was not capable of functioning well in this new arena. Because PI was ill equipped to service the oceanographic customer, it was thought that there could even be repercussions in its more traditional field. Parker was unwilling to risk the company's established reputation in this way. However, while he preferred not to represent

EI in the oceanographic field, he worried about a "one market, one distributor" mentality at EI.

The Current Visit

George Parker had strong personal sentiments for EI as a company. In his opinion, however, some concrete action was required if the business relationship was to survive, let alone prosper.

Parker recognized the good sales of EI products, but also took note of shrinking profit margins over the last few years due to the increased costs PI faced with the EI product line. Since EI was slow to respond to service and other problems, PI had been putting things right and absorbing the associated costs more and more frequently. However, these costs could not be absorbed forever. Parker had been willing to help tide EI over the last difficult year but expected a more positive response in the future.

George Parker hoped that Bruce MacDonald would bring good news from Canada. Ideally, he hoped to drop the oceanographic line and rebuild the "bridges" that used to exist between his firm and the manufacturer. A return to the close and helpful relationship that once existed would be welcomed. However, he wondered if EI's management wanted to operate in a more formal and distant "buy and sell" manner. If this were the case, George Parker would have to give more serious thought to the EI distributorship.

1. Discuss the role of overseas distributors and the value they contribute. What benefits can be realized using overseas distributors compared to other methods?
2. What is meant by "commitment to international marketing"? What is meant by "lip service to marketing"?
3. What should be done in the situation described in the case?

*This case was prepared by Professor Philip Rosson of Dalhousie University, Halifax, Nova Scotia.

30   LeClair Chemical Company*

"What the heck was I thinking . . . What did I get myself into . . ." Joe Foster wondered to himself as he prepared for the long drive from Montreal to Toronto. This was a trip that Joe was destined to become very familiar with.

Six weeks ago, Joe decided that his marketing career was stuck in the proverbial rut. He'd spent almost 25 years in the medical products industry. He'd begun as a salesman, and worked his way up to Eastern Division Sales and Marketing Manager for the Canadian branch of a large British firm. Joe had built strong relationships with the organizations of some of the largest hospitals from southern Ontario to St. John's, Newfoundland. He had built a solid reputation of being truly focused on his customers' needs. It was that reputation that led to the offer from LeClair.

LeClair Chemicals is a global chemicals company. Its Canadian headquarters are Toronto, Ontario. LeClair manufactures a well-known polymer known as "Plaston." Stanley Easterbrook, the business manager of LeClair's Plaston Division, was looking for ways to pull his "production-oriented" department into the 90s with more of a customer orientation. Through time, the Plaston division had developed the mindset that the only way to make money in the chemical industry was to concentrate on reducing manufacturing costs by continuously improving technology and keeping a sharp eye on fixed costs. Unfortunately, this led to a kind of "marketing myopia" that saw the division completely losing sight of the fact that it even had customers.

Stanley had heard of Joe's reputation through a golfing buddy, and decided to make Joe an offer to join his team. This would be the first step in Stanley's refocusing strategy. Financially, the offer looked quite attractive to Joe. But more importantly, it was a chance to try something completely different—almost like a new lease on life!

The Business of By-Products
"Joe, I think I have the perfect opportunity for you to demonstrate to our organization the power of the customer-oriented approach. And let me tell you something else, this is a tough problem that we really need to get resolved. So there are a couple of good reasons for getting you involved as soon as possible.

"You know, although Plaston has been around for many years, it is still widely used and the market is growing as new applications continue to be found. However, the growth is not rapid and Plaston is viewed as being well into the maturity phase of its life cycle."

Joe became more excited as Stanley finally began to get to the meat of his new adventure.

"There is a by-product in the manufacture of Plaston. It is a weak organic acid known in the industry as 'Triple A.' For many years, Triple A was treated as a waste product, and burned as fuel or simply disposed of in water sources. Several years ago, it was discovered that with minimal processing, Triple A could be converted into a useful product known as 'Solvent E.' Over these past few years, demand for Solvent E has grown rapidly, and LeClair now converts every pound of Triple A to Solvent E. There is an excellent margin on Solvent E, even higher than those received on the sale of Plaston.

"LeClair has enjoyed a position as the only manufacturer of Solvent E in North America. The European market for Solvent E is saturated by LeClair's Plaston competitors, and LeClair holds a small fraction of that market; the Asia-Pacific market is in its infancy. Now, one of LeClair's Plaston competitors in N.A. has announced that it will begin converting its Triple A to Solvent E and introduce it to the market. We expect that we will lose a significant amount of market share, and that there will also be an erosion in price.

"It has also been discovered that with no processing, Triple A can be sold directly for a rapidly growing environmental application. The margin on Triple A at this point is significantly lower than on Solvent E, but the market is growing rapidly.

"Due to the growth in concern for protection of the environment, simply burning or disposing of Triple A is not desirable—heck, it may not even be acceptable! You know, burning the stuff makes carbon dioxide which contributes to the greenhouse effect; and treating it means using lots of energy and still ending up with a final product to dispose of! Also, the Kyoto protocol makes it even more important to reduce greenhouse gas emissions. So, Joe, I want you to spend some time at our manufacturing facility in Montreal. All of our production and R&D folks are located there. They're good people—their focus is just oriented towards finding better ways to make Plaston and Solvent E. Work with them, Joe, make them part of the solution."

Highway 20 was now turning into the 401 just outside of Cornwall as Joe Foster's mind began to reflect on more recent events: his first meeting with the Plaston by-products team, the experts in the technology and production of Triple A and Solvent E.

The Production Team
Joe had started the meeting: "Guys, I've pulled this meeting together for a few reasons. First of all, I wanted to meet all of you face to face. We'll all be working together for a while, so a voice on the telephone or a name at the bottom of an e-mail is just not enough to build a relationship on—not in my books. Second, I wanted to gather together all of the information on the market situation around Solvent E and Triple A. I think we all have little pieces of the puzzle, and hopefully, today, we can pull it together. And finally, I'd like to talk about some potential strategies for proceeding. . . ."

"Well, I'll tell you what, you want some pieces in the puzzle, I'll give you a couple of the biggest ones," said Jim Pankhurst, the Solvent E production manager. "No matter what Easterbrook may have told you, the boys in Toronto don't give a fiddler's diddly about Triple A or Solvent E. LeClair's whole world revolves around Plaston. All of the company's energies are focused on Plaston. And every penny that's spent in Montreal is spent on improving the way we make Plaston. Triple A is an unfortunate necessity, and Solvent E is an opportunity for some publicity to make the environmentalists happy. We pulled together the Triple E manufacturing facility on a shoestring budget, and we haven't put a nickel into it since it was built."

"Don't let Jim scare you, Joe. He only talks that way because manufacturing managers are supposed to be rough and tough and most of all, grumpy!" There was a chuckle from the crowd as Linda Dubinski broke some of the tension created by Pankhurst. Linda was the technical specialist assigned to the Triple E unit. She had a great relationship with Jim and the rest of the team, so she could get away with a remark like that. "The reason that the Triple E plant was built on a shoestring budget is that it's quite simple to produce. I'm sure I could make it in my backyard with old oil tanks and some moonshine stills. As a matter of fact, the tollers who make 50 percent of Canada's Triple E product and all of the American product are basically 'Mom and Pop' chemical companies who do it in their backyards with second-hand equipment and dirt cheap labour."

"Yeah, there's a couple of key points in what you just said, Linda," responded Joe. "First, 90 percent of North America Plaston production is done by tollers. These companies take the Triple A and convert it to Solvent E at an agreed upon cost per pound. Even though it's sold as 'LeClair's Solvent E,' it was produced by the tollers. The second key point is that the barriers to entry into Solvent E production are almost nil!"

"Well, that second point isn't exactly correct, Joe," said Ron Wu, R&D specialist for Solvent E and Triple A applications. "Although anybody could make Solvent E, they need to have Triple A to start with. And the only people who have Triple A are the other Plaston producers. There isn't a snowball's chance in hell of new companies entering the Plaston business now—the economies of scale are much too large and the technology is much too complex. One other thing, Joe, is that I don't think we should too quickly disregard Jim's comments about the way Toronto looks at these by-products businesses."

Market Size and Production Capacity
"Thanks for the clarification, Ron," said Joe. "Can you give us a little more info on the production of Triple A and Solvent E that would help in our decision- making process?"
"Sure, Joe. I hate to steal any marketing thunder away from you, but some of the market numbers are key in understanding why the technical points are so critical."
"Seems to me that Ron just wants to show off his newly acquired MBA, don't you Ron?" joked Linda.
"Of course, Linda. I need to make sure that Jim knows about it when he starts handing out the raises in the spring!"
Jim half-smiled, as he knew that Ron was only half-joking.

"Anyway, let me continue. The global market for Plaston is about 500 million pounds a year. LeClair presently holds approximately 200 million pounds a year of that total market share. For every pound of Plaston produced, .01 pounds of Triple A are produced. So the global capacity for producing Triple A is 5 million pounds a year. Each pound of Triple A produced can be converted to 1 pound of Solvent E, so the global availability of raw material for producing Solvent E translates to 5 million pounds a year of potential Solvent E production." You could see Ron bursting with pride as he displayed his business knowledge.

"That's good information, Ron," said Foster. "Now let me add some info that I got from Stanley this week. The existing global market for Solvent E is approximately 1.5 million pounds. 0.5 million is in Europe and is being satisfied by European producers. LeClair has a production facility in Europe which is serving a small portion of the European market. The Asian Pacific market is approximately 0.25 million pounds. One of LeClair's Plaston competitors is serving approximately 0.10 million pounds of that market, and LeClair expects to have over 0.20 million pounds of production capacity in the Far East within the next two years."

"I wouldn't hold my breath on that Far East production capacity, Joe," said Jim Pankhurst, now trying to play down his "grumpy" image. "That's the Indonesia Plaston project, which is in the process of being one of the biggest screw-ups in LeClair history . . Then again, I don't think that matters a whole lot. I was always of the impression that the North American market was kind of independent."

"That's right, Jim," added Ron, "and the North American market for Solvent E is 0.75 million pounds and is presently served entirely by LeClair. LeClair's N.A. competitor is introducing almost 0.25 million pounds of Solvent E into the market this year."

"Well, I don't have an MBA," said Linda, "but I do know something about what's out there in terms of competitors: globally, there is about 5 million pounds a year of available Triple A, which translates into 5 million pounds of potential Solvent E production. All of the Plaston producers are under the same pressure from environmentalists to find more environmentally friendly ways to deal with their Triple A, so the market for Solvent E and the potential market for Triple A both look as if they will become extremely competitive in the next few years."

"Ron, is there any way to differentiate our Triple A and Solvent E?" asked Joe.
"Well, not significantly. We can make minor reductions in the levels of impurities in both products, but I don't know if our customers would see any value in it."

The Customers
Joe saw his opportunity at this point to shift the conversation toward the customers. "You know, as we've been talking, we've looked at the size of the market, and we've even alluded to some of the applications for these products, but we haven't really talked about our customers. What do we know about them?"

"Joe" said Linda, "I have had several opportunities to deal with Solvent E customers in resolving quality issues. I think I could give you a little insight into their wants and needs."
"Go ahead, Linda," said Joe.
"Well, nobody uses Solvent E in the kind of volumes we make. We have many, many customers who use small amounts of Solvent E. We sell the solvent in bulk loads to three or four distributors, who then put it into drums and bottles to be sold to the final users. The distributors do all the sales. We simply provide them with technical data and they try to match the product with the user—as well as giving the sales pitch about Solvent E's 'environmental superiority.' "

"And who are the final users?" asked Joe.

"Well, it's the same people who buy any kind of organic solvent—you know, companies who paint or coat things. The last one I visited put plastic coatings on clothes hangers. When you visit these places, you can smell all the other coatings they use—the acetone, methyl-ethyl ketone, iso-propyl alcohol—it's kind of gross, actually."

"That's the best thing about Solvent E, Linda," interrupted Ron. "It has similar solvent properties to those other chemicals you mentioned, but it doesn't evaporate as easily. This reduces the amount of volatile organic compounds—VOCs—that make their way into the atmosphere."

"Was that what you were referring to, Jim, when you mentioned that LeClair got good publicity out of Solvent E?" asked Joe.
"That's right, Joe. The Solvent E goes a long way to providing the coaters with some good enviro publicity, but the bottom line is still the bottom line. We've lost customers before when we've driven the price too high—just remember that there are plenty of low-cost alternatives out there. They'll pay an environmental premium, but only to a certain point!"

"Good point, Jim—those industries are really competitive and margins are really tight," said Joe, excited to see the team shifting their focus toward their customers. "That will be extremely important when competitors start driving their Solvent E into the market. Now, what do you guys know about Triple A?"

"I've been involved with some of the applications research for Triple A, Joe," said Ron. "It's a weak organic acid, so industries use it to control the pH in the water used to scrub contaminated air before it leaves their plants. It's the heavy industries like steel making and copper and nickel smelting that use it to scrub their effluent gases."

"So, what added value does Triple A bring to these industries," asked Joe.
"Well actually, not a heck of a lot. There are many, many low-cost alternatives out there that will do the same job. That's why the margins are so much lower than what we see in Solvent E. However, the total volume of organic acids used in these industries is incredible. If we could make Triple A the acid of choice," added Ron, "we could easily sell every drop of it."
"Do we also sell Triple A through distributors?" asked Joe.
"No," said Pankhurst. "At least I don't think so. We're not really selling any of it right now, but for the trial runs, we shipped in tank trucks directly from our plant. Remember, they use tons of this stuff. The guy you replaced, Jack Burns, set it all up with the two steel mills where we ran the tests."

Strategic Options
"OK guys, I'm starting to get the picture now. What do you think are some of our options?" asked Joe. "Ron, you already talked about trying to sell all of the Triple A to the industrial scrubbing market. What else can we do?"

"Well," said Linda, "if this company really wants to show what it's made of, I would suggest we invest in our own manufacturing facilities. We could reduce our variable costs by eliminating the fees we pay to tollers, and it wouldn't increase our fixed costs. The lower production costs would allow us to go head to head with our competitors and hold on to a big share of the Solvent E market." Linda was always a risk taker. "You know what else bugs me, is that we let distributors sell our Solvent E. These guys are also selling all of the alternative solvents that compete with Solvent E. We need to spend some money on promotion, Joe."

"Another option is to put some money into finding new applications for one or both products, so that we can expand the total market," added Ron. "Or along that same line we could see if we could find ways to process Triple A so that it's differentiated from all the other organic acids out there."

"All of those things cost money, guys," said Jim. "Joe, let me tell you what you've got to do, first and foremost: you've got to get Easterbrook to define exactly how LeClair is going to look at by-products. If we're a waste-processing division, then we can take low margins, or even stand to lose a few bucks. Our strategy would be quite different than if we were a real SBU, with profit objectives and all that stuff! I have a feeling that the strategy will come down to deciding on the mix of Solvent E and Triple A to make in order to minimize the amount we have to burn. By the way, we have to pay a penny a pound to burn Triple A, so the environmentalists are not our only concern here."

"What about lobbying for legislation to reduce VOCs so that coating industries will be forced to use more Solvent E?" asked Ron. "I saw this kind of strategy in a case study in a marketing course I just completed."

"That's not a bad thought," answered Joe. "But it sounds kind of risky—we're going to ask the government to force our customers to increase their operating costs. If I were them, I'd be sending LeClair a very clear message by buying any Solvent E I needed from somebody else!

"Guys, I've got to get back to Toronto tonight. Let me bring your ideas back to Easterbrook to see how he reacts, and we'll have another go at this next week. Thanks a lot for your help, and it's been great meeting all of you."

Joe had to stop for gas in Belleville, where he started mulling over all the information he received from the production team that day. "The team had some great ideas, I really must tell Stanley that these guys are a lot further along than he believes. I need to know if anyone will be willing to spend the kind of money those guys were talking about. I wonder if we can reduce our costs enough to keep our competitors out of the Solvent E market and let them fight over the 'Triple A scraps' ? What about playing 'wait and see,' and responding to our competitors' moves . . . or what about some market research to see if we can differentiate ourselves through customer service . . . LeClair's got some good experience in coatings . . . I think . . . man . . . all of a sudden, I'm longing for the smell of hospital hallways!"

1   Should LeClair invest in facilities to manufacture their own Solvent E?
2   Should there be any changes in promotional activities or channels of distribution?
3   Should there be an increase in R&D expenditure to find new applications or new users for Triple A and Solvent E to expand their total market?
4   Is differentiation for this type of product a possibility?

*© 1996. Faculty of Administration, University of Ottawa. This case was prepared by Joe Menchefski under the supervision of Dr. David S. Litvack, who at the time of its preparation was associated with the University of Ottawa.

31   The Parks Canada Dilemma*

Jennie Sparkes, the national visitor-risk management specialist, was in her office trying to develop her recommendations for the future course of public safety communications at Parks Canada (www.parkscanada.ca). A client-oriented approach required identification of which segment(s) of the population should be targeted and the types of message themes which would be most effective in creating awareness and encouraging changed behaviours in the segment(s) leading to fewer occasions requiring the intervention of Parks Canada Public Safety Specialists.

After reviewing the many reports on her desk, Jennie understood the meaning of being stuck between a rock and a hard place.

It is estimated that more than 25 million person visits are made annually to Canada's 38 national parks, 4 national marine conservation areas, 129 national historic sites and 9 historic canals. It is expected that the number of visitors will almost double over the next ten years. Part of the increase will be due to the opening of new national parks, bringing the total to more than 50 covering more than 2 percent of Canada's land. These new parks are, for the most part, located in wilderness areas, away from communications and Parks Canada resources. The balance of the increase in visits will come from the aging population, who will spend more on recreation, and from federal government initiatives to encourage domestic and foreign tourists to visit Canada's heritage areas.

In spite of the projected increase in visitor activity, Parks Canada has experienced significant reductions in funding and personnel. Additional cuts will occur over the next few years.

In 1986, Parks Canada adopted a policy whereby responsibility for public safety is shared between visitors and Parks Canada. Parks Canada is responsible for visitor risk management and public safety planning, building and maintaining facilities (such as trails, hazard signs and overpasses to prevent wildlife from crossing in front of traffic), and working with other government departments and non-governmental agencies to provide trip planning and safety information, as well as search and rescue services.

The visitor also has a responsibility. While some visitors recognize the risks involved in outdoor recreation, and are prepared for their adventures, many others don't know what they're getting into. That means they're unable to choose effectively between taking a smart risk and a foolhardy one.

This policy does not negate any legal responsibility that the government may have but actively solicits the visitor's participation in the safety process (see Exhibit 1 for a generic example). Parks Canada recognizes that a generic safety message may only be accepted by some people, and may not be recognized and acted on by those people who can benefit the most from the information.

Risk management is a science that takes into consideration many factors including:
- The frequency of the incident occurring.

- The extent of the potential loss (consequences).
- The costs of search and rescue efforts.
- The costs of activities to prevent or reduce the occurrence of the risk.

Some types of risks can be eliminated or significantly reduced by education, training and the use of suitable equipment. However some incidents are completely unpredictable and are considered acts of God (see Exhibit 2 for examples of incidents that may be reduced).

Since Parks Canada does not have the resources to address all possible risk situations, the risk management factors need to be included in the decision as to which market segment(s) to concentrate on. That cost–benefit analysis is a key factor in prioritizing potential risk reduction strategies.

As the result of effective risk management activities, benefits should accrue to both visitors and Parks Canada.

    (a) Increased visitor satisfaction because of fewer incidents of loss or physical injury and an increased sense of personal control or management over the activities pursued.

    (b) Reduced costs to Parks Canada in mounting search and rescue efforts and less need to provide physical barriers to protect visitors. That is, increased visitors' responsibility will translate into reduced visitors' loss incidents and therefore into reduced search and rescue costs.

    (c) Reduced risk of lawsuits.

One might think that presenting messages that relate to shared responsibility for personal safety would not have any competition. This is far from the truth.

One frequently featured type of competing media message promotes risk as glamorous and sexy. This type of message is often implied in lifestyle advertising (e.g., beer and car advertisers frequently target youth with messages that risk is attractive and sexy). Similar messages often appear in movie and TV program situations, where the risk takers almost always succeed and in addition gain the admiration of others, especially attractive people of the opposite sex.

A second type of conflicting message is based on promoting risk as part of the total product experience. Adventure vacations such as white-water rafting and wilderness treks often feature risk. Not only is the type of message often in conflict with safety messages, but the use of expert guides and special equipment tends to mask the danger of these activities for those who are not as skilled or well equipped.

Similarly, some marketers of outdoor gear portray their products as a means to control personal risk. That is, the products represent a "quick" means of obtaining an experience that once required the development of an extensive skill set.

Finally, competition comes from other organizations, which also promote safety. The multitude of safety-related messages may impact in two negative ways. First, the multitude of safety messages may produce wear-out of all safety messages (i.e., people will ignore the existence of all safety messages). Second, different and sometimes conflicting messages may produce confusion and interfere with people adopting the desired behaviour. For example, the Parks Canada message that you are responsible for avoiding trouble is very different in meaning and implication from messages from other organizations, which proudly proclaim that we are there to help you if you get into trouble.

Over the years, Parks Canada has looked at many possible ways to segment the visitor market. Although marketing research studies have profiled some possible market segments, Parks Canada has not, at this time, commissioned a specific definitive segmentation project for a public safety communications strategy.

The following section outlines some of the possible segments considered by Parks Canada:

(a) Male/Female

- Statistics indicate that although the types of incidents vary by sex, the sexes appear almost equally in the list of Parks Canada interventions.

(b) Age

- Older people, say over 40 years of age, tend to participate in less risky and less strenuous activities. However, aging baby boomers are now in this life cycle stage and will constitute the largest single market segment. Park wardens are already reporting an increased number of rescues involving knee problems (associated with aging). In addition, mountain bikes allow the general public to access areas previously visited only by people in top physical condition.
- Young people 16 to 24 years of age have the highest rate of accidents per 1,000 visitors to Parks Canada. This is consistent with other research findings by the Smart Risk Foundation and the Canadian Red Cross (Drowning Reports). These people often feel immortal—death happens to older people—and take unadvisable risks. As a group, this age category tends to resent authority and is less likely to read and follow safety information.

(c) Type of Experience Sought and Activity

In general terms, there appears to be five types of visitors:

- Extreme Recreational Adventurist
  - These individuals seek a high degree of risk as an element of their experience and tend to participate in activities requiring physical fitness, preparedness, skill and ability. Typical activities include mountain climbing, ice climbing, and ski mountaineering.
- Active Recreational Adventurist
  - Individuals in this category expect various degrees of risk in their activities and are often experienced and well-prepared for personal challenges. Participants in this category engage in moderate risk activities, such as rock climbing, back country hiking, and skiing.
- Recreationalist
  - Recreationalists tend to favour high-use activities where facilities are provided and where a sense of security is evident. Seeking educational, discovery, and personal growth experiences, these visitors participate in less

adventurous activities, such as boating, swimming, and back-country hiking and camping.

- Passive Recreationalist
  - o These visitors participate in leisure activities in scenic nature or interesting cultural settings. Seeking relaxation, fun, and entertainment, this group tends to rely on information and Park facilities in predominantly high visitor use areas.
- Touring Recreationalist
  - o These visitors seek the company of others, security, convenience, and facilities in low-risk activities where little preparation is required. Activities typical of this group include bus tours, educational group hikes, pleasure driving, and special events.

(d) By Education Level

- It might be reasonable to assume that the higher a person's level of education (and IQ) the more likely is the individual to be risk adverse. This is not true. A disproportionately large number of people who visit heritage areas are highly educated. Because they are not really mentally challenged at school and work, they seek out physical challenges sometimes resulting in injury and death.

Exhibit 1 Examples of Situations Involving Parks Canada Personnel

Peer Pressure Leads to Tragedy
Maligne Canyon at Jasper National Park is rugged, steep, and deep. At places, the edges of the canyon narrow and are very close together. At one spot in particular, young thrill seekers have been known to dare one another to jump across. Some visitors dared a 12-year-old boy to jump. He jumped, slipped, and fell to his death.

A Tense Night in the Woods
A mother and her two children were hiking by the ocean at Long Beach. When they tried to return to their campsite, they missed the signs indicating the trail and became lost in the dense bush. When the hikers did not return, Parks Canada launched a search with a helicopter and searchers on the ground. The three lost hikers were found the next day cold but alive, after spending the night huddled together in a rainstorm.

Unforgiving Lake
Lake Superior is well known for its treacherous conditions, as demonstrated by the experience of four canoeists. In two canoes, they rounded a headland on a late August afternoon and encountered large waves. By the time they realized the conditions outmatched their expertise, both canoes were swamped and capsized. Fortunately, the visitors were outfitted with PFDs and good floatation gear and were able to withstand the cold water long enough to be rescued by Park Wardens.

Dishwasher Dies
In the spring of 1993, three young men attempted to climb a steep slope west of the waterfall on Cascade Mountain. The three friends, employees of a nearby hotel, climbed

through the thinning forest toward the base of a large cliff, led by the one with the most scrambling experience. The two inexperienced scramblers fell behind and the group was eventually separated. One straggler slipped on the shale and tumbled 130 m to his death.

Swept Away

In 1992, a family from Great Britain was visiting Pacific Rim National Park. The father and his two sons, unaware of the power of the ocean, went down onto the rocks to get a better look at the monstrous waves that were pounding the beach. They had worked themselves out onto a dangerous and exposed area when a large wave swept the three out to sea. Luckily, the father and the younger son were tossed back onto the rocks on the next wave. They then had 10 to 15 seconds to scramble to safety before another wave hit. Unfortunately, the man's other teenage son was not as lucky. He was pulled out to sea. Despite an intensive multi-agency SAR comprising Parks Canada, the Coast Guard, and the RCMP, the boy was never found.

The $50,000 Search

A woman hiking in the Rainbow Lakes trail area of Wood Buffalo National Park became lost and failed to return to her car. An intensive search was launched involving park personnel, the RCMP, GNWT Renewable Territorial Five Centre personnel, GNWT Department of Highways workers, and local volunteers. The search involved a helicopter outfitted with an infrared scanner, ground search teams, and specially trained search dogs. In order to increase the chances of locating the woman, search coordinators used the Mattson Consensus technique to plot the most likely search areas. The woman was found alive and in good condition, after a 75-hour search that cost $50,000.

Broken Ankle

A woman hiking in the vicinity of Edith Pass broke her ankle after slipping on an exposed tree root. Several hours passed before friends notified the Warden Office. The subsequent rescue required wardens to transport her several hundred metres by stretcher and then by heli-sling to the highway and a waiting ambulance.

A Needless Death

A 19-year-old Quebec man stumbled over a cliff and fell more than 60 metres to his death in Banff National park while trying to retrieve his diary. The man was part of a group who were descending the steep back side of Tunnel Mountain. Somehow the person's pack, including the diary, went over the edge. He started to scramble down to look for it and slid over a steep edge and was killed.

According to a Public Safety Warden, people hike up Tunnel Mountain every day without mishap. But a growing number of adventure-seeking hikers, usually young men, stray off the well-travelled path and venture onto the exceedingly steep, forested slope.
Source: Visitor Risk Management Handbook, 1994, Parks Canada

At the other end of the scale, there is an education/ skill category referred to as "the Pot Scrubber" by Parks Wardens. This describes a young person, often a school drop-out with no skills, who gets a job in or near a Park (often doing dishes in a restaurant) so that he/she can do exciting activities in the Park. The lack of skills and education make him/her a prime candidate to become a statistic.

Exhibit 2 Socio-Cultural Profile of Young People (15–24 years)

Key descriptions include:
- take risks for the thrill of risks
- interested in the novel/unusual
- free to act as an adult
- accepting of violence
- adaptable to complex challenges/difficulties
- hedonistic
- sexually permissive
- confident in technology, business, and advertising
- more influenced by emotion than by reason

Issues of no interest include:
- health
- mortality
- fear
- family
- financial concerns

Source: Selected Marketing Research Results from Parks Canada Studies

After reviewing the segments, it became apparent that these segments are not mutually exclusive and perhaps there are other possible segmentation bases which may be relevant.

Exhibit 3 Self-Reliant Message Example (responsibility of park users)

You are responsible for your own safety We expect that you:
- are aware of the natural hazards
- are properly equipped and provisioned
- have the adequate knowledge, skill and fitness level
- are prepared for emergencies

Do you need information? We'd like to help you with:
- hazards information
- back country trip planning
- route information and advice
- voluntary safety registration for high risk activities

Source: Parks Canada Posters

Jennie looked out of her office window and saw the sun shining on the tree-lined Ottawa River and, in the background, on the House of Commons. She realized that she could not leave work today without reaching a decision on which segment(s) to concentrate on, and why.

1   Which market segments are in most danger?

2   What are the possibilities of changing the behaviour in each market segment? Which segments should be targeted and why?

3   What type of message themes are most appropriate for each such segment? Why do you say this?

*This case was written by Maurice Borts and Jim Mintz. The authors acknowledge the advice and encouragement of Per Nilsen, Head Appropriate Activity, Assessment and Risk Management, Department of Canadian Heritage. At the time of the case's preparation, Maurice Borts was associated with McGill University, and Jim Mintz was Director, Marketing and Partnership Division, Health Canada. Copyright 1996 Marketec Business Consultants Ltd. All rights reserved. No portion of this case may be reproduced by any means without the prior written permission of Marketec.

32   Sure-Grow Fertilizers*

It was a cool, rainy day in March 2004, and Len Dow, manager of Sure-Grow Fertilizers, was sitting in his office looking over the past season's records. Volume in 2003 was 10,000 tonnes (see Exhibit 1) and the profit margin was approximately 6%. In spite of this good performance, Len was not completely satisfied; he wanted to increase the volume and profitability of the outlet, but was not sure what direction he should take.

The Company

Sure-Grow Fertilizers is located in Goodland, a town in the middle of a major corn and potato producing area of Ontario. Sure-Grow does most of its business within a five-mile radius of Goodland (60%); however, it does have some sales and distribution extending 20 miles from its plant (35%), and a very small wholesale market over 100 miles away in Northern Ontario (5%). At the present time, Sure-Grow is involved only in the sale of fertilizers and related services. Dry bulk blends and bagged blends make up the majority of Sure-Grow's fertilizer volume (9,000 tonnes) with 28% liquid nitrogen making up a much smaller portion (1,000 tonnes). Potato and vegetable farmers purchase almost 60% of Sure-Grow's production, corn and cereal farmers account for 33%, and sod farmers purchase the remaining 7% (see Exhibit 2). Sure-Grow's dry fertilizer plant has a peak season capacity of approximately 10,000 tonnes under ideal conditions.

Sure-Grow sells a custom application service for bulk fertilizers and rents application equipment to farmers who wish to apply their own fertilizer. Since Len purchased the organization, he has cut the full-time staff from seven to five including himself. One of his newest employees is a young agricultural university graduate who spends most of his time in a sales capacity calling on present and potential customers in the area. Len also spends some of his time making farm calls. Of Sure-Grow's 85 local customers in 2004, five are merchant dealers who resell to farmers. These five dealers account for 2,000 tonnes of Sure-Grow's business and range in volume from 100 to 1,000 tonnes each. For the most part these dealers are located on the fringes of Sure-Grow's 20-mile trading area. Of the remaining 80 local customers, Len's records show that 70 are within five miles of the Goodland plant and ten are at a greater distance. Almost all of these customers are large farmers who purchase more than 50 tonnes of fertilizer a year from Sure-Grow.

Exhibit 1: Sure Grow Fertilizer Sales

Year	Liquid and dry fertilizers (tonnes)	Micronutrients (tonnes)
1999	10,000	—
2000	10,000	—
2001	7,000	—
2002	8,400	10
2003	10,000	100

Sure-Grow sold 10 tonnes of micronutrients in 2002 and over 100 tonnes in 2003. Micronutrients are basic elements that a plant requires in relatively small amounts, compared to the larger amounts of nitrogen, phosphorus, and potassium found in most regular, blended fertilizers. Micronutrients have been proven by university and industry research in the U.S. to improve the quality and yield of crops. Commercial trials carried out in Ontario have indicated similar positive results.

The Market and Competition

The total market for fertilizer in Sure-Grow's trading area has been remarkably stable at approximately 50,000 tonnes for the past several years. This is not expected to change significantly in the future although some shifts in types used are possible. Within five miles of Goodland there are four major fertilizer outlets competing with Sure-Grow for approximately 25,000 tonnes of fertilizer business, and within 20 miles there are an additional three fertilizer outlets competing for the remaining 25,000 tonnes. Len estimates that there are approximately 550 farmers within a five-mile radius of Goodland.

Although the market for fertilizer is very competitive, Len feels that he has been able to better his competition by offering excellent service, by remaining open extended hours, by offering advice and timely delivery to his customers, and by knowing how to deal with the large farmer. Len quickly came to realize that farmers place service ahead of price when deciding where to buy fertilizer as long as the price is close to that of the competition. Len feels that by offering a superior service, he has nurtured a high level of dealer loyalty in his customers which has resulted in a lower turnover relative to his competition.

Exhibit 2: Sure-Grow Fertilizer Sales By Farm Type

Farm type	Percentage of dry fertilizer sales	Percent of acres served
Potato and vegetable	60%	35%
Corn and cereals	33%	60%
Sod	7%	5%

Growth Opportunities

Although the business has been doing well, Len realizes that growth is essential to future success. He therefore has been giving this matter considerable thought the past couple of months. So far, he has been able to identify several avenues of growth; now his problem is to evaluate each and arrive at a plan for 2004 and beyond.

Liquid nitrogen

Len has been toying with the idea of getting into 28% liquid nitrogen in a bigger way. He estimates that a total of 4,000 tonnes of 28% liquid nitrogen were sold in his 20-mile trading area in 2003, of which Sure-Grow sold 1,000 tonnes to three large corn farmers. Because of its ease of handling, liquid nitrogen is of particular interest to larger farmers.

Although the price per tonne of liquid nitrogen is usually less than the price per tonne of nitrogen in a granular form such as urea, comparisons between the two can be made only after adjusting for the percentage of actual nitrogen in each form. Because liquid nitrogen contains 28% actual nitrogen and urea contains 45% actual nitrogen, a farmer would need to purchase a greater volume of liquid nitrogen than urea to reach the same level of actual nitrogen applied to his crop.

Liquid nitrogen is very corrosive, which means that the farmer must purchase a stainless steel sprayer costing about $2,000 if he is to use 28% liquid nitrogen. This relatively high initial capital outlay is another factor restricting use to fairly large farmers. Of the 400 corn farmers in his trading area, approximately 200 have sufficient acreage to be possible 28% liquid nitrogen users, and Len estimates that about 20 farmers were using 28% liquid nitrogen in 2003. Price is the major purchase criterion since the product is a commodity and little service is involved. Len felt that well over half of the 28% liquid nitrogen in the Goodland area is sold in December for delivery in the spring (see Exhibit 3 for prices, costs, and margins).

Exhibit 3: Fertilizer Prices and Margins

	Dry fertilizer $/tonne	%	LN winter $/tonne	%	LN spring $/tonne	%	Micronutrients $/tonne	%
Selling price	$248	100	$138	100	$170	100	$700	100
Cost of sales	$203	82	$131	95	$136	80	$595	85
Margin	$45	18	$7	5	$34	20	$105	15
Fixed costs	$260,000		$15,000				$5,000	

Sure-Grow's current holding capacity for liquid nitrogen is 10,000 gallons or 50 tonnes. If output is increased, additional storage and nurse tanks would have to be purchased, as well as another pumping system. A pumping system costs $4,000, storage tanks cost 15 cents per gallon, and a 1,400 gallon nurse tank costs $1,000. Len feels that one additional pumping system, one more 10,000 gallon storage tank, and two more nurse tanks should be sufficient to allow for a large increase in sales.

No matter what Len decides to do, he wants to stay ahead of his competition by at least two years. Because he feels that 28% liquid nitrogen could be a big thing in the future, he is excited about this possibility. Recently, he saw a new type of potato planter which required only liquid fertilizer. If this type of planter became popular, the potential for liquid fertilizer could increase dramatically.

Despite these positive feelings about this market, Len was concerned about the relatively low liquid nitrogen margins and the slow growth of this market in the past.

Micronutrients
Another opportunity confronting Len was to try to expand micronutrient sales in a major way. Currently, Sure-Grow is a dealer for the Taylor Chemical Company, which produces and sells a complete line of micronutrients. Included in their line are manganese, zinc, iron, copper, molybdenum, boron, calcium, and sulfur. These materials are sold separately or in various combinations designed to treat specific crops. An example of the latter is the

company's vegetable mix, which contains magnesium, sulfur, copper, iron, manganese, and zinc in fixed proportions. The individual materials and mixes are sold in two forms: (1) dry for mixing by the dealer with other fertilizer products, and (2) liquid for spray application by the farmer on the foliage of the growing crop. Although foliar application is more bother for the farmer, and may result in some leaf burning, some farmers prefer it because they can postpone micronutrient application until visible signs of deficiencies are present. Also, there is some research which indicates that micronutrients can be most effective if absorbed through the leaves at the peak growth period of the plant. Despite the apparent advantages of foliar application, Len has not sold any micronutrients in this form during his first two years in this business. If properly applied, he feels that liquid micronutrients offer the most value to his customers, yet he has noticed some reluctance and scepticism on the part of even the most progressive farmers in his area to try this product form.

Sales of dry, mixed micronutrients have grown considerably over the past year, and it appears that the product offers real value to customers. One of Len's customers applied micronutrients to half of a large potato field, and none to the other half. The treated portion yielded 327 hundredweight of potatoes compared to only 304 hundredweight on the untreated portion. This 23 hundredweight gain resulted in a $111.55 per acre revenue increase for the farmer when computed at the current $4.85 per hundredweight price for potatoes. Unfortunately, the University of Guelph, which many farmers look to for technical information, is not promoting or even recommending the use of micronutrients (see Exhibit 4). Their soil testing service, which analyzes soil samples and makes fertilizer use recommendations, doesn't even include an analysis for micronutrients. Len feels that competitors do not want to get involved in this business unless there is a very high demand and not being involved starts to affect their other fertilizer business.

Of the 100 tonnes sold in 2003, 75 went to six large potato farmers representing 3,500 acres, 10 tonnes went to vegetable farmers, and 15 tonnes went to corn farmers (see Exhibit 5 for rates and costs per acre). Len has been receiving excellent service and advice from the company distributing the micronutrients. He feels that the use of micronutrients is becoming accepted by the farmers using them, and that sales should rise in the future. Len chuckled to himself as he recalled the day two very large potato farmers who were brothers were sitting in his office and the subject of micronutrients came up. One of the brothers, Jack, asked the Taylor sales rep if he thought they should be using micronutrients. The sales rep related all of the advantages of using micronutrients to them, whereupon Jack turned to his brother Peter and asked, "Well, what do you think?" Peter replied, "Yes, I think we should be using them." With that Len landed a micronutrients order worth several thousand dollars.

Exhibit 4: No Substitutes for Rotation

This past year there has been a lot of interest in Perth and Huron counties about micronutrients. There are numerous plots out this year with different formulations and mixes and ways of application, both on corn and beans. We are sure there will be a lot of discussion this winter about the subject.

Some things are becoming evident about micronutrients, at least we think they are. The first is that you cannot expect dramatic yield increases with individual nutrients on small areas.

Secondly, none of the micronutrient sales staff has been able to explain to us the problem of over-applying micronutrients. They suggest if you put on too much potash you may tie up magnesium. If you put on too much phosphorus, you may need to put on more zinc and manganese. We believe, with our variable soils, in some fields you can put on too much zinc and manganese.

Finally, these micronutrients seem to be most attractive to growers with poor crop rotations. Some of your neighbors have gone to poor crop rotations and their yields have dropped. (You know they are the ones that think Pioneer corn followed by Cargill corn is crop rotation.) Now they are searching for something to pull their yield back to former highs. Micronutrients appear to them to be an answer.

What puzzles us is why some of you are willing to spend large sums of money on products you are not sure will work: shotgun micro-nutrients. We both know what the problem is. You have to get more crops into the rotation, especially perennial forages. I suppose the bottom line is when you hear your neighbor talking about all the micronutrients he is using. That's just a polite way for him to tell you he has a terrible crop rotation.

Exhibit 5: Micronutrient Sales By Crop Application, 2003

Crop	tonnes sold	Acres	rate	Cost/Acre
Potatoes	75	3,500	50#/acre	$15.90
Corn	15	1,300	25#/acre	$ 8.00
Vegetables	10	400	50#/acre	$15.90

Len was convinced that micronutrients had potential in his area. His major concern was how he could convince farmers to spend an additional $10 to $15 per acre on a product for which there was no objective basis for determining need.

Northern Ontario

Len also was considering expanding sales in Northern Ontario. Currently he has three dealers selling bagged fertilizer for Sure-Grow in Sault Ste. Marie, Thunder Bay, and Sudbury. Sure-Grow's current volume in Northern Ontario is approximately 500 tonnes of bagged fertilizer only. Several Co-op outlets have most of the market in this area. Prices are very competitive and there appears to be some farmer loyalty to the Co-ops. There are many small farms in the region with 75 to 100 acres of workable land per farm. The crop types in the area are mixed grain, barley, hay, and a few hundred acres of potatoes near Sudbury. On the average, farmers in Northern Ontario who use fertilizer purchase 2 to 3 tonnes of bagged fertilizer per year and do their purchasing in the winter months. Because the retail price of fertilizer in Northern Ontario is similar to that around Goodland, the margins to Sure-Grow are reduced by about $17 a tonne, the sum of the $12 dealer commission and the $5 freight cost. The lower margins are offset to some extent by lower personal selling costs, since dealers are used. Although the growing season in Northern Ontario is only two to three weeks behind that of Goodland, because most sales occur in the winter months, Sure-Grow's ability to service the Goodland area in the spring is not affected by what they do in Northern Ontario.

In addition to the lower margins earned on sales in Northern Ontario, Len is also concerned about possible credit problems, particularly because the cost of collection could run very high due to the distance involved. On the more positive side, Len is quite optimistic about the long-run potential growth of this market. He feels that there is a total industry potential in this market of 60,000 tonnes of dry fertilizer, of which less than 20% has been developed at the present time.

Agricultural chemicals

So far, Sure-Grow's product line consists only of fertilizers. Len observed, however, that all of his competitors were carrying insecticides, herbicides, and fungicides as well. Although he always believed that concentrating on one line was the way to go, lately he has wondered if he shouldn't be getting into the agricultural chemical business. By doing this, he would be able to better meet the needs of some customers who prefer to purchase more products from the same supplier. It could also be a way for Len to attract new customers that he could sell fertilizer to as well as agricultural chemicals. In the past, Len sized up his customers as not wanting to buy everything from one dealer, so he was satisfied to receive all or most of their fertilizer business and to leave agricultural chemicals to other dealers. Increasingly, he has wondered if this assessment was correct.

Agricultural chemicals are very competitively priced, leaving small margins in the neighbourhood of 5% to 10% for the dealer. The set-up costs for carrying chemicals would be approximately $20,000 for warehouse upgrading. No other direct costs would be attributable to the chemical line, but Len knew that servicing the line would take valuable time away from servicing and selling the fertilizer line, which could possibly result in lower sales and profits. Len estimated that the average farmer in his trading area spent $3,000 to $5,000 per year on agricultural chemicals.

Exhibit 6: Results of Fertilizer Marketing Research Study

1. Only 7 percent of total crop acreage in southern Ontario is not fertilized at the present time. This acreage is almost entirely in soybeans, pasture, and forages.

2. The average fertilizer application rate for southern Ontario farmers is 384 pounds per acre. Most farmers use soil test recommendations from the University of Guelph to determine the application rate. There is some tendency for farmers to apply more fertilizer than recommended by their soil tests.

3. The major types of fertilizer used by southern Ontario farmers are dry bulk blends and liquid nitrogen. Of lesser importance are dry bagged fertilizers, anhydrous ammonia, and liquid mixes (N-P-K). Liquid nitrogen fertilizers are almost exclusively used by very large farmers.

4. Most farmers find the quality and availability of fertilizers to be very good.

5   In southern Ontario as a whole, a relatively small percentage of farmers purchase a large percentage of the fertilizer products sold. The breakdown is as follows:

   a.   About two-thirds of all dry fertilizers are sold to farmers in April and May. Only one-third of liquid fertilizers are sold in the spring.

   b.   Thirty percent of Ontario farmers use dealer custom application services, while 70 percent apply the fertilizer themselves using rented dealer application equipment. There is some tendency for larger farmers to be more inclined to want custom application services.

6   In the course of a year, farmers discuss their fertilizer program with a number of parties to get information and advice on various aspects of fertilizer use and dealer selection. The influence groups most widely consulted are the local fertilizer dealer, other farmers, and family members. In addition to these influence groups, fertilizer company representatives, agricultural extension officials, and university scientists are consulted by some farmers. In the case of company representatives and university scientists, proportionately more larger farmers visit these people than smaller farmers.

7   Farmers also obtain fertilizer information from soil test results, various government publications, company-sponsored farmer meetings, dealer demonstration plots, and company and dealer displays at farm shows and fairs.

8   Over 60% of all farmers contact more than one fertilizer dealer before making a purchase. Larger farmers have a tendency to contact more dealers than smaller farmers.

9   Over 50% of all farmers reported receiving an on-farm call by a fertilizer dealer in the last year. Larger farmers reported receiving more dealer calls than smaller farmers.

10   In addition to fertilizers, southern Ontario farmers purchase, on the average, more than three other products from their fertilizer supplier. Of these, the most common are herbicides, insecticides, general farm supplies, and seeds. Large farmers are more likely to purchase herbicides and insecticides from their fertilizer supplier than small farmers.

11   Six dealer services were identified as being essential to all but a very small proportion of farmers: application equipment that is available when needed and in good repair; custom application services; custom fertilizer blending; fertilizer information through a well-informed staff, brochures, newsletters, and farmer meetings; soil testing; and demonstrations.

12   Other dealer services that were reported as being important to smaller groups of farmers were crop management assistance, help in securing expert assistance with problems, and custom herbicide application.

13   Dealer location, price, and availability of product when needed are the major factors farmers consider when selecting a fertilizer dealer. In general, dealer location and availability of product when needed are more important to smaller farmers, while price is more important to larger farmers.

14   Over 45% of all farmers purchase fertilizer from their nearest dealer. On the average, farmers purchase from dealers located less than five miles from their farms.

15   Thirty percent of all farmers purchase from more than one dealer. Larger farmers have a greater tendency to spread their purchases over more dealers than do small farmers.

16   Analysis of dealer switching showed that one-third of the farmers made no dealer changes in the past five years, one-third made only one change, and the remaining one-third made two or more changes. Those farmers making several dealer changes are the larger, younger farmers.

Exhibit 6 Results of Fertilizer Marketing Research Study (continued)

Size categories	% of farmers	% of purchases
Under 25 tonnes	30%	10%
26–50 tonnes	35%	25%
51–100 tonnes	20%	20%
Over 100 tonnes	15%	45%

1   Only 7 percent of total crop acreage in southern Ontario is not fertilized at the present time. This acreage is almost entirely in soybeans, pasture, and forages.

2   The average fertilizer application rate for southern Ontario farmers is 384 pounds per acre. Most farmers use soil test recommendations from the University of Guelph to determine the application rate. There is some tendency for farmers to apply more fertilizer than recommended by their soil tests.

3   The major types of fertilizer used by southern Ontario farmers are dry bulk blends and liquid nitrogen. Of lesser importance are dry bagged fertilizers, anhydrous ammonia, and liquid mixes (N-P-K). Liquid nitrogen fertilizers are almost exclusively used by very large farmers.

4   Most farmers find the quality and availability of fertilizers to be very good.

5   In southern Ontario as a whole, a relatively small percentage of farmers purchase a large percentage of the fertilizer products sold. The breakdown is as follows:

6   About two-thirds of all dry fertilizers are sold to farmers in April and May. Only one-third of liquid fertilizers are sold in the spring.

7   Thirty percent of Ontario farmers use dealer custom application services, while 70 percent apply the fertilizer themselves using rented dealer application equipment. There is some tendency for larger farmers to be more inclined to want custom application services.

8   In the course of a year, farmers discuss their fertilizer program with a number of parties to get information and advice on various aspects of fertilizer use and dealer selection. The influence groups most widely consulted are the local fertilizer dealer, other farmers, and family members. In addition to these influence groups, fertilizer company representatives, agricultural extension

officials, and university scientists are consulted by some farmers. In the case of company representatives and university scientists, proportionately more larger farmers visit these people than smaller farmers.

9   Farmers also obtain fertilizer information from soil test results, various government publications, company-sponsored farmer meetings, dealer demonstration plots, and company and dealer displays at farm shows and fairs.

10   Over 60% of all farmers contact more than one fertilizer dealer before making a purchase. Larger farmers have a tendency to contact more dealers than smaller farmers.

11   Over 50% of all farmers reported receiving an on-farm call by a fertilizer dealer in the last year. Larger farmers reported receiving more dealer calls than smaller farmers.

12   In addition to fertilizers, southern Ontario farmers purchase, on the average, more than three other products from their fertilizer supplier. Of these, the most common are herbicides, insecticides, general farm supplies, and seeds. Large farmers are more likely to purchase herbicides and insecticides from their fertilizer supplier than small farmers.

13   Six dealer services were identified as being essential to all but a very small proportion of farmers: application equipment that is available when needed and in good repair; custom application services; custom fertilizer blending; fertilizer information through a well-informed staff, brochures, newsletters, and farmer meetings; soil testing; and demonstrations.

14   Other dealer services that were reported as being important to smaller groups of farmers were crop management assistance, help in securing expert assistance with problems, and custom herbicide application.

15   Dealer location, price, and availability of product when needed are the major factors farmers consider when selecting a fertilizer dealer. In general, dealer location and availability of product when needed are more important to smaller farmers, while price is more important to larger farmers.

16   Over 45% of all farmers purchase fertilizer from their nearest dealer. On the average, farmers purchase from dealers located less than five miles from their farms.

17   Thirty percent of all farmers purchase from more than one dealer. Larger farmers have a greater tendency to spread their purchases over more dealers than do small farmers.

18   Analysis of dealer switching showed that one-third of the farmers made no dealer changes in the past five years, one-third made only one change, and the remaining one-third made two or more changes. Those farmers making several dealer changes are the larger, younger farmers.

More sources on the fertilizer industry in Canada:
Fertilizer Institute of Canada: http://www.cfi.ca/fertfacts.cfm?itemid=52

Dry fertilizers

An alternative Len thought particularly attractive was to expand dry fertilizer sales in his local trading area. Although he had a substantial share of this market already, he felt it would be possible to pick up additional business through aggressive marketing. As part of his strategy to do this, he was thinking about adding another person to his staff who would act as a second salesperson and develop and offer a comprehensive crop management service to interested farmers. He was also considering the possibility of developing a local advertising program aimed at developing more awareness and interest among farmers outside his immediate 5 mile concentrated area. The total cost of the new sales specialist would be about $35,000 per year, and the local advertising would cost about $10,000 per year. Since he was near capacity now, expanding dry fertilizer sales would require an addition to his plant that would cost approximately $60,000.

The decision

Len knew he would have to make a decision soon if he were to make some changes for 2004. Although he had identified what he thought were several good opportunities for future growth, he knew he could not pursue all of them right away and that he would therefore have to establish some priorities. To help in this assessment, he recently wrote away to the University of Guelph and received a publication entitled Farmer Purchasing and Use of Fertilizers in Ontario (see Exhibit 6 for a summary of this study). With this new information, plus his own size-up of the situation, Len began the process of planning for 2004 and beyond.

1   Which of the possible opportunities should Len pursue? Which should not be followed up?

2   On what are you basing your decisions?

33   New Brunswick Telephone Company Limited*

Rising above the 130,000 residents of greater Saint John, New Brunswick, is an office tower decked in satellite dishes. The roof is illuminated by the brilliant blue logo of NBTel, the New Brunswick Telephone Company Limited. When Eleanor Austin arrived at NBTel in the summer of 1996, she found that her cubicle was located on the nineteenth floor. The location had an air of mystery, since the elevator buttons indicated that the eighteenth floor was the highest floor in the building. As NBTel's first and only behavioural research specialist, Eleanor would be working in the Planning and Marketing Department. And while the department's location would later be explained as an underestimation of the growing company's need for space, the secretive nineteenth floor would add to the mystique of the élite team of which Eleanor was to become a member.

NBTel and the Changing IT Industry.
In recent years, the history of the telecommunications industry has been a history of realignment, and telephone companies (telcos) have often found themselves at the eye of a storm. In 1984, the American telco giant, AT&T, was ordered to break up to curtail monopolization. Less than ten years later, telcos were realigning not through conglomerate breakup but through small business acquisition. In Canada, business diversification and technological convergence were bringing their own share of threats and opportunities. The Radio-television and Telecommunications Commission (CRTC) was dealing with cross-competition between telcos and cable companies and with the invasion of communications services via satellite. Adding to the uncertainty of CRTC policy revision and changing markets was the explosion of Internet services into the public imagination.

NBTel executives have decided to take advantage of converging technologies by discarding the telco's image as a telephone service provider and re-envisioning it as an electronic services integrator. A new vision is only a beginning. Executives share the widely held belief that the public is losing patience with the sheer amount of information being broadcast toward it through communications technologies. Members of the public want particular information to help them do the things they want to do. They want useless, time-consuming information screened out of their information sources. NBTel's new commitment is to buy when possible, create when necessary, the applications that will help its customers find desired information packaged in a way that makes it ready for use.

NBTel is the keystone company in the telecommunications group owned by Bruncor. To further its renewed commitment to service provision, NBTel has formed and has cooperated in forming several small businesses that fall beneath the Bruncor umbrella. These businesses develop and provide products and services, which NBTel in turn makes available to its customers. Businesses are responsible for developing and implementing business plans to make them self-sufficient, plans which include selling products and services to other telecommunications service providers in other markets.

The new corporate vision is part and parcel of a process that began years earlier. As a traditional telco directly employing over 2,000 New Brunswickers across the province, NBTel had developed and maintained highly structured departments and processes that fit their respective functions. However, executives have responded to the growing argument for a matrix structure of teams by applying new team concepts to the top-down, management-by-function structure of the old organization. On Eleanor's arrival, NBTel's organizational structure appeared to be a network of cross-functional teams stretched across a framework of departments divided by function, a hybrid of the old and the new. Organizational change was evident, but she did not know how the changes would affect her position and her position's relationship to teams and team members.

The Planning and Marketing Department has necessarily changed, as well. At the birth of the information technology (IT) industry, the new-product-development process tended to follow a model common across industrial sectors. A generalized, seven-step, linear model consists of (1) a new product development strategy, (2) idea generation, (3) screening and evaluation, (4) business analysis, (5) development, (6) market testing, and (7) commercialization. A post-purchase evaluation often follows to identify gaps between consumer expectations and experience with the aim of improving product quality based on gap analysis results. (Crane, F.G., Grant, E.S., & Hartley, S.W. (1997), Marketing Canadian Insights and Applications, Toronto: McGraw-Hill, pp. 218, 472–3.) The department has moved away from this model to keep pace with the IT industry and to support application development for business transactions over computer-moderated networks, which are being referred to increasingly and generically as electronic commerce (EC). Planning and Marketing works closely in product development with other Bruncor companies and with Future Services, which is the department charged with the in-house development of new products.

Eleanor's new position is symptomatic of a major shift in regard to how market research is incorporated into an EC application's development. As recently as ten years ago, engineers across technological industry sectors would have been familiar with the process whereby they developed new products, which marketers then tested with focus groups until they found a marketable use for the product. In general, major development and marketing decisions took place before the product was introduced to its market. This generalization is useful to show why the behavioural research specialist's challenge is unique and entirely new.

The new method of application development requires the technical developer and the marketer to work side by side. Major application development and marketing decisions are often made after the product has been introduced into the market. If the old model could be described as a process spiralling upward toward the development of a marketable application, in the new model the spiral has been compressed, with development, marketing, and market reaction feeding off one another to speed application development. In the new model, the seven traditional steps are followed, but less time is afforded them. However, commercialization becomes a new process in itself. Initial commercialization is followed by an analysis of market reaction. Based on this new information, the product is developed further. Dramatic changes to the product lead to another commercialization process. These steps are repeated until the product manager determines that there is no longer value in continuing them.

The Position

Planning and Marketing management has decided that a new model calls for a new kind of researcher to help NBTel get the most out of the new processes. Eleanor has come to NBTel with no formal business education or traditional business experience. She was hired in part because of her fourteen years of journalistic experience, much of it in radio, where research, interviews, and new program development were major responsibilities. By conducting in-depth interviews with customers, Eleanor would acquire knowledge that would be put back into the product development process.

The position of behavioural research specialist was created to help NBTel's marketers and planners learn what their customers want to do and how they want to do it. This information will enable the department to recommend the purchase or creation of products that are most likely to increase use of NBTel integration services. The department has directed Eleanor to share research findings and her expertise with application developers working within or for NBTel. Eleanor describes the sense of adventure and trepidation that comes with her position as that of being asked to find the best way through "a field of tall grain through which no one has cut a path before."

The first "field of tall grain" to which Eleanor has been assigned is the customer base of the Vista 350 and its applications. The 350 is a telephone equipped with a small liquid crystal display screen and several buttons added to a standard touch-tone keypad. The visual display and recorded, structured audio messages enable users to access telco applications such as caller identification and a callers' log; "window-shop" from a menu of advertisers that they create themselves; electronically transfer bank funds into other accounts or pay utilities; and entertain themselves by listening to horoscopes or by checking winning lottery ticket numbers. Nortel produces the Vista line of screen phones, and applications are developed by New North Media, a company originally supported by Nortel and NBTel to develop the business case for Vista 350 rentals and services.

NBTel marketers already know which functions are used, and how much, through quantitative research based on company records. What they do not know is why some functions are used and others not, and what things their customers might like to do with the 350 if it were possible. They do not know what customers need—the gap between what customers want and what NBTel currently offers. Eleanor's job is to create the process through which to discover this information, execute the process, record and interpret research results, and disseminate this information in a way that ensures it will be incorporated into future application purchase or development.

The Vista 350 Research Project

Eleanor's position evolved naturally out of the environment that NBTel has built in New Brunswick. The province's population of 750,600 has grown accustomed to their province's reputation as a LivingLAB™ for telecommunications network applications (LivingLAB is a trademark of NBTel). Time to market is reduced because the small population's access to a state-of-the-art network makes New Brunswick both a test market and an implementation site, supporting the compressed model for application development. The province's demographics are typical of the age, gender, income, and urbanization mix throughout

Canada and many parts of the United States. The Vista 350 and its applications had been first implemented in New Brunswick and had achieved 16 percent market penetration. At the time of Eleanor's project, 80 percent of Vista 350 application business was being generated outside of New Brunswick, supporting the theory that what is implemented in New Brunswick can be marketed for export quickly.

Eleanor began her project by phrasing a simple question that she wanted her research to answer. The classic technology/business question is, "Will people buy what I build?" She modified the question to match the new environment: What do people want to buy that I can build?" Since she was asking this question about applications already on the market, she chose to go to the people using the products to gather her information. Which applications did they choose to use, choose not to use, and why? What would make them want to use applications more? What would they like to be able to do with their phone, and how would they like to be able to do it? And to get underneath people's understanding of themselves and to discover deeper motivations of which they might be unaware, Eleanor asked other, less direct questions. How is the phone used in the home? What other objects are located near the phone? How do users feel about the phone? And of particular significance, how does the phone make them feel?

Eleanor determined that 36 subjects would represent a significant sample and that twelve interviews from each of three targeted segments would reveal themes consistent for each segment's population. This qualitative information would be quantified and statistically tested to ensure that the results were significant. In Saint John, twelve respondents were chosen, aged 55 and over, to represent the growing "grey market" of ageing people who have, as a group, significant disposable income. Another twelve people, aged 34 to 54, were chosen to represent the most significant current demographic group, the baby boomers. To test her findings in Saint John, Eleanor selected twelve more random users in Fredericton, one of the three largest cities in the province.

Groups of potential Saint John respondents were targeted for selection, but individuals ultimately self-selected. Eleanor attended community meetings to let Vista 350 users know about her project and made some preliminary telephone interviews as determined by telephone number prefixes. Prefixes tend to be a reliable indicator of whether telephones in greater Saint John are located in urban, suburban, or rural areas, so Eleanor was able to keep her sample representative of where users live. Selection for the major interviews was based on how well individuals demonstrated their willingness to share information about themselves.

The major interview took place in the user's home and began with an explanation of the project. Eleanor asked respondents to show her how they operated 350 applications. If a respondent so desired, Eleanor demonstrated how to operate unused functions. Respondents were then asked questions about their family, friends, and lifestyle. These questions led to others about how they perceived the role the 350 played in their lives, the sorts of things they would like to be able to do but couldn't, and whether the 350 could somehow be used to help them do what they wanted to do. Interviews lasted an average of two hours. Eleanor later mailed letters to respondents to inform them that they had received long-distance gift certificates for their co-operation. The final contact, Eleanor believed, caused respondents to see the gift as a reward instead of a bribe to cooperate, and she used occasional calls as an opportunity to follow up any issues arising out of the interviews. For instance, she learned that use of previously unused functions increased after she showed respondents how to operate them.

The Results

"The results of this study have reinforced two truths for me," says Eleanor. "First, behind any marketing statistics are living, breathing human beings engaged in very active relationships with other human beings, using our technology in ways we hadn't imagined. Second, the lure of technology has been the same since the invention of the wheel: people want control over their environment, and technology is a tool for control." Throughout the interview process, Eleanor was struck by the openness of respondents to share their life experiences with her, the delight in walking another person through their daily routines, and the thoughtfulness of their responses. Most respondents felt that Vista 350 technology brought them control: control in deciding whether and how to answer the phone, control in knowing who was calling and why, and control in choosing access only to those information or financial services which were useful to them. The elderly and parents of young children, for example, saw the telephone as a home security device that gave them the ability to monitor who was calling their home, whether or not they were at home at the time the call was made.

Respondents were particularly aware of the messages they sent to others by the way they used technology. If you return a call that was made to your number in your absence, hasn't the caller received the message that you are aware of what goes on around your home even when you are not there? If you abruptly interrupt a telephone conversation to talk to a second caller on another line, haven't you been rude to the first caller? If an information service helps you find information valuable to your friends and family, do they not see you as a knowledgeable, helpful person? Users indicated that the kind of technology they choose and how they choose to use it impart a whole set of character traits—a public persona that influences how others see them.

Translating Results into Action

Eleanor's confidence in her research methods has been supported by market researchers with whom she has attended conferences. Other researchers representing major players in the IT industry have envied the level of intimacy she has achieved with customers in the small-town, "down home" atmosphere of New Brunswick. Eleanor understands her organization's market in ways that would be impossible for organizations in major centres across North America. This level of intimacy and understanding outweighs any concerns about scientific weaknesses in the sampling process.

Eleanor has been able to put the knowledge gained from her project to use for the Planning and Marketing Department. She has contributed to the decision-making process for the purchase of a new customer service, and she has provided advice and written copy for the telemarketing of telco products. Her research has also been used in positioning the Vista 350 in new markets. But before she prepares for her next research assignment, she wants to ensure that NBTel and its application development partners take full advantage of her research results.

Application development teams acknowledge the flattened development spiral that requires ongoing product development, but their reward systems tend to focus on the development of new applications. Team members are typically rewarded for developing new concepts, for turning those new concepts into usable applications, and for the profit the new applications reap for the company. Development teams are a particular challenge for Eleanor, not because they fail to cooperate but because she does not yet see how her role fits into the processes they follow. Current practices do not give her an opportunity to measure her effectiveness in, and contribution to, product development and improvement.

Another perennial battle between quantitative and qualitative researchers is whether the sampling methods and subsequent sample sizes of qualitative research meet the rigours enforced by quantitative research. Qualitative researchers respond to questions of reliability by arguing the validity of their sample size and the robustness of the quality of responses gleaned from smaller samples.

1   To ensure that the telco and its technology partners benefit from the full value of the behavioural research specialist's position, should structural changes be made to current new-product-development processes?

2   How can new marketing information be integrated back into the development spiral when application development teams are already working on the development of new applications?

3   How can research results be put to best use?

4   How can the product development process be assisted and how can the impact of new information be measured?

*This case was written by Mark Henderson, who at the time of its preparation was associated with the Electronic Commerce Centre of the University of New Brunswick at Saint John. Based on interviews with Eleanor Austin, NBTel, conducted 7 August and 5 September, 1997. Although NB-Tel was merged into Aliant in 1999, the underlying case is a valuable insight into behavioural factors.

34   Rocky Mountain House Co-op*

Frank Gallagher, general manager of Rocky Mountain House Co-op (RMHC), was sitting in his office reviewing the performance of his organization when Milt Zirk, petroleum manager of the company, hurried into the room. "Frank, I'm afraid I've got some bad news," exclaimed Milt. "The word is out that United Farmers of Alberta (UFA) is planning to open a new petroleum outlet in Rocky Mountain House. The petroleum end of our business has been going fairly well for us over the past couple of years. This could really mess things up! You know they are very aggressive marketers, and because they are a co-op like us, they could really eat into our market share. Frank, I'm worried! We're going to have to make sure we're ready for them. We've got to develop a plan to minimize their impact on our sales and profits."

Rocky Mountain House Co-op

Rocky Mountain House Co-op is a retail outlet located in Rocky Mountain House, Alberta, approximately 80 km west of Red Deer, on Highway 11. Rocky Mountain House is a community of approximately 6,000 people with both an agricultural and a commercial economic base. The area is characterized by mixed farming, with most farms being relatively small and having at least some livestock. Industry in the area includes general business, trucking, construction, oil exploration, and logging.

The trading area served by RMHC is much larger than Rocky Mountain House itself and contains the following communities: Alder Flats, Alhambra, Caroline, Condor, Leslieville, Nordegg, Rocky Mountain House, and Stauffer. The trading area has an approximate population of 16,000 people and a radius of 50 km, although the trading area on the west extends nearly 100 km to the Rocky Mountains.

Exhibit 1: Product Line Breakdown

	Home centre	Shopping Centre	Petroleum
Sales	$4,620,000	$11,044,000	$2,550,000
Less: cost of good sold	$3,536,000	$8,418,000	$2,294,000
Gross margin	$1,084,000	$2,626,000	$256,000
Less: operating expenses	$931,000	$2,106,000	$189,000
Contribution	$153,000	$520,000	$67,000

RMHC is a co-operative type business. Co- operatives are like regular businesses except that they are owned by their users, who purchase shares in the business. Instead of earning "profits," co-operatives earn "savings," which can be returned to members through "patronage dividends." RMHC is owned by 7,332 active members. For the most part, these "owners" are people in the trading area who have become members by purchasing shares in the organization. Each share is valued at $1.00, and a minimum of five shares must be purchased to become a member. The main reason for being a member is to share in the savings of the business through patronage dividends. Patronage dividends are based on the amount of business a member does each year and have amounted to about 5 percent of purchases at RMHC over the past several years. In addition, members have a voice in the affairs of the co-op through their right to elect a board of directors to represent their views.

RMHC is involved in a number of retail businesses, which they classify under three divisions: Home Centre, Shopping Centre, and Petroleum. The Home Centre consists of building materials, hardware, animal health products, livestock feed, livestock equipment, and twine; the Shopping Centre consists of food, hardware, clothing, and a cafeteria; and the Petroleum Division consists of bulk fuels, propane, oil/lubes, cardlock, and a gas bar. Despite the fact that Rocky Mountain House is in a significant grain-producing area of the province, RMHC has elected so far not to sell crop supplies. Sales, cost of goods sold, and gross margins for each division for 2003 are shown in Exhibit 1. Exhibit 2 shows the operating statement of RMHC for the same year.

In 2003, RMHC received patronage dividends of $683,000 from Federated Co-operatives Limited in Saskatoon, the large wholesaling co-operative, which is owned by several hundred local co-ops like RMHC across western Canada. Like most other local co-ops, RMHC used Federated Co-op as their main source of supply for all products they sold. The patronage dividend they received from Federated was based on a percentage of purchases. In the same year, RMHC allocated $614,000 in patronage dividends to local owners. This, together with current savings, left RMHC with retained savings of slightly more than $1 million. This represented funds the organization could use for future expansion.

Exhibit 2: Operating Statement

Sales	$18,214,000
Less: cost of goods sold	$14,248,000
Gross margin	$3,966,000
Less: operating expenses	$3,226,000
Contribution	$740,000
Less: indirect interest expense	($96,000)
Less: general overhead	$432,000
Savings	$404,000
Patronage dividends from federated co-ops	$683,000
Retained savings	$1,087,000

Petroleum Division
The petroleum division of RMHC has always been a tough business. Margins in the petroleum division are much lower than in other areas of the company, largely due to intense competition and the commodity-type products being sold. In the Rocky Mountain House trading area alone there are six major oil companies competing for a total fuel market of approximately 26.9 million litres. Exhibit 3 lists the major petroleum companies with facilities in Rocky Mountain House and their approximate fuel sales.

Most of the 26.9 million litres of petroleum sold in the Rocky Mountain House trading area went to commercial accounts. Commercial accounts purchased 18.3 million litres in 2003 compared to 6.1 million litres to farm accounts and 2.5 million litres to consumers.

Although precise market shares were not known, Milt estimated that Co-op and Esso were the major petroleum suppliers in the area, followed by Shell, Petro-Canada, Turbo, and Husky. Exhibit 4 shows approximate market shares for each company by type of account.

Exhibit 3: Competitive Petroleum Suppliers

	Estimated Litres
Co-op	5,900,000
Esso	7,500,000
Shell	4,000,000
Petro-Canada	3,500,000
Turbo	3,500,000
Husky	2,500,000
Total	26,900,000

Exhibit 4: Approximate Market Shares by Type of Account

	Farm	Commercial	Consumer	Total
Co-op	34%	17%	30%	23%
Esso	31%	27%	27%	28%
Shell	13%	15%	16%	15%
Petro Canada	6%	17%	4%	13%
Turbo	12%	13%	13%	13%
Husky	4%	11%	10%	9%
Total	100%	100%	100%	100%

Exhibit 5: Financial Summary for Petroleum Products

	Fuels	Propane	Oil/lubes	Gas bar	Total
Sales	$2,016,000	$41,000	$126,000	$367,000	$2,550,000
Cost of goods	$1,829,000	$34,000	$106,000	$325,000	$2,294,000
Gross margin	$187,000	$7,000	$20,000	$42,000	$256,000

Exhibit 6: Petroleum Department Expenses

Depreciation	$5,600
Utilities	$500
Insurance	$4,900
Repairs & maintenance	$9,000
Taxes & licenses	$4,600
Total standby costs	$24,600
Employee benefits	$18,000
Staff discounts	$1,600
Training	$1,800

Salaries & wages	$99,000
Uniforms	$1,500
Total staff costs	$121,900
Advertising & promotion	$5,600
Delivery trucks	$29,000
Other expenses	$7,900
Total operating costs	$189,000
Contribution	$67,000

RMHC currently sells four product lines in petroleum: bulk fuels, propane, oil/lubes, and gas bar (self-service pumps at the Shopping Centre). Sales, cost of goods sold, and gross margins for these products in 2003 are shown in Exhibit 5. Exhibit 6 shows the petroleum department expenses for the same year.

Like most petroleum suppliers in the area, RMHC sells five types of petroleum products: premium gasoline, regular gasoline, clear diesel, marked gasoline, and marked diesel. Exhibit 7 shows 2003 sales of the five products in each of the major markets, while Exhibit 8 shows current pricing for each product in each major market. Marked gasoline and marked diesel are dyed a purple colour to distinguish them from clear product. This is done to identify these products as tax exempt because they are used for off-road purposes and not subject to normal fuel taxes. At the moment, marked fuels sell for approximately $0.09 per litre less than clear fuels, which are intended for on-road use and subject to a road tax. The prices established by RMHC are very similar to those of other petroleum suppliers in the area. Only Turbo and Husky sell petroleum at lower prices than other companies in the area, and in both cases, the differences are very small.

Margins on petroleum products do not vary by type of product, but do vary by type of customer. Current margins in the farm market are $0.049 per litre; in the commercial market, $0.034 per litre; and in the consumer market, $0.063 per litre.

In the petroleum end of the business, RMHC deals with three main types of customers: farms accounts, commercial accounts, and consumers.

Exhibit 7: Petroleum Sales by Market

	Farm	Commercial	Consumer	Total
Premium gasoline			16,500	16,500
Regular gasoline	200,000	1,173,000	666,500	2,039,500
Clear diesel		1,154,000	63,000	1,217,000
Marked gasoline	949,000	50,000		999,000
Marked diesel	937,000	736,000		1,673,000
Totals	2,086,000	3,113,000	746,000	5,945,000

Exhibit 8: Petroleum Prices by Market

	Farm	Commercial	Consumer
Premium gasoline			$0.870
Regular gasoline	$0.725	$0.715	0.749
Clear diesel	0.585	0.575	
Marked gasoline	0.635	0.625	
Marked diesel	0.505	0.495	

Exhibit 9: Types of Commercial Accounts

Type of Account	Percent
General business	29%
Loggers	11%
Truckers	18%
Construction	17%
Oil company contractors	22%
Institutional	3%

At the moment, RMHC has about 350 farm accounts, which purchase 2,086,000 million litres of fuel. Although the average farm account purchases about 6,000 litres of fuel each year, some purchase much larger amounts and many purchase much smaller amounts. The largest RMHC farm account purchases nearly 20,000 litres of fuel a year. Farms in the RMHC trading area are somewhat smaller than typical Alberta farms. A very high proportion of these farms have livestock as their principal operation.

Commercial accounts represent the major proportion of RMHC petroleum business. At the moment, RMHC has 175 commercial accounts, which together purchase approximately 3,113,000 litres of fuel and range in size from 5,000 litres per year to as much as 300,000 litres per year. The average commercial account buys 18,000 litres. Exhibit 9 provides a breakdown of commercial accounts into various types of businesses.

The final category of customer is individual consumers, who currently purchase 746,000 litres of fuel. About 80 percent of consumer sales are through the gas bar at the Shopping Centre, and the remaining 20 percent are through the cardlock system described below.

Although all three types of accounts (farm, commercial, and consumer) can use the cardlock system, it is very popular among commercial accounts. The cardlock system allows approved buyers to have 24-hour access to bulk fuels at the main RMHC petroleum outlet. To obtain fuel, the buyer inserts a card into a metering device, which then pumps the requested amount of a certain type of fuel into the user's tank. The user's name and the amount of the purchase are recorded electronically for future billing. Use of this system is growing very rapidly among farm and commercial accounts because of convenience and cost savings. The price of fuel purchased through the cardlock is generally $0.008 per litre less than bulk delivery. Although RMHC has a good, very clean cardlock operation, there are two problems that make it less than ideal. One problem is that currently it does not sell marked gasoline and does not have the capability of adding this product into the existing system. This undoubtedly prevents some potential customers from using the RMHC cardlock. Another problem with the cardlock is that access to the facility is a little more difficult than some customers would like.

At the moment, the marketing program used by RMHC is fairly similar to that used by other petroleum suppliers in the area. In 2003, less than $6,000 per year was being spent on advertising petroleum products. Most of this was for ads placed in local papers highlighting special deals on oils and lubricants. In addition to advertising, a substantial amount of selling is done by Milt on the farm, at the offices of commercial accounts, and on the phone. Milt maintains contact at least four times a year with most customers, and more often with larger customers. Some very large customers are contacted on a weekly basis. In addition, he spends a considerable amount of time calling on prospective customers. Milt's philosophy is that regular contact with prospects will put him in contention for their business if there is ever a reason for a customer to switch. History shows this to be a good strategy, as RMHC has picked up a number of new customers each year when they became dissatisfied with their present supplier. Customer loyalty in petroleum, however, is very high. Milt figures that less than 10 percent of customers change suppliers each year. Milt also follows the practice of driving the delivery truck himself on occasion so that he can have more contact with customers.

Frank and Milt have long thought that the success of RMHC in the petroleum business was due to a number of factors:
- The company provides excellent service. All people working for RMHC are topnotch individuals committed to providing good service. In addition, the company prides itself on clean, modern facilities and prompt attention to detail. Any customer who needs fuel can expect to receive it the same day an order is placed. RMHC currently spends more than its competitors on staff training.
- Co-op products are quality products that are produced under strict quality control measures.
- Patronage refunds provide customers with "cash back" at the end of the year based on their volume of business. For many customers this is a real incentive to do business with a co-op.
- The company has an excellent highway location in Rocky Mountain House. This provides excellent visibility in the community.
- RMHC offers a very wide range of products, making "one stop shopping" possible for customers.

United Farmers of Alberta

United Farmers of Alberta (UFA), like RMHC, is a member-owned co-operative. UFA has approximately 30 outlets in Alberta in which they sell petroleum and a complete line of farm supplies. In addition, they operate approximately 90 outlets in which only petroleum products are sold, through bulk plants, cardlocks, and gas bars. UFA has shown considerable growth in recent years through very aggressive marketing. This growth has come both from an increase in the number of retail distribution points and from an increase in the volume sold through existing outlets.

Recently, UFA was granted a development permit to build a farm supply facility in Rocky Mountain House. The permit allows UFA to construct a facility that contains the following: a 2,200 square foot building, a bulk petroleum plant, a gas bar, a cardlock, and a farm supply distribution facility. It is expected that UFA will sell a complete line of both crop and livestock farm supplies through this facility. It is also expected that UFA will construct a cardlock facility that is larger than any other in the area and will sell a complete line of fuels.

The entry of UFA into this market has the potential of causing significant problems for RMHC, for a number of reasons:

- UFA is a co-op like RMHC and therefore very similar in structure and philosophy. As a result, they may be considered a good alternative by many current RMHC customers.
- The fact that they are building a complete farm supply outlet may be attractive to many current RMHC customers who would like to purchase crop supplies where they buy petroleum.
- UFA's facility will be much newer than that of RMHC. This is of particular concern for the cardlock.
- UFA currently has a number of commercial accounts on the fringes of the RMHC trading area. This gives them a foothold into the market.
- In similar situations, UFA has demonstrated a willingness to enter new markets in a very aggressive manner. Often this entails aggressive pricing, introductory advertising in local media, a direct mail campaign targeted to larger potential customers, and special introductory deals.
- UFA traditionally supports its marketing efforts with a high level of excellent service. This includes the availability of skilled technical experts who can answer questions and help customers make informed buying decisions, attention to detail in all aspects of the business, and frequent sales calls (either phone or in person) with key customers.

Decision

Although at first Frank was not overly concerned about the situation, as he considered it in more detail, he began to worry about the potential effects it might have. RMHC had worked hard over the last ten years to build a strong customer base and some of this investment in time and marketing dollars appeared to be at risk. To determine the seriousness of the situation, and to develop some plans to counteract it, Frank called a meeting with Milt for early next week.

The meeting began with Frank raising the issue of what impacts the entry of UFA might have on RMHC. After some discussion, the two men agreed that if RMHC did nothing to soften the impact, it was conceivable they could lose a significant portion of both their farm and their commercial business, especially the larger accounts that were more price sensitive. Although it was hard to come up with specific numbers, they felt that up to a quarter of their present volume might be at risk. What was even more alarming was the fact that RMHC had three very large commercial customers who each purchased 300,000 litres of fuel a year. Losing these people alone would result in a very large sales decline. Although these large commercial accounts had been with RMHC for a number of years, and Milt provided a high level of personal service through almost weekly contact, it was conceivable they could switch allegiance if they perceived greater value in an alternative supplier.

Given the seriousness of the situation, they then began to discuss alternative courses of action they might pursue to counteract the problem. A number of possibilities were identified and briefly discussed.

1   The first idea that came to mind was to pursue a pre-emptive pricing strategy. Under this strategy, RMHC would begin immediately cutting prices and margins to existing customers. The idea behind this strategy, of course, was to solidify business relationships with customers to the point that it would be very difficult for UFA to be successful in taking customers from RMHC.

2   A second strategy they discussed was to match UFA's promotional programs dollar for dollar and engage in a substantial amount of local advertising and direct marketing themselves. Although neither Frank nor Milt had a precise idea of what UFA would spend entering the Rocky Mountain House market, they felt that $30,000 was not an unrealistic amount. They considered stressing two main points in the promotion: their excellent staff, and their outstanding record of providing patronage dividends. Frank envisioned ads and direct mail pieces with pictures and human interest stories about the staff, as well as charts showing the steady growth in patronage dividends over the past few years.

3   Another idea they considered was to develop a program in which the rate of patronage dividends would vary by department. Under such a scheme it would be possible for the petroleum division, for example, to announce a patronage dividend of 8 percent where some other division's dividend might decline to 3 percent. They felt this might be particularly effective in the short run to meet a competitive challenge.

4   Yet another alternative they were considering was to get into the fertilizer and ag chemical business. On the assumption that some RMHC customers might be attracted to UFA because they had a complete line of crop and livestock supplies, this might provide existing customers with enough reason to stay with RMHC. It would, however, be a major investment for RMHC in a business they knew little about. Frank estimated it would require an investment of approximately $600,000 in facilities and working capital.

In addition, two new full-time people would be required to run the business and work with farm customers. An additional five seasonal employees would be needed for a couple of months each year to help during peak sales seasons. Total additional labour costs would amount to approximately $150,000 plus another $50,000 in administrative costs. Margins on fertilizer were typically in the 15 to 20 percent range on product that sold for an average price of $250 per ton. Although an average farmer in the Rocky Mountain House trading area currently used only 25 to 30 tons of fertilizer a year, use appeared to be growing fairly rapidly as more farmers were starting to use fertilizer and those already using fertilizer were increasing application rates. Ag chemicals were not widely used in the Rocky Mountain House trading area, so this would be considered a break-even business that simply provided a complementary service to farmers who purchased fertilizer. Presently there are three fertilizer suppliers serving the 1,200 farmers in the Rocky Mountain House trading area. One of these suppliers is a large, independent farm supply outlet specializing in crop inputs; the other two are smaller operations, one of which is the local Esso dealer.

5   The final alternative Frank identified was to move up construction of a new bulk petroleum facility. The current facility was old and starting to show its age. Of particular concern was the fact that the cardlock system had reached its capacity and could not add a tank and pumping system for marked gasoline. Frank knew that the new UFA facility would be "state of the art" and have ample capacity for the present and for future expansion. Although Frank had hoped to get another five years out of the present facility, he felt that one option was to invest immediately in new facilities so that they would be ready at least by the time the UFA facility was built. A new facility that would include a new bulk plant, an expanded sales area, and a new and expanded cardlock would cost $300,000 to construct.

Frank and Milt concluded the meeting wondering what to do. They agreed to consider the options more fully and do some real thinking about the consequences of each option and then meet again in a week to make a decision.

1   How serious is the threat posed by the imminent entry of UFA? What impact could this have on RMHC sales and profits?
2   Carefully analyze each of the options Frank and Milt have outlined, and any others you can identify, in terms of their pros, cons, and financial implications.
3   What should Frank and Milt do? What will be the likely outcome of such a decision?

35   Chalaga Mussel Farms*

In July 2002, mussel farmer Malcolm Wilson was examining the mussel industry in Atlantic Canada. As a mussel farmer, he was concerned about competition from two areas. One was the United States, particularly Maine, since it appeared to control the low end of the market. The other was Prince Edward Island, where "Island Blue" mussels were positioned at the high end of the market. Wilson was searching for an appropriate strategy that would make Chalaga Mussel Farms more competitive.

Malcolm Wilson's Background in Mussel Farming

In the late 1990s, while attending the Marine Institute in St. John's, Newfoundland, Malcolm Wilson worked part time for a small mussel farming operation. He quickly saw potential for the mussel industry and conducted some secondary research on the industry. His findings indicated that there was a future in owning and operating a mussel farm. However, he realized that several marketing issues needed careful attention. For example, Wilson felt that Newfoundland was not a viable location since there were difficulties with respect to distribution that, in turn, affected marketability. Wilson particularly wanted to enter the Minneapolis market since a previous visit to that region had been very encouraging.

In January 2002, he relocated to Halifax, Nova Scotia, and he and a partner, who had some previous entrepreneurial experience, bought some mussels and equipment and started Chalaga Mussel Farms on the eastern shore of Nova Scotia.

Chalaga Mussel Farms was a small operation, and the two partners realized that they needed an increased sales volume in order to survive in an increasingly competitive marketplace. They felt that a steady supply of good-quality mussels was necessary for survival and to enhance market share. However, distribution posed a problem. One way to improve profit margins would be for them to own their own processing plant to clean, grade, and bag mussels, since this would permit them to market directly instead of being required to sell to others who had the ability to process.

The growing cycle of mussels requires approximately two years before the product can go to market, and Chalaga Mussel Farms needed to develop appropriate inventory and distribution channels in order to be competitive. By June 2003, Chalaga Mussel Farms had begun production on a larger scale and was also examining distribution and pricing strategies. Chalaga Mussel Farms bought the appropriate equipment and set up a processing plant.

By late 2003, Chalaga Mussel Farms had sold 175,000 pounds of mussels directly to supermarkets, local brokers, and brokers in Quebec City, Montreal, and Toronto. The operation began to show a small profit, and plans were made to increase production by 15 to 25 percent a year for the next three years.

Wilson was convinced that he would continue working in the mussel farm business, and he felt that having the right products in the right markets was the key to success. He then began to seek out more information on the mussel industry in Canada and the United States.

Research on the Mussel Industry

Wilson obtained several consulting reports, book and magazine articles on the mussel industry, and information from the Department of Fisheries and Oceans and Canadian Aquaculture Magazine. To supplement his secondary research, Wilson conducted several interviews with mussel growers, brokers, and retailers in Canada and the United States. He also set up focus groups comprised of individuals from Newfoundland, Nova Scotia, and Prince Edward Island who were knowledgeable about the mussel industry.

Data concerning mussel meat yield varied, but Wilson came up with an average percentage: whole mussel meats (16 percent recoverable yield) and broken meats (2 percent recoverable yield). Broken meats are often thrown away, but Wilson felt that they could be used for chowders and soups in the food service or institutional markets. From his research, Wilson decided that priority should be given to the development and expansion of Chalaga Mussel Farms' product line. For example, whole meats could be individually quick frozen (IQF) or sold in one-pound block form; a mussel salad could be developed to compete with other mussel salads currently on the market, such as Limfjord and Marina; smoked mussels could also be considered to compete with M'Lord brand; a yogurt pairing campaign might be undertaken (in Europe, cream-based and yogurt-based mussel salads are common) and recipes developed that paired mussel salad with yogurt.

Exhibit 1: 2002 Canadian Production of Mussels by province (000's $)

NFLD	PEI	NS	NB	QUE	CAN
5,500	22,202	2,288	801	550	31,341

Source Canadian Aquaculture Statistics 2002

Exhibit 2: Canadian Mussel Exports January to December 2002

Quantity	Value (000's$)	Average Price/kg
8,528 tonnes	25,671	$3.01

Source: Department of fisheries and Oceans, domestic exports of selected commodities

Exhibit 3: Canadian Mussel Imports January to December 2002

Quantity	Value (000's$)	Average Price/kg
1,988 tonnes	8,348	4.20

Source: Department of fisheries and Oceans, imports of selected commodities

The information Wilson gathered generally segmented the mussel market in three ways: geographically (American and Canadian cities, Europe); by product type (wild, long-line cultured, and bottom-cultivated); and by sector (institutional or food service and restaurants versus consumer or retail); overall, 75 percent of fresh mussel product goes to the food service sector and 25 percent to the retail sector.

The volume consumed by the food service sector versus that consumed by the retail sector varied considerably by city. According to one of the studies that Wilson had reviewed, markets with a large retail sector volume offered good opportunities to long-line mussel growers because the retail sector catered to sophisticated consumers who could distinguish between the different types of mussels.

Another study suggested that the growth in North American demand for mussels in the 1990s could in part be traced to the dietary preferences of yuppies: mussels were high in protein, low in calories and cholesterol, and considered chic to eat. Mussel consumption was clustered around large North American cities. Growth was anticipated in the restaurant sector of these cities because mussels were trendy and their high markup, particularly of bottom-cultivated mussels, made them attractive to restaurant managers. The retail trade was expected to have much slower growth.

The Canadian market, by industry sector, consisted of approximately 70 percent in the food service industry (mainly restaurants) and 30 percent in the retail trade (supermarkets, etc.). The retail trade was directed mainly at ethnic populations residing in large cities. The type of mussel consumed varied from city to city (see Exhibit 1).

Even though Quebec purchased a good deal of Prince Edward Island mussels, the "Buy Quebec" preferential purchase policies limited the market potential. Other market segments Wilson considered were value-added products and export markets. Even though transportation costs limited the potential of these markets, Wilson knew that Island Blues were already being flown to Los Angeles and other American cities. He had to find a way to distribute his product more economically. Government research indicated that Europe was a mature market with few prospects for export; however, Wilson felt that there was still potential in Europe, particularly in the Baltic States and the Moscow region of Russia.

Mussel Processing
There are basically three types of mussels marketed: long-line cultured, bottom-cultivated, and wild. Since the marketing approach for each type of mussel varied, Wilson had to pay particular attention to the different growing methods.

Chalaga Mussel Farms used the long-line suspension method of growing cultured mussels. This method involves the suspension of mussel "seed"—small mussels from intertidal zones, stuffed in "socks" about three metres long. The socks are suspended on a line supported by buoys at the surface and attached to the bottom by weights. After harvesting, fresh whole mussels are brought to the processing plant, which often houses two separate processing areas in one building: primary processing (fresh product) and secondary processing (value-added product). Tote boxes are used to carry the mussels, with approximately 80 to 100 pounds per box.

The first stage of production includes declumping, grading, and debyssing (the mussel attaches itself to surfaces by means of tough filaments called byssal threads). The mussels are manually shovelled into a hopper that leads to the declumper, where they are drum-rotated to break up the clumps. Next, they are separated by use of a bar grader and carried by conveyor belt to the debysser, constantly being sprayed with water during this process. The mussels are then debyssed and are again put in tote boxes while awaiting further processing or packaging for the fresh market.

Exhibit 4: Price per kilogram 2000

	Wild	Bottom Cultivated	P.E.I.	Long-Line Cultured Newfoundland	Nova Scotia
Wholesale	na	$1.80	$1.80	$1.75	$1.80
Retail	na	2.20	2.21	2.03	2.03

All prices are in Canadian dollars. Prices were obtained from a survey of wholesalers and retailers. Seasonal price fluctuations were wide.

Secondary processing requires that the mussels be cooked in a large steam kettle. This takes place in a separate area of the plant. Approximately 80 to 100 pounds are steamed for about 15 minutes per kettle load. The cooked mussels are then dumped onto a shaker that vibrates rapidly, thereby separating the meat from the shell. Mussel meats are then collected and placed in a tub of salted water where the meats float and the shells and other debris sink to the bottom. Finally, the mussel meats can be either marinated for a retail mussel salad product or stored in a chill room for later processing.

Compared to other types of mussels, the long-line mussel is cleaner (no pearls or grit) and has a nicer shell and a higher meat yield. The market price for these mussels tends to be higher than the price for wild or bottom-cultivated mussels.

New methods developed in 1989 improved growing yields and increased the industry margin of long-line cultured mussels between 30 and 35 percent at current wholesale prices.

Wild mussels were harvested from in-shore areas using bottom dredges. The mussels were then picked by hand from the dredged material. Like bottom-cultivated mussels, wild mussels had a reduced meat yield and a higher content of sand and pearls than long-line cultured mussels. Quebec consumed a high proportion of wild mussels. Once harvested, all mussel types had a shelf life of 7 to 14 days if properly stored. They had to be processed for market (cleaning, sorting, etc.) and handled carefully during transport. Mussels shipments usually constituted part of a mixed load of seafood products.

From his interviews with retailers, Wilson discovered that even though its shell was cleaner and the meat yield higher, to the average consumer, the long-line cultured mussel was difficult to distinguish from the wild mussel and the bottom-cultivated mussel whether in or out of the shell.

American markets

In 2003, the American food service sector accounted for 80 percent of mussel demand while the retail sector accounted for 20 percent. The type of mussel consumed also varied from city to city.

Canadian Supply

In 2002, 31,341 tonnes of mussels (mostly long-line mussels) were produced in Canada. Exports represented 28 percent or 8,528 tonnes. In addition, 1,988 tonnes were imported. Almost all of the imported mussels were bottom-cultivated mussels. All of the Canadian supply of mussels came from Atlantic Canada, but there were problems with distribution and not only to Canadian destinations. Canadian west coast production still faced large technical difficulties.

Wilson had seen the mussel industry grow at a fast rate. He knew that the American and Canadian markets were large, but he also felt that he was missing out on many opportunities for export. A biologist's report mentioned that the environmental conditions in the Atlantic region could lead to a long-line cultured mussel capacity of 50,000 tonnes a year. This figure could double if bottom-cultivated methods were considered.

American Supply

Bottom-cultivated mussels grown by Maine companies dominated the American mussel market. Maine mussels also had a strong presence in the Canadian market. In 2003, American growers produced over 60,000 tonnes of mussels. Recent developments in the Maine industry concerned Wilson. Bottom-cultivating had been the prevalent growing method in the industry, but some growers were experimenting with long-line technology in anticipation of a more educated and demanding consumer. Most of the 20 American producers were on the east coast, and four major operations (three in Maine) dominated the industry.

The Mussel Scare

Since 1989, mussel farming has been an industry plagued by inconsistent quality standards, seasonal supply, environmental hazards, and problems of mussel toxicity. The efforts of most of the private growers and producers who Wilson knew were directed toward preventing a repeat of the crisis of December 1987, when two deaths and 134 cases of illness were attributed to toxic molluscs from Prince Edward Island. On the American east coast, the "Red Tide" (a marine condition that makes mussels toxic) had created havoc in the mollusc industry. Even though water temperature and other environmental conditions made the Red Tide a threat to Prince Edward Island waters but not to Nova Scotian waters, consumers assumed that all Atlantic products were at risk.

Industry self-regulation and government authorities had made improvements in quality control. The federal government had revamped its Shellfish Monitoring Program, which included testing of water quality by Environment Canada, testing of the product by the Department of Fisheries and Oceans, and policing of growing areas by various agencies in order to prevent harvesting in closed areas. Wilson was prepared to support these activities, but he also needed to make decisions concerning product line and what markets to pursue.

1   What type of products (growing methods) should be adopted by Chalaga Mussel Farms? What markets should be pursued?
2   What pricing strategy must be adopted, given the products and markets that are selected?

*This case was prepared by Dr. Christopher Vaughan and Dr. Julia Sagebien of Saint Mary's University as a basis for classroom discussion and is not meant to illustrate either effective or ineffective marketing management. The case is based on material gathered by Ian McLeod for his master's research project at Saint Mary's University, together with material from a case previously published by Dr. Julia Sagebien and copyright by the Atlantic Entrepreneurial Institute. Used with permission from the authors.

36   Argon Carpet Cleaning Company*

The company's fiscal year end on March 31 was six weeks away. Bill Sartoris, the founding owner/manager, and his wife, Bena, had worked day and night for over six years building the company. He now felt he was at a turning point in his life. He had just reached his 56th birthday and was still working 60 hours a week. But while his company was making a good profit, he believed that success was eluding him. At breakfast that morning, his wife raised the thought that perhaps he should sell the company and do something else.

Introduction
The company, Argon Carpet Cleaning Company Drapery & Upholstery Cleaners Limited, was founded in January 1995 as a sole proprietorship. Starting with little more than a vacuum cleaner and a scrub bucket, Mr. Sartoris targeted building managers and apartment building owners as his primary customers. In order to set himself apart from the usual "mop and pail" operators in the industry, he offered extra free services, cleaning entranceways or common areas at no charge whenever he was called on to provide apartment cleaning services. Six years later, he had become relatively successful with sales approaching $1 million.

The Cleaning Industry
The company is in an industry that has enjoyed solid growth over the last decade. The building services sector, including office, plant, and apartment maintenance, renovations, and restoration, has grown at an average annual rate of 12 percent each year since 1986, with little indication of a decline.

Up until the late 1950s, most office, apartment, business, and manufacturing operations performed their own cleaning and maintenance with in-house staff. For example, Cadillac-Fairview during the early 1960s maintained a staff of 50 people to look after the apartment complexes it was developing in Toronto. By the mid-1970s, the cleaning and maintenance of rental housing (already approaching 10,000 rental units in the Toronto market) was causing at least one major property management company no end of problems in staffing, and it replaced its staff of over 200 full and part-time employees with outside contracting services. This started a trend toward using building service contractors in Canada.

Today the service to buildings and dwellings sector (NAIC 56121) of the business services industry exceeds $2.5 billion in revenue and employs over 100,000 people in Canada. From 1986 to 1996 total revenues increased from $1.09 billion to $2.07 billion, an 89 percent increase over a ten-year period, with almost 11,000 firms in 1996.

Exhibit 1: Canadian Janitorial (Cleaning) Services, Industry estimates (Dollars)

	Total revenue (in millions)	No. of firms (Businesses)
1990	1,662	8,923
1991	1,775	9,562
1992	1,837	10,194
1993	1,898	10,791
1994	1,971	11,750
1995	2,059	12,487
1996	2,070	10,887

Source: Statistics Canada

The average company does about $190,000 in annual sales (see Exhibit 1). The more typical firms—that is to say those which earn less than $2 million in revenue—average only $123,000 per year in annual sales. These smaller companies make up 99 percent of the industry. In fact, there are fewer than 100 firms in Canada doing more than $2 million annually.

The industry in British Columbia has also experienced considerable growth, most of it in the last few years. From 1990 to 1996 total revenue grew at an annual rate of 18 percent to $450 million, most of it in the greater Vancouver market, where it is estimated that the industry will reach $605 million for 2004. There are 1,900 companies competing in the B.C. market. Most of these are small operators. Only a few earn $6 million in sales.

The Building Services Market

Most of the building services market in British Columbia is in the commercial or business sector, accounting for 78 percent of all revenues. Government institutions—schools, offices, and other facilities—represent 18 percent while private households take up the balance.

Market Cleaning Segments

Offices	2.95 million sq. ft.
Hotels	30,000 units
Retail	40 million sq. ft.
Restaurant	5 million sq. ft.
Shopping malls	8 million sq. ft.
Plants and warehouses	1 million sq. ft.
Rental apartments	110,000 units

Within the business sector, there are seven segments:
- Drapery and blind services
- Window cleaning
- Walls and ceilings
- Carpet cleaning and service
- Floor cleaning and service
- Restoration (flood and fire)
- Other

Within these, there are seven markets, which include:

Office cleaning

There are almost 5 million square feet of office space in the greater Vancouver area. The market is relatively competitive for cleaning services; prices range from $2.07 per square foot in the suburban areas to $1.26 for larger, downtown buildings. The costs for repair and maintenance range from $1.56 in the downtown area to $1.44 in the outlying areas. This indicates an annual sales volume of $14 to $16 million (based on BOMA statistics), with an additional $16 to $32 million from other office markets. The total potential is about $41 million annually.

Hotels

There is not a great deal of statistical information on cleaning services in the hotel and accommodation sector. There are an estimated 30,000 units in the Vancouver area, but many such establishments hire their own staff to service the rooms and do the cleaning. However, excluding cleaning services and using office costs as a guide, the potential for carpet repair services could reach $5 million a year.

Retail stores

There are roughly 50 million square feet of commercial retail space in Vancouver, with much of this contracted out to cleaning services. Here, approximately 15,000 stores are expected to spend $65 to $100 million for cleaning. The likely average is $80 million a year.

Restaurants

Most restaurants employ their own staff to clean the premises. However, taking into account repair and replacement for draperies, blinds, and so on, the estimated income potential runs about $5 million a year.

Shopping malls

Malls (including both stores and common areas) account for about 12 million square feet, or $30 million in revenue potential.

Plants and warehouses

There are few reliable sources of statistics for this market sector. Most production plants and warehouses use their own employees for cleaning, but specialized services such as cleaning and repairing draperies and blinds could result in sales between $3 million and $10 million.

Apartment rental units

There are 110,000 rental units in the greater Vancouver area (Refer to CMHC Published Statistics), representing over $20 million in cleaning services. This market has been growing significantly in the GVRD and is expected to double with the addition of condominium services in the next decade.

Summary Market Potential

There is a potential for this sector of $615 million in British Columbia. Assuming that the GVRD accounts for 60 percent of this value, the total revenue potential that is calculated using comes to $369 million.

Competition

There are five or six big players and a thousand "mop and pail" operators in Vancouver and the Lower Mainland. Statistics Canada listed 2177 firms in 1996. The top few account for 38 percent of the volume, while the balance (2170 firms) have annual sales of $275 million, or about $127,000 each. Argon is expected to reach just under $1,000,000 for the 1993–94 period, making it one of the larger organizations in the market.

There are about 200 competitors listed in the Vancouver Yellow Pages that compete with Argon. However, taking into account the company's 14 percent annual growth, there is little reason why the firm should be concerned with competitors at this point, particularly since Argon Carpet Cleaning accounts for less than 1 percent of the market. However, there is a considerable amount of guerrilla warfare taking place in the market. A number of larger firms have expressed concern about the "mop and pail" competition. In one contract bid situation, a big company's $2,500/month bid for a government contract was given to a "mop and pail" for about $1,000/month, or the cost of labour.

Exhibit 2: Revenue Sources

1. Offices	5 million sq. ft. (BOMA)	$12 to $41 million
2. Hotels	30,000 units	$5 to $10 million
3. Retail	60 million sq. ft.	$65 to $100 million
4. Restaurants	5 million sq. ft.	$5 to $10 million
5. Shopping malls	12 million sq. ft.	$30 million
6. Plants and warehouses		$3 to $10 million
7. Rental apartments		$8 to $20 million
8. Other		$30 to $50 million
Total		$158 to $271 million

Argon's Competitive Advantage

Most companies, mainly rental property managers, have a favourable attitude toward Argon. A typical observation is that managers actively seek out high-quality cleaning contractors. They rely on outside services for all carpet cleaning, drape and blind service, and renovations, and there are a number of important components that influence the buying decision.

1.   Availability, regardless of the time.
2.   Company personality—the ability to get along with tenants.
3.   Reliability and consistency.
4.   Value for price. In this respect the evaluation goes beyond quality of workmanship, which is an expectation.

Argon has been very sensitive to these elements and has incorporated them into their selling strategy. Consequently, the company has been able to develop a positive, professional reputation and is able to inspire confidence in tenants and managers alike.

Most managers prefer to establish a long-term relationship with their outside contractors. Argon already has a good customer base representing over 400 building complexes and managers, including some of the larger real-estate management firms such as North American Management, Viam Group, Bristol Management, Continental Realty, Nacel Properties, and Ranch Realty.

As it expands its operations and continues to provide that same sense of value, there is little reason why it should not expect good, solid growth.

History of Argon Carpet Cleaning Company

From 1995 to 1998, Mr. Sartoris barely managed to break even as he learned the business and began to establish a network of customers and suppliers who could help him grow. In 1998 the cleaning side of the business began to earn a profit with sales of $286,000 and gross profit of $60,000, increasing to $630,000 in sales for the first ten months of 2003.

Allocation of revenue sources:

Cleaning services	56%
Drapery and blind sales	11
Flood and restoration	18
Carpet repair and installation	15
	100%

During the 2003-2004 period (fiscal year end is March 31), the company operated as a mixed service organization and responded to whatever orders were called in by building managers. In one respect this is a positive aspect of the business. Their reputation as a reliable, consistently available cleaning company has offset the need for a sales force to generate orders.

The company operates from a 6,000 square foot plant in New Westminster, centrally located to serve its Lower Mainland market. The company has a lean administrative staff consisting of an administrative manager, a coordinator, a receptionist-dispatcher, and an accounts clerk.

The company originally started its business in cleaning carpets, flooring, and other areas of offices and apartments. Starting with a single van, the company progressed to ten truck vans and expects to add two in the coming year. Each vehicle is self-contained and has $5,000 worth of equipment, and each operator manages the vehicle as a small business. Argon Carpet assumes responsibility for the vehicle, its upkeep, operations, and supply of cleaning chemicals. The operator realizes a 26 percent commission.

The company schedules jobs for each of the ten cleaning operators, who are also required to perform other services. Typically, they pick up and deliver drapes and window blinds that have been cleaned, repaired, or newly supplied by Argon Carpet. They are encouraged to do other jobs at a site if approached by the building manager, and end each job by filling out a quality checklist that is used to assess the cleaning job and prospects for other cleaning and repair opportunities. The vans return each night to the plant, where the equipment and vehicles are serviced, and where supplies are restocked for the following day.

Drapery Manufacturing

The company supplies drapes and Venetian blinds to apartments and offices on an intermittent basis. It has recently moved into full-time production of these products in answer to a need by building managers for quick, consistent, and reliable service. The company has two people on sewing operations, including a supervisor, and is now producing 10 to 15 sets per week. The production department is located on the second floor of the plant in 1,000 square feet of space.

Flood and Restoration

The company would like to expand this part of its business portfolio. The attraction to this market is the relatively high markup for providing fast, quality cleanup of homes and businesses following a flood or fire. Offsetting the good profitability is the 90 to 120 day aged receivable period, since the bills are paid out of insurance claims. However, Argon has factored these "hidden costs" into the selling price. The company uses its coordinators to look after these projects, which draw on one or more cleaners from the company's regular cleaning operation.

Carpet Installation

This is a very profitable part of the company. In the past this service was provided to customers as a courtesy. However, the business is now continuous and flows from Argon's cleaning service. The company maintains a list of reliable carpet layers, who are scheduled as the jobs come up. It purchases its own materials, usually based on a standard for the installation. The company's main inputs to this service are scheduling and purchasing. Labour is contracted to do the job.

Dry Cleaning Operations

Argon owns a soon-to-be-obsolete dry cleaning plant. This 1,200 square foot operation is separate from the main business, and after B.C. government regulations covering perchloride emissions are implemented at the end of 2004, it will be redundant. During the last fiscal year, this operation received approximately $5,000 worth of business monthly from Argon, in addition to doing $300 daily in walk-in trade. The plan is to consolidate this operation and to purchase an environmentally acceptable dry cleaning business.

Operating Costs Annual ($)

The company's past experience provides a solid basis for establishing the costs of future operations. Operating costs have been established as follows:

1. Rent and business taxes	42,000
2. Plant overhead: shop expense, training, equipment leases, misc.	13,600
3. Depreciation	15,000
4. Maintenance	6,900
5. Utilities	7,000
6. Vehicles: insurance, fuel, repairs	54,700
	(10% increase)
7. Vehicle leasing	18,300
	(20% increase)
8. Payroll (includes office)	333,400
	(10% increase)
	490,900

Company Operations

Also, administration and marketing costs include accounting, advertising, bad debts, consulting, insurance, damage, office expense and supplies, telephone, travel, and entertainment. These costs are projected at $92,600 for 2004 and are expected to increase 20 percent annually.

Comparative Performance Statistics: Argon Carpet Vs Industry Cleaning Company Averages

Cost of goods	3%	17%
Salaries, wages	61	43
Rent	1	3
Repair and maintenance	1	1
Advertising	1	2
Depreciation	1	2
Occupancy expense	3	3
Others	23	17
Profit margin	6	12
	100%	100%

Source: Stats Canada, Cat: 63-232

There is a considerable difference between the Argon Carpet operations and the average firm. First, the company is twice as profitable. Second, it generates more value-added content through its repair and replacement activities (high cost of goods sold). Part of the company in fact does manufacturing.

Organization

Bill's son Fredericci looks after the company's accounting, while his wife Bena looks after the banking. The company payroll is managed by the bank. Fred doubles as a coordinator and project boss when floods and other emergency cleanup jobs come into the plant on weekends and evenings.

1   What marketing strategy would you employ to double the company's sales?
2   What are the some of the problems that will have to be addressed if the firm is to grow?
3   As a consultant to the company, what would be your detailed recommendations in regard to marketing and operations management?
4   Should Sartoris sell the company?

Argon Carpet Cleaning Company, Drapery & Upholstery Cleaners
Balance Sheet
December 1, 2003

Assets			Liabilities		
Current Assets			**Current Liabilities**		
Petty cash	0.58-		Loan-line of credit		74,000.00
Cash clearing	0.00		Accounts payable		2,206.03
Royal Bank	25,363.86-		Misc. accrued payables		4,153.37
Bank of Montreal	1,406.39		Vacation payable		6,980.63
AAA Fuels	72,155.32		Corp. income taxes payable		292.65-
Accounts receivable	155,505.75		UIC payable	58.23-	
Advance receivable	455.00		CPP payable	22.00-	
Receivables: net		204,158.02	Federal income tax payable	63.592	
Prepaid exp. and deposits		7,694.92	Rec. gen payable: total		143.82-
Prepaid vehicle insurance		5,842.20	Misc. deductions		13.25
Deferred finance charges		6,934.39	WCB payable		5,834.12
Total Current Assets		224,629.53	Shareholder's loan		203,183.03
			GST charged on sales	4,558.98	
			GST paid on purchases	2,127.56-	
			GST owing		2,431.42
			PST payable		390.51
			Total Current Liabilities		298,755.89
Fixed Assets					
Vehicles	98,368.94				
Trailer	12,758.00				
Accum deprec: vehicles	5,159.032				
Vehicles: net		105,967.91			
Cleaning equipment	135,735.62				
Office furniture & equip.	24,480.07				
Accum deprec.:			**Long Term Liabilities**		
furn & equip	16,518.902		Cond. sale contract—11		20,837.89
Drapery-making			Cond. sale contract—9		19,436.38
equipment	5,782.31		Royal Bank loan—vehicle		36,689.00
Shop equipment	32,292.69		Drycleaning sale contract		6,900.00
Furniture & equipment: net		181,771.79	**Total Long Term**		83,863.27
Computer	14,579.40				
Accum. deprec.					
–computer	1,436.91-		**Total Liabilities**		382,619.16
Computer: net		13,142.49			
Dry cleaning equip.		8,056.00			
Dry cleaning goodwill		12,000.00	**Equity**		
Total Fixed Assets		320,938.19	Common shares		100.00
			Total Share Capital		100.00
Total Assets		545,567.72			
			Retained Earnings		
			Retained earnings		67,480.47
			Current earnings		95,368.09
			Total Retained Earnings		162,848.56
			Total Equity		162,948.56
			Liabilities and Equity		545,567.72

Argon Carpet Cleaning Company, Drapery & Upholstery Cleaners
Income
April 1, 2003, to January 31, 2004

Revenue			Expense		
Service Revenue			**Cost of Goods**		
Dry cleaning		3,918.91	Service equipment rental		842.84
Area rug cleaning		1,325.51	Cleaning supplies		16,790.03
Carpet cleaning		330,841.85	Dry cleaning supplies		4,317.05
Blind cleaning		11,35 2.88	Repair supplies		5,178.00
Flood/restoration		36,51 2.25	Carpet and underlay material		56,704.59
Scotchguard/deodorizer		5,560.12	Drapery materials		36,013.45
Pressure washing		12,29 7.50	Blind materials		2,271.20
Drapery cleaning		35,99 1.01	**Total Cost of Goods Sold**		122,117.16
Upholstery cleaning		5,254.56			
Drapery sales		82,64 7.61	**Operating Expenses**		
Blind sales		969.96	Shop expense		2,637.14
Carpet repair		13,38 6.39	Technician courses		1,382.37
Lino and carpet installation		93,379.60	Accounting		5,192.00
Blind repair		334.31	Advertising		11,308.10
Drapery repair		70.00	Equipment repair and maint		5,761.40
Pet odour control		1,024.00	Bad debts		215.00
Service call	6,043.69		Bank charges and interest		7,542.07
Labour on flood/rest.	40,985.26		Consulting/legal fees		9,792.35
Equipment rental	36,815.00		Insurance		3,770.72
Underlay supplied	10,871.92		Miscellaneous		1,139.51
Misc. material supplied	2,406.12		Damaged goods or property		531.54
Total flood/restoration		97,12 1.99	Office expense		12,858.34
Miscellaneous revenue		1,233.50	Office supplies		5,174.65
Total Sales Revenue		733,221.95	Rent and taxes		35,097.17
			Telephone		20,335.87
			Travel and entertainment		4,246.76
Total Revenue		733,221.95	Utilities		5,872.83
			Shareholder's wages	41,800.00	
			Wages	257,547.44	
			UIC expense	9,379.40	
			CPP expense	5,172.53	
			WCB expense	5,732.77	
			Payroll expense: total		319,632.14
			Vehicle, gas and oil		20,536.57
			Vehicle insurance		10,149.55
			Vehicle, repairs and maint.		14,908.59
			Vehicle, lease payments		15,251.52
			Equipment lease payments		2,440.51
			Total Operating Expenses		515,736.70
			Total Expense		637,853.86
			Income		95,368.09

*This case was written by Dr. Ken Blawatt, who at the time of its preparation was associated with Simon Fraser University as an Adjunct Professor at the University College of the Cariboo.

37   Columbia Chrome: A Joint Venture with India*

Columbia Chrome Industries Ltd. is engaged in repairing, rebuilding, and manufacturing of hydraulic and pneumatic components on various types of mechanical equipment. In their 40,000 square foot plant in Langley, British Columbia, the company offers fully integrated services with cutting edge technology in hard chroming, honing, grinding, machining, welding, and so on. Customer experience reveals that rebuilt rods, pins, and valves wear much longer than the originals; yet the cost is only one-third to one-half of the price of new ones, resulting in savings of hundreds of thousands of dollars on new equipment.

Columbia Chrome services machines used in a number of industries, but the main target market is mining companies that use various types of mining equipment. The strategy is to offer customers the best in quality control and fast service, at competitive prices. This strategy has enabled the company to outperform its rivals. Sales and profits have steadily increased over the years; current combined sales exceed $15 million.

The company has eight branches in western Canadian mining towns. Its head office and production plant are in Langley, B.C. In the United States it has expanded into the mining states of Colorado, Wyoming, Arizona, Nevada, and Washington.

The next natural expansion was to markets outside North America. Pursuing an aggressive international marketing program, Columbia Chrome set up joint ventures with Malaysia, Papua New Guinea, Australia, Thailand, and Indonesia in the Asia Pacific, and also made direct sales of turnkey plants to Colombia and Peru in South America.

Foreign expansion is a priority for the company, and the company's international marketing strategy is to go global—that is, go where the markets are. This strategy involves simultaneous entry in entirely different markets—and through different entry modes, if warranted. The latest expansion is a joint venture with India. Also, discussions are under way for joint ventures with three other countries—the People's Republic of China, Kuwait, and Ireland. To facilitate such expansion, an international subsidiary called Colco International Industries Ltd. has been created. President of the new division is Mr. John Jansen, who was previously president of Columbia Chrome. Mr. Jansen trots around the globe making new deals and overseeing projects in various stages of completion.

The India Partner

Colco's partner in India is an engineering firm, Concast India Ltd., which in reality is a holding company under the Concast name with head offices in Mumbai (formerly Bombay). The Concast group offers a variety of engineering services and products to the Indian market such as steel plant equipment manufacturing, continuous casting machines, and pollution control systems. The technology for some of these services and products has been acquired through foreign collaborations.

Concast is owned mostly by Mr. Narinder Nayar, the managing director, who started the business in 1983 and singlehandedly built the Concast group of companies. They employ 225 people, including project planning teams, technical consultants, marketing personnel, and service engineers. In spite of keen competition, sales have grown steadily to their present level of 400 million rupees, or about 16 million dollars. As local technology in hard chroming is outdated, Concast has been on the lookout for foreign collaborators for some time.

In 2003, an equity joint-venture agreement was signed between Concast and Colco. The new enterprise was named Columbia Chrome India Private Ltd. A private limited company incorporated in India has restrictions on the right of transfer of shares—it cannot have more than 50 shareholders or make public issue of its shares or debentures.

The primary objective of the joint venture is to obtain a competitive edge in the marketplace in high-precision technology applications in hard chroming and maintenance of hydraulic cylinders. The long-term plan is to use the experience gained from the first plant to build a chain of service facilities in key markets in India.

The main target market of Columbia Chrome India Pr. Ltd. is the mining companies. To this end, Goa, a seaport on the west coast of India about 500 kilometres south of Mumbai, has been selected as the location for the first plant. Goa (which was once a Portuguese colony) and the nearby states of Karnataka and Andhra Pradesh contain vast deposits of iron ore, copper, bauxite, and manganese, which are presently mined with old equipment and outdated technology. So there is immense scope not only for chroming technology, but also for the upgrading and optimizing of mining operations as a whole, to make them competitive in terms of quality and cost.

The Pattern of Negotiations
Initial contacts between Colco and Concast started in 1999, soon after the Indian government abandoned its old model of a "mixed economy" and opened up the country for large-scale foreign investment. A year after liberalization, Barton Biggs, chairman of Morgan Stanley Management, stated that "India is an interesting example for foreign investment because the overall economy will grow 5% to 6% a year even though the mass of the economy is the agricultural and government sectors . . . as we calculate it, the private sector's real GNP growth is about 10% a year. It is a dynamic story."

The economy has posted an average growth rate of 6% since 1990, slowing down somewhat in 2003 to 4.3%.

Concast initiated the venture through networking with the Canadian Trade Commissioner in India as well as the Canada-India Business Council. After an exchange of visits by senior executives of the two firms, a detailed feasibility study was undertaken. It showed excellent short-term as well as long-term potential for profit.

Concast is the major shareholder in the joint venture, with 60 percent of equity. Colco has 40 percent. Five directors are appointed, three from the Indian side and two from Canada. The project's implementation, day-to-day operations, and marketing will all be looked after by Concast personnel; no expatriates from Canada will be required. However, initially a group of technicians from India will go to Canada to acquire training of three to four weeks' duration in chroming technology. Their visit will be facilitated by the Canadian International Development Agency (http://www.acdi-cida.gc.ca/index-e.htm).

Between the initial stages of searching for a partner and the signing of the final agreement, four years elapsed. Both parties wanted to proceed faster with an agreement; however, the Indian bureaucracy turns its wheels slowly. Interestingly, in a poll conducted on governmental bureaucracy by Roper Starch Worldwide, the Indian government received low ratings. More than two-thirds of those polled said that the bureaucratic challenges of doing business in India were greater than in other developing countries.

Also contributing to the slow pace of negotiations was the variance in management styles between the two countries. In comparison to Canada, decision making in India, generally speaking, is slower, and once decisions are made, implementation also is slower. Besides, Indian managers work in an environment characterized by scarcity; many are not yet used to thinking in terms of efficiency, quality, core competency, and the like—the common parameters of a successful business in a competitive environment.

The joint venture is now at the implementation stage. Land has been acquired in Goa, and a project team from Concast is overseeing the plant construction. However, during the long negotiation period, some of the competing companies have acquired chroming technology with foreign collaboration; hence, Concast may have lost its competitive advantage. To be on the safe side, Concast and Colco are now contemplating a project with a smaller scope than originally envisaged.

1   Evaluate the economic, cultural, and political risks Columbia Chrome took in its decision to set up the joint venture in India. What are some of the typical problems investors encounter?

2   What opportunities does India offer to market North American products and services?

*This case was written by Dr. George Jacob, who at the time of its preparation was associated with BCIT.

38   Ecolad Incorporated*

Ecolad Inc. is a family-owned business incorporated in 1996. The firm is located on Ouellette Avenue, the heart of the business district in Windsor, Ontario. The president of the firm is Gary Awad, and he works with his three brothers, who are actively engaged in the business. Ecolad employs a secretary and an artist.

A Family Business

After the business was established in Windsor, Gary Awad was able to convince his brother, Tom, to join the new firm. Previously, Tom worked for twelve years with General Motors as an industrial engineer. He then set up his own firm and bought a custom framing shop, called Noon Day Graphics, in the same building occupied by Ecolad. Roger is also part of the family enterprise and was working for Chrysler Canada before joining the other family members. Roger Awad, the third brother, is now in Toronto trying to establish Ecolad's presence in Canada's largest city.

Finally, Richard Awad, a school teacher by training, will move shortly to London, Ontario, to manage the Ecolad franchise, which recently had been repurchased by the company. In the last few years, the London franchise had not done very well and it was in poor financial health. The family is now the main source of financing for Ecolad.

Ecolad's Mission

Ecolad is primarily in the business of selling advertising space to any firm or organization wishing to advertise on the side of a litter container. The litter containers are located in high-traffic areas in those cities and shopping malls where Ecolad is able to obtain territorial exclusivity. For example, the greater Windsor area has over 120 litter containers owned and maintained by Ecolad.

Presently, Ecolad supplies free of charge the containers to any participating city or mall. In return, the company asks for a three to five year contract granting Ecolad the exclusive right to offer such a service in the area. It hopes to expand the number of available locations to include schools and university campuses, as well as recreational areas such as campgrounds, golf courses, sports clubs, and so forth. Ecolad feels that its litter containers are a service to the public at no cost to cities or firms that are willing to permit their display. According to Gary Awad, "Ecolad is also in the business of fostering good litter habits among consumers."

Understandably, most city administrators are very receptive to the arrangement proposed by Ecolad. Gary Awad, the president, and Tom, VP, are the family members most actively involved in seeking contractual permissions to locate the litter containers in approved locations. Once permission is granted, they and other commissioned sales representatives attempt to sell advertising space available on the four panels of the litter containers.

Ecolad's advertising media service is not a new idea, at least in the greater Windsor area. The idea of providing advertising space on litter containers was first introduced in the city in the late 1960s. Unfortunately, that original provider went bankrupt because the containers available then were of poor quality and were easily damaged. As a result, they had to be replaced too often and their high replacement cost led to the company's demise. In the United States, such a business venture was successful right at the beginning because the litter containers used were much heavier and sturdier, and did not have to be replaced as often.

Initially, Ecolad began importing American-made litter containers. Later on, Gary Awad secured an agreement with Alcan of Canada to make the containers. The aluminum is poured into a special mould that was developed in accordance with Ecolad's specific needs. As a result, these containers are now sturdy enough to take abuse and are resistant to oxidation. The top part of the container has a movable aluminum flap on which is inscribed "Waste Only." Each container cost Ecolad about $300. The potential advertising revenue per container varies between $50 and $100 per panel per month, depending on its location. Thus, a litter container can generate as much as $400 per month (assuming all four sides are used).

Ecolad feels that the service it provides accomplishes two functions. First, with its free containers, Ecolad provides a free waste management program to any city, mall, or other organization willing to participate. Second, this advertising medium is less costly compared to most other established media, including outdoor. Ecolad offers small and medium sized companies an affordable advertising medium.

The approximate size of each panel is 60 by 90 cm (or 2 by 3 feet). The artist produces all the panels according to customers' advertising specifications. Each panel is laminated to protect it from the elements. The actual cost of preparing each panel advertisement varies widely, from $50 to $400 or more, depending on what is to be done and the quality of the colour reproduction desired.

All maintenance of the litter containers is done by Ecolad. The firm cleans and washes the containers on a weekly basis. Ecolad repairs and replaces those containers as necessary. Such quick servicing is not available for billboards, for which repairs can take up to one month and which are cleaned only a couple of times a year. Ecolad gives advertisers free exposure time equivalent to the time lost while the container was out of use. As an added service, a new Ecolad advertiser is given up to one week of free advertising time on a company truck, which has space reserved for such a purpose—a service unmatched by any other outdoor media firm. However, emptying the containers is the responsibility of the city, the mall, or the organization under contract with Ecolad.

The Ricky Receptacle Awareness Program
Ecolad is now in the process of changing the moveable flaps on the containers to ones that have the inscription "Ricky Receptacle says Thank You." The containers are now only available in the Windsor area, but Ecolad hopes to expand the program to all other markets it serves. The reason for the change is to make the litter containers more user friendly—to give the containers human qualities. It is hoped that the new inscription on the flap will personalize the containers and help promote Ecolad's image of being an ecologically responsible firm.

Gary Awad is confident that the new Ricky Receptacle initiative will further enhance Ecolad's corporate image, especially in those cities which have yet to grant Ecolad's need for exclusive distribution rights. Ecolad is also hoping that the new Ricky Receptacle program will create goodwill among current advertising users. More importantly, Tom Awad is convinced that the new program will add credibility and goodwill to any business buying advertising space on Ecolad's containers.

Advertisers will want to associate themselves with a firm that has such a favourable image in the community. All the other Awad brothers expressed the same feeling that the Ricky Receptacle inscription on the litter containers will be a big boost to their business. Irrespective of this new initiative, Ecolad has always faced the drawback of trying to convince advertisers that a garbage container can be used to help promote their goods and services. Tom Awad prefers to call Ecolad's litter containers "pollution control devices" so as to minimize any negative connotations that advertisers or consumers associate with garbage cans.

The Ricky Receptacle program was launched in Windsor and was not only aimed at Ecolad's prime market but also at kids. An Ecolad spokesperson, taking the role of "Ricky Receptacle," visited kindergarten classes and other educational institutions and gave advice to kids on the benefits of litter control. Children were able to talk to Ricky and were able to ask him questions about pollution and the consequences of poor waste management habits. As part of this pollution awareness campaign, Ecolad made it possible for children to send letters to Ricky Receptacle, which were answered. It also sent questionnaires to parents to find out if their children's litter habits had changed as a result of Ecolad's efforts to promote sound litter habits. The educational litter awareness program aimed at kids was very successful in that it received wide media coverage with the CBC and the CTV networks. It also enjoyed much local press and radio coverage. This free publicity for Ecolad made the firm the talk of the town and had a favourable impact on Ecolad's business.

Some Problems for Ecolad
City administrators and mall operators request far more containers than Ecolad is willing or capable of supplying. Ecolad's distribution policy of litter containers is based on the amount of advertising space it can sell in the area, not on the number of litter containers needed by the city or a mall. For Ecolad, there is an optimum number of containers that can be distributed in a given area. This number is always lower than the total number of litter containers a city or mall needs.

Also, the Ricky Receptacle program is becoming far too costly for Ecolad to manage. Using Ecolad people to educate the public about litter issues was not the most efficient way for those people to generate sales for the company. Gary Awad thinks that the best way to solve this problem is to obtain municipal grants or some other form of government financial assistance to keep the litter educational awareness program going.

1   Is there any conflict of interest in Ecolad's mission of serving its own needs while at the same time attempting to serve the needs of the community?

2   What business is Ecolad in?

3   Is Ecolad's demand for exclusive distribution rights for litter containers appropriate?

4   Should the Ricky Receptacle program be extended to all Ecolad's markets?

5   To what extent will the new inscription on the container's flap affect consumers?

6   What should Gary Awad do with the Ricky Receptacle awareness program?

7   Can Ecolad change the litter habits of kids? What about adults? What about a community, or society in general?

*This case was written by Dr. Robert Tamilia, who at the time of its preparation was associated with UQAM (University of Québec at Montreal).

	39	**Maritime Trading Company**

In February 2004, Kent Groves sat in a coffee shop thinking about his company's new site on the World Wide Web. As president of Maritime Trading Company, a small business he started in 1998, he still made most of the decisions for the company.

Maritime Trading had had a Web site since 2000. Until recently, there had been no real strategy for the site. In 2000, some friends of Kent's, who had developed skills in Web site development, offered to create one for MTC for little cost. Kent's attitude toward this was "let's throw it up and see what happens." From that time until the end of 2003, co-op students from a local university maintained it. The only purpose of the site was to be an on-line extension of the company's catalogue, giving people using the Internet access to the products.

In January 2004, Kent had the site redesigned to appear more professional and include complete, secure on-line ordering. He wanted to entice people to visit and order on-line. Kent wondered how to both draw traffic to the Web site and encourage customers to come back. His goal was to provide the most interactive and secure on-line shopping experience in Atlantic Canada.

Company Background

Maritime Trading began as a mail-order company specializing in foods and consumables unique to Nova Scotia. Its first catalogue was published in 1998 and products were marketed only in Canada at that time. Between 1998 and 2000, new products were added and subsequent versions of the catalogue were produced. Exhibit 1 provides a synopsis of the company's development.

Exhibit 1: Synopsis of MTC's Development

Year	New products	Other developments	Sales
1998	Gift boxes, jams, maple products, fruit syrups, fruitcake, hand-made soap, herbal oils and vinegars, balsam Christmas wreaths	First catalogue published	N/A
1999	Clothing, dried flowers, coffee, oatcakes, lobster pate	Retail store opened in Halifax Second catalogue produced	N/A
2000	More titles of East Coast music	More emphasis on Canadian East Coast music Vender kiosk opened on Halifax Waterfront East Coast music catalogue produced Expansion of retail store Third catalogue produced Started to explore the Internet	$350,000

2001	Toys, books, home décor items, King Cole tea, Ganong chocolates, live lobster	Retail expansion continued Fourth catalogue published Hired co-op students to do new Web site design	$500,000
2002		Full-page colour catalogue published More advanced Web site; all products on-line Expanded into wholesale	$700,000
2003	Jewellery, art, smoked salmon, maple syrup	Sixth catalogue produced Relationship with Icom Alliance began New Web site launched in December	$750,000

MTC had been keeping track of its customers and sales in a database for several years. Although the company had customers from all walks of life, the typical customer had remained the same. Women in their late 30s to 50s, with considerable disposable income, were the greatest consumers of the company's products. When it came to mail-order sales, this typical customer was generally restricted from shopping in person either by geography or time constraints. Maritime Trading had never done very much prospecting for new business; eighty percent of its business had come from repeat customers over the last two years.

The company broke even in 2000. Kent felt this was appropriate, "It takes five years to build a critical mass in a direct-to-consumer venue." Maritime Trading had moved away from just marketing its products to the rest of Canada. Its new slogan, "Delivering Atlantic Canada to the World," clearly expressed its new scope.

Competition
Maritime Trading was in the gift business, selling predominantly via mail-order. The competition was almost any gift store and catalogue, anywhere. Three other organizations promoted regional Canadian products by mail-order and the World Wide Web: Beautiful BC, Canadian Geographic, and Images of Canada. Kent considered these three organizations as competition in only the loosest sense of the word.

Although several entrepreneurs had tried, no one had been successful in creating direct competition for MTC in the sale of Atlantic Canadian products. Kent believed these ventures did not have enough capital to be successful and did not anticipate any threats to his business in the near future.

Distribution Channels
Maritime Trading Company was a retailer and wholesale distributor for many small Maritime manufacturers and several medium-sized companies. It sold products from a retail

location, a catalogue, and the Web site. Orders from the catalogue and Web site were received by mail, fax or telephone. Products were also sold wholesale to other retail outlets.

Retail outlet
The peak sales period for the retail store was August and September, the prime tourist season in Halifax. Approximately 75 percent of the store's sales came from visitors to the area.

The VP of Retail Marketing, Stephen Simpson, was responsible for the development of retail operations. Stephen, aged 36, had joined Maritime Trading Company from a position as a general manager in automobile sales. The level of opportunity for retail expansion was considered quite high and a major goal was to open a retail location in Boston within three years.

Kent preferred to spend his time with the mail-order side of the company. Although he preferred to leave it up to Stephen, Kent realized retail was an integral part of mail-order sales. Tourists coming into the store would be encouraged by the staff to register to receive a catalogue. The retail presence of Maritime Trading directly drove mail-order sales.

Catalogue
In 2000, 20 percent of mail-order sales came from the U.S., while less than three percent came from the Atlantic Region of Canada. Seventy-seven percent of mail-order sales were from customers across the rest of Canada.

November was the busiest month for the mail-order business. This was the result of past visitors and Atlantic Canadians buying holiday gifts. The catalogue had developed greatly over the past few years and was currently a full format design (8.50 x 110) with 24 full-colour pages.

Wholesale
Kent was constantly searching for products to broaden the company's offering, especially for wholesale distribution, which made up approximately 15 percent of the company's sales. The challenge of this process was to find products that had sufficient margins for wholesaling to be worthwhile.

Wholesale customers included Alder's, a company that owned gift shops in several Maritime airports, and Clearwater Fine Foods. Kent saw the wholesale business as a definite growth area. However, the most popular high-margin products were fish products, which were sometimes in short supply. Kent was wary of sales growing to the point where he would be unable to meet the demands of his existing customers.

Web site
Kent viewed electronic commerce (the sale of products and services on-line) as the future of the Maritime Trading Company. With the new Web site in place, Kent was intent on increasing sales with the use of Internet technology. Kent did not see the Web site as a replacement for the current distribution channels but an extension of them. His focus was on

an integrated marketing strategy, allowing the customer to order products via any desired channel. He was afraid that if Maritime Trading wasn't offering its products on the Web, some customers might be dissuaded from buying.

Maritime Trading Company on the World Wide Web
The Web site had evolved since 2000. Initially, it had been just an experiment. It was inexpensive and entertaining to see if a few people would fill out the on-line order form or print it and fax it in. It was completely insecure, with no protection for those who entered their credit card numbers on-line. Orders came occasionally but far from regularly.

At the time, the company's domain name was unknown and virtually impossible to remember. In 2001, the site was linked to the sites of a few of the Maritime Trading Company's suppliers.

In 2001 and 2002, information management co-op students from a local university were hired to redesign and maintain the Web site. In 2002, Maritime Trading acquired the domain name maritimetrading.com. The site was largely unchanged until December 2002.
By this time, Kent was no longer satisfied with the site. He felt it was too static; it did not make use of the interactive aspect of the Internet medium. He contracted Icom Alliance to redesign the site. Icom was a small, Halifax-based, information technology services company specializing in electronic commerce and Web-enabled business solutions.

Maritime Trading agreed to pay Icom Alliance $2,500 for the initial design and a floating percentage of gross on-line sales (12.5 percent, on average). These payment terms were not typical but they involved a far lower up-front cost than the standard payment terms. Under standard terms, a site like the new Maritimetrading.com would have a start-up cost of approximately $10,000 and monthly updating fees of $150. Kent thought that he was getting a better deal with Icom Alliance. Furthermore, he knew the Icom managers personally and felt comfortable doing business with them.

The Future of Maritimetrading.com
Kent felt he had some good ideas about what the new Web site could accomplish. He believed that his own three-step marketing strategy for the company—acquisition, retention, and extension—was applicable to the Web site as well. Acquisition meant getting customers to visit the site for the first time. Retention referred to keeping the customer coming back. The third step, extension, was motivating customers to buy across a broad range of product offerings on the Web site.

Kent viewed this three-step process as the building of relationships with customers. He felt that relationship building was the only way to make the new Web site successful. His ultimate goal, of course, was to increase sales above and beyond what the catalogue brought in. In the meantime, Kent wanted to get customers comfortable with the Web as a shopping medium and provide a place where they could get useful and current information about Maritime Trading and its products. He was not exactly sure how he would know if the Web site was generating sales that would have come in from the catalogue anyway.

Site promotion

In 2003, the URL was promoted on all business cards, letterhead, envelopes, and gift cards. It was also printed on all private labels, inserts, and hang-tags. The address was published on every second page of the general merchandise catalogue and in the music catalogue. On-line promotion included links from suppliers, promotion by Icom Alliance, and targeted e-mail. Kent's goal was to incur few or no additional promotional costs for the Web site.

In the past, Kent supported the idea of registering with search engines but he felt quite differently about it by 2004. It was more than a matter of submitting a site, it became an issue of ranking (how close to the top would a site be listed in a search result). Ranking he found out depended on three related factors, how popular the site was or in other words how much traffic was generated, how many links there were to other sites, and finally how relevant the site was to the search parameters.

Kent also felt uneasy about using on-line promotion such as links from other sites and banner ads. At first, he didn't want very many links or any ads on the Maritime Trading site because he thought they would lead people away and advertising links did not fit with an online store.

Maritime Traders did not have many links to its site from other web sites. There were links on the pages of a few suppliers and on Icom Alliance's site.

It was for these reasons that Kent strongly felt traditional or offline promotion was the way to go for the new Web site. He didn't want to pull customers onto the site who had never heard of Maritime Trading. He wanted customers to see the URL on products and in the catalogues and then go to the site. This way, they would be familiar with Maritime Trading before they arrived at the Web site.

Keeping people coming back was part of the retention step of the marketing strategy. Kent was still wondering how to retain customers effectively. In order to make a purchase or enter a contest on the Web site, the customer had to fill out an on-line registration form, which included his or her e-mail address. The form included a question asking customers whether they would want to receive news and offers from the company. This gave Maritime Trading a way to make contact at a later date and build a relationship. This would also give him the opportunity to send out a regular newsletter that would include interesting articles as well as special promotions and new products.

The site also used "cookies," or pieces of information saved on the visitor's computer that allowed the company to record how often a particular computer accessed the site and what kind of pages the visitor looked at while there.

Cookies and unsolicited e-mail were a current issue of debate. The Canadian government was reviewing bill C-54, "an act to support and promote electronic commerce by protecting personal information that is collected, used or disclosed, in certain circumstances... ." This bill meant banning the use of information collected on-line for any purpose other than what the customer intended.

It was clear that any steps taken in the use of cookies and e-mail would have to be careful ones. The permission of the customer was obviously important.

Goals

In January 2004, the new site had 10,000 visits. Kent hoped to have 50,000 visits per month by the end of 2004. Sales on the old site had been roughly $500 per week. The new goal was to have weekly sales of $1,000-$2,000 by the end of the year.

Kent didn't have figures on the length of the average visit but he knew that longer visits meant more interest and more time for a relationship to be built. Catalogue requests had been fairly good in the past since they did not require a credit card number to be given on-line. However, Kent hoped for more activity with the new site.

Kent felt these goals were important as consumers became more comfortable with the idea of electronic commerce. He anticipated sales would become a significant measure of site effectiveness in the long term.

Gathering his thoughts

As Kent sat in the coffee shop, he began to organize his thoughts about the Web site. Although his off-line promotion of the site was quite extensive, he wondered if there was anything he could do to make it more effective on the shoestring budget he had for Web site promotion. The site had to be profitable in order to be worthwhile—it was already quite expensive and he needed cost-effective ideas. Kent was pretty sure off-line promotion was the way to go but was a bit concerned after hearing that someone wanting to visit the site could not find it because they had not been exposed to the promotion of the URL.

Kent felt that building a relationship on-line should be the main focus of the Web site. He was not sure how he could do this most effectively. The new site used cookies and the database of customers was growing. He really wanted to figure out how to build strong, lasting relationships with on-line customers. He knew he needed to give them something of value in order to keep them coming back.

Kent also realized that e-business could be more than just a Web site, but he wasn't exactly sure what else he could do. The office used accounting software for invoices and inventory management and much of the internal communication was done using e-mail. Kent was puzzled as to how he could use e-business when dealing with suppliers, since only around five percent even had a fax machine, let alone Web-based ordering systems.

Kent was meeting with Icom Alliance next week. He had some thinking to do. He flagged down a waiter. "Can I get a refill on this coffee?"

*Case by Shelley MacDougall and Martha Lawrence, F.C. Manning School of Business Administration, Acadia University, Nova Scotia, Canada.

Although his firm had been successful for a number of years providing marketing and sales training for agricultural companies, Tom Jackson, President of Agri Train, was   wondering if the time was right to introduce a major new product line. Since the company's inception in 1982, all training programs had been conducted in face-to-face, classroom type settings. Agri Train was very good at this traditional method of delivery having a number of long term, highly satisfied clients. Tom was not thinking of dropping this service, but was contemplating the introduction of a new service using online delivery of training programs. Given the rapid expansion of Internet use, Tom thought it might be time to move in this direction. He was unsure, however, of whether the market was really ready for this approach and how he should proceed with the idea.

Agri Train Inc.
Tom Jackson established Agri Train Inc., located in Milton, Ontario, in 1982 to provide marketing and sales training programs for agribusiness. Over the 17 years the company had been in business, revenues grew from just under $100,000 in the first year to $1,200,000 in 1999. In addition to Tom, Agri Train employed three full time trainers and one full time administrative assistant.

Agri Train's product line consisted of programs in marketing and sales. All of the company's programs were custom designed and offered for clients in all parts of North America. Current clients consisted of both large and small company's in the seed, chemical, machinery, animal health and feed industries.

A typical Agri Train program was three days in duration and normally held at a central location such as a hotel or a company's training center. Although participants included middle and senior management, most were sales representatives. The usual number of participants at a program varied from 15 to 25.

Although Agri Train programs were custom designed for individual clients, they were built around standard course modules. The customization usually consisted of changing the mix of course modules used and some cosmetic changes such as use of the client's logo on visual materials.

Two Agri Train programs were very popular and accounted for nearly 75% of the company's revenue. The first of these was called Principles of Agri Marketing (PAM). This program was targeted at sales reps and designed to provide basic marketing skills. As in all Agri Train programs, the method of instruction consisted of lecture/discussions and case studies. PAM topics normally included:
- Marketing Strategy Planning
- Financial Analysis for Marketing Decisions
- Marketing Products and Services
- Building a Marketing Mix
- Customer Buying Behavior

A second Agri Train program was called Strategic Agri Selling (SAS). This program was also targeted at sales representatives and designed to develop basic selling skills. In addition to lecture/discussions and case studies, this program involved role-playing sales situations. SAS topics normally included:

- Preparing for a Sales Call
- Opening a Sales Call
- Probing for Information
- Presenting Features and Benefits
- Handling Objections
- Closing the Sale
- Follow-up Service

The Online Opportunity

Agri Train had always relied heavily on computer technology in developing and presenting programs. It was one of the first training companies to adopt computer-generated graphics in the late 1980's when this technology was first developed. More recently, Tom experimented with digital video in presentations. For years the company used analog video in taping role-plays for subsequent analysis and discussion.

In July 1999, Tom attended an American Marketing Association conference on the use of online educational programs. Although the conference was designed mainly for university people that might want to start teaching online, Tom immediately recognized that this approach might be appropriate for the type of training programs his company conducted.

Online educational programs utilized the Internet as a delivery mechanism. Instead of face-to-face lectures, narrated PowerPoint presentations were used to deliver conceptual material. Various conferences were designed in chat rooms to allow participants to discuss cases or exercises. Assignments were completed using word processing programs and sent to the instructor as attachments. Tom was absolutely amazed at the versatility of this approach and began to think about how he might use this approach in his own company.

In October 1999 Tom signed up for a four week online training program offered by the Ontario Agricultural Training Institute (OATI) entitled: Achieving Exceptional Customer Satisfaction. It was during this course that Tom really began to appreciate the power of online delivery. Although the course only attracted eight participants, that was a sufficient number for Tom to see the ability of online delivery to facilitate participant interaction. Each week the participants were given case studies to read and discuss and it was not uncommon for there to be a hundred or more interactions among the eight people. Not only were there numerous interactions but, in Tom's opinion, the quality of the interactions was superb. Tom was also very impressed with the quality and quantity of individual feedback provided by the instructor. Based on this experience, Tom became convinced that the online method of delivery was a viable alternative to more traditional methods.

After completing the OATI course, Tom began to investigate the feasibility of adopting this approach for Agri Train. He started to assemble information on the costs associated with online delivery as well as the potential market for this product.

Because online training was a new concept, cost information was difficult to estimate. Based on information gleaned from a number of sources, Tom developed the following cost estimates:

- Course development costs could range anywhere from $30,000 to $50,000 for a single course. This included the development of teaching material, software development and programming. Once a course was developed it would cost at least $10,000 each year to update material and technology.
- Getting involved in online training would require more administrative support than the company currently had available. Tom felt this would cost an additional $50,000 each year.
- Because of the method of delivery, instructors for online course could be retained on a per course basis. Hiring the type of people required would probably cost Agri Train $150 per hour of instruction time. Tom estimated that it would take approximately 30 minutes per student per week of an instructor's time to provide basic instruction and feedback. Higher levels of individual feedback would require much greater instructor involvement, perhaps as much as one hour per student per week. Although the three people on staff at the present time were excellent in delivery face-to-face training programs, Tom was not sure they were the proper people to deliver an online program. In addition, they were all fully occupied with current duties.
- Several Internet providers were willing to support online training. Their fees for hosting a course were in the vicinity of $15 per week per participant. This included Internet access as well as some technical support for participants.
- The cost of teaching materials varied a great deal depending upon the subject matter. Tom felt that $15 per participant per week would be a high estimate.

Although Tom had been involved in the training business for a number of years, online training was so new that he did not have a feel for this market. Consequently, he decided to do some marketing research prior to making decisions about this new venture. He retained the services of Kelso Marketing Research to conduct a telephone survey of 50 randomly selected agribusiness organizations in Canada and the United States. The main objectives of this research were to:

- Determine the size of the market for training in general
- Determine the type of training currently undertaken
- Determine the likely demand for online training

Summary results of this study are presented in Appendix A.

Tom's Decision

Armed with the cost and market data, Tom started to think about how he might expand his business to include online training. It was fairly apparent that the major short run opportunity would be in sales training. Most agribusiness companies used sales training for their employees and there appeared to be some dissatisfaction with existing programs.

Tom thought his first product would be a six-week introductory sales training course targeted at new sales reps. He thought this course could be offered on both a public and private basis. The public offering would be available to people from any agribusiness that might want to take it. The course would be scheduled to run eight times a year and people from any agribusiness company could sign up. This would result in a group of participants from different companies. The private courses would be sold to individual companies and customized to some extent to meet their specific training needs.

Both the public and private courses would contain essentially the same content as the current three-day sales training courses offered by Agri Train. Lectures would be in the form of narrated PowerPoint presentations. Agri Train would develop a number of video clips showing parts of sales calls that could be critiqued and discussed by participants in online conferences. An instructor who would monitor the discussion in the conferences would provide feedback. Participants would be expected to devote five hours a week to the sales training course. This made one week of online experience more or less equal to a half day of face-to-face training.

Marketing the courses was a major consideration. Agri Train had not done much marketing in the past because there was a lot of repeat buying by satisfied clients. Moreover, word-of-mouth was an effective method in getting new clients. Tom knew he would have to develop an effective marketing program in order to be successful with the new online venture. Ideally, the online courses would be sold to new clients so as not to cannibalize existing face-to-face courses.

There appeared to be a number of ways he could develop a marketing program for the online product. One method was to hire one or more full time sales reps for the company. Reps would use a combination of telephone and personal contact with prospects. A full time sales rep would cost Agri Train approximately $100,000 annually including all benefits and expenses.

A second method was direct mail. A nice direct mail piece could be designed and mailed to prospects for approximately $20 a contact. This included all the design work as well as the costs of distribution. Tom noticed that many companies were using CD's in direct mail. The advantage of a CD was its ability to demonstrate how the online learning system actually worked. Adding a CD to the direct mail would increase costs to approximately $25 a contact and would result in a one-time production cost of $30,000.

A third method was to use media advertising. The most logical publication to use was Agri Marketing Magazine. Sales and marketing executives in virtually all agribusiness companies received this magazine. One full-page color ad in this publication costs $6,000. Agri Marketing Magazine was published monthly throughout the year.

Regardless of the communication media used, a key issue was how to position the new product. Tom was not sure how to deal with this issue, but felt the marketing research would provide some insight.

In addition to developing a communication program for the online product, Tom also had to establish a price. This was a key issue. Normal industry practice was to establish prices on a per participant per day basis. This, of course, was not appropriate for online training, so Tom had to think of other alternatives.

With all this in mind, Tom wondered if this was the right move for Agri Train at the present time. Online training seemed like the way of the future, and if he could get established in the area before competition he would have a real advantage. On the other hand, was the time really right for this move? Was the market ready to accept a fairly radical departure from current practice? If Tom invested a considerable sum in both marketing and course development and sales did not materialize, he could lose a substantial amount of money.

* This case was prepared by Tom Funk of the Ontario Agricultural College at the University of Guelph. Much of the data in the case was developed by a group of undergraduate students at the University of Guelph as part of a project undertaken for international marketing competition hosted by the National Agri Marketing Association in Kansas City, Missouri. The case is designed for classroom discussion and not intended to illustrate either effective or ineffective handling of administrative problems.
Copyright 2000 by Thomas Funk.

Appendix A
Market Research Summary

The objectives of this research were to determine the size of the market for training in general, the type of training currently undertaken and the likely demand for online training. In total, 50 companies representing different sectors of agribusiness were interviewed in Canada and the United States. Company names were randomly selected from a listing of 2,500 agribusiness firms found in the annual Marketing Services Guide published by Agri Marketing Magazine. It was felt that the 2,500 companies encompassed virtually all agribusiness organizations in North America. The survey consisted of three sections. Section A focused on characteristics of the individual companies. Section B identified the various training programs currently used by these companies. Section C was designed to gain information on how people perceived online training and whether or not they saw this as a viable alternative to more traditional methods.

Section A

The first section focused on the companies themselves in terms of what they did, how large they were, and the number of employees participating in training programs. The purpose of this section was to get some idea of market composition and size.

How many employees does your company have?

Each company was asked to provide data on the number of people they employed. The responses from the sample companies varied greatly with the smallest having ten employees and the largest having 85 000 employees. The average company in the sample employed 410 people with 10% being involved in sales and marketing. All sales and marketing employees receive some training over the course of a year.

What business is your company involved in?

Respondents were then asked to list the type of business they were involved in. Possible responses were feed, seed, fertilizer, agricultural chemicals, farm equipment, financial services and grain handling. Tabulation of the results revealed a good distribution among all of these sectors.

Approximately how many sales and marketing employees have access to computers and the Internet at home and at work?

Respondents were asked to provide the number of sales and marketing employees that had computer access at home or at work. Results showed that 64% provide computer access to all of their sales and marketing employees, another 12% provide computer access to more than 50% of their sales and marketing employees, while the remaining 24% provide computer access to less than 50% of their sales and marketing employees. These statistics decreased slightly when respondents were asked to give the number of employees who also had access to the Internet at home or at work.

Section B

The purpose of this section was to identify the different training programs currently in use. Information such as the styles of teaching, length and frequency of the course, cost, amount of feedback provided and level of satisfaction were explored

What are some internal and external training programs that you have provided to your sales and marketing employees on either an individual or group basis over the last two years? What are some of the characteristics of these programs?

The main types of training programs used by companies, in order of popularity were:

- Sales Training
- Product Training
- Marketing Training
- Time Management

The majority of programs appeared to be customized to the needs of the individual companies. Only a small percentage of the programs were generic. Almost all of the programs were purchased from external suppliers as opposed to being provided in-house. The sample companies listed a large number of external suppliers.

Respondents were also asked to state the methods of instruction used in training courses. The most common methods were:
- Lecture
- Video
- Case

Most of the training programs were either one, two or three days in length. The remaining programs were all less than one week in duration. Most of the courses were held either annually or biannually.

The range in the costs of these programs was $3,000 to nearly $30 000. The cost per participant per day varied from a low of $250 to a high of $600. The average was $500 per participant per day. These costs included:
- Fees and expenses paid to the training supplier
- Travel, food and accommodations for participants
- Facilities for the program

The costs do not include the value of time away from work for program participants.

Not surprisingly, the number of participants in each course varied greatly. In most companies all sales and marketing people took some training each year. As a result, the number of potential participants can be directly linked to the number of people employed in sales and marketing.

Most respondents confirmed that their training courses provided some feedback. This feedback took many forms including individual follow-up by the trainer, tests and role play sessions. All respondents stated that feedback was something they valued a great deal and was an area that needed considerable improvement.

The data showed that while most respondents felt that training programs were effective, many stated that there was definitely room for improvement.

Are there other programs that you would like to see? How would they be structured?

When asked to list any training programs they would like to see, most people responded by saying that they would like to see more customized programs related to their company, products and people. Virtually all respondents stressed the fact that sales training programs were the highest priority training activities in their companies.

In your company, what are the biggest problems you have faced with the training of employees?

This question was asked to determine limitations with traditional methods of training. The most frequently cited responses to this question were:
- Time required to do training and have people away from their work
- Costs associated with travel, lost production and the training program itself
- Finding training programs that meet the needs of the individual
- Identifying the skills that require improvement
- Finding time to complete the training and getting everyone into one central location
- Lack of ability to measure the impact of training on an individual or group basis
- Lack of individual feedback to participants during and after a training program. Many companies were concerned that individual participants did not receive proper evaluation of their performance and, as a result, the value of the training was not as great as it should be.

Section C

The last section of the questionnaire was designed to gain information on people's perceptions of online training. This information included awareness, benefits, concerns and price.

Prior to this interview, have you ever heard of or have you used online training?

Two-thirds of the respondents confirmed they had heard of online training. 20% stated they had heard of and had actually investigated online training. Only 8% of the respondents stated they were using online training at the present time.

Where did you hear about online training?

The most common ways people had become aware of online training were:
- Internet
- Magazines and newspapers
- Universities
- Training suppliers
- Colleagues
- Other companies

List the benefits you think online training might provide your company.

The most significant benefits identified were:

- Lower costs
- Increased convenience
- Can learn at own pace
- Flexible to needs and schedule
- Superior feedback and interaction

List any concerns you think you might have with online training.

The most significant concerns identified were:

- Not enough interaction with other participants or the instructor
- Motivating trainees to actually do the program
- Participants may not have the required technology or feel comfortable with this technology
- Difficulties in monitoring performance
- May be hard to provide good feedback

Assuming that online training in sales and marketing were available at a reasonable price, would your company be interested in trying this method of delivery?

In responding to this question
- 12% stated that they definitely would try online training
- 20% stated that the probably would try online training
- 36% stated that they may or may not try online training
- 28% felt the probably would not use online training
- 4% said they definitely would not use online training

Would you expect this type of training to be less expensive, as expensive or more expensive on a per student basis than traditional training?

Nearly 72% of the respondents felt online training would be less expensive than traditional training; another 20% felt that online training would cost the same as traditional training; while the remaining 8% felt online training would be more expensive.

41   Hannas Seeds

Patricia Hannas and Warren Stowkoski were engaged in a heated debate concerning the future direction of distribution at Hannas Seeds. Patricia, daughter of the founder, Nicholas Hannas, and current president of the company, was a strong supporter of further development of the company's dealer distribution, while Warren, sales manager, was more inclined to favor direct distribution. As they sat in the company's head office in Lacombe, Alberta, Patricia commented, "Warren, I appreciate that direct distribution has a place in our company, but I cannot see building our long term plans around this method of distribution. It's just too limiting in scope and would require hiring more people and incurring more marketing costs. In addition, it would take years to reach the volume objectives we have for the company." In reply, Warren commented, "I appreciate your point of view, Patricia, but further development of our dealer system will require more people too. And, of course, it means we have to compensate our dealers for selling our product. This is a costly activity. And our dealers are always complaining about something. Just last week, a couple of dealers mentioned again that they were not adequately trained to provide technical advice to customers. And we are getting more and more complaints about not protecting dealer territories. It just isn't worth the hassle." And so the debate continued as Patricia and Warren argued the pro's and con's of dealer versus direct distribution.

Company Background

In 1956, Nicholas Hannas purchased Lacombe Seeds, which was a retail store selling forage seed (alfalfas, clovers and grasses) for use as hay or pasture to area farmers. Shortly after buying the company, Nicholas changed the name to Hannas Seeds and continued to operate in Lacombe. For the next 15 years, the company consisted of both a garden center that supplied packaged seeds, bulbs, tools and chemicals to local customers, and a warehouse for forage seeds that were sold to central Alberta farmers. The marketing program during this period consisted of the distribution of forage seed price lists by mail or by customer pickup up at the store. Advertisements were placed in the local newspaper during the busy spring season. Sales came from repeat customers, referrals, walk-in traffic and telephone inquiries. Little or no effort was devoted to aggressively generate new business. The company did not own a delivery truck so all sales were picked up by customers.

The 1970's were a time of significant growth for Hannas Seeds. Sale revenues and volumes increased substantially as a result of the well-established presence of Hannas Seeds in Lacombe, the continually expanding client base and the absence of significant competition in the area. In 1973, a grain cleaning and processing facility was purchased in the Peace River region of northwestern Alberta and converted into a processing facility for creeping red fescue seed. Creeping red fescue was a primary component in packaged lawn grass mixtures sold for residential lawns, playgrounds, golf courses and parks. The demand for creeping red fescue was substantial, so the purchase of this facility provided Hannas Seeds with the ability to produce and market a product that could be sold into world markets. During this period, there were only a handful of companies in the creeping red fescue market. Export sales were generated through the use of commodity brokers so there was no need to market one's own product. Brokers would approach a seller of creeping red fescue with a bid from a prospective buyer. If interested in selling one or more loads of seed, the seller would agree or counter the bid. Conversely, the seller may approach the broker first with an offer and the broker would then search for an interested buyer. The identities of both the buyer and seller remained undisclosed until a transaction was completed. As there were only a small number of fescue processors and exporters, demand tended to be greater than supply and the sellers could be assured that they would attain very attractive margins.

The successful entry of Hannas Seeds into the export market was accompanied by similar rapid growth in the domestic market. In the early 1980's, the company began developing a dealer network to complement retail sales. Despite this growth, marketing and sales efforts remained more of less the same as in earlier years with the exception of targeting golf courses, oil and construction companies and parks and recreation departments as well as the traditional farm customers. Occasionally an employee would be assigned the task of contacting potential customers by telephone, but this was never a sustained activity.

The retail side of the business continued to develop in the early 1980's although not at the same pace as in earlier years. Several new seed companies sprang up in Alberta and large eastern Canadian seed companies also sought to establish a presence in the province. Many of these companies entered the lucrative fescue market attracted by the possibility of attaining very high margins. Consequently, it was not long before the fescue market became saturated and margins declined accordingly.

Even with the entrance of new competition, Hannas Seeds did not alter its low key approach to marketing. More advertising vehicles were used, such as radio, local newspapers and telephone yellow pages, but there was no formal marketing program nor was any individual hired or assigned to concentrate exclusively on marketing. The company continued to rely on its springtime mailing campaign to generate direct sales, and there was a small dealer network. Hannas Seeds dealers generally sold forage seed as a sideline to their existing farm or business operations and tended to order seed as they received orders from customers. Only a few dealers inventoried Hannas Seed products and attempted to sell them aggressively.

In the early 1990's, it became apparent that more effort should be devoted to marketing. In 1990 a Customer Appreciation Day was created where customers were offered discounts on their forage seed purchases. That same year the company purchased a custom designed display booth for use at various farm, turf, seed industry and horticultural trade shows. Most competing seed companies had been attending such shows for years and it was felt that Hannas Seeds should established its own presence at these shows in order to reach more prospective customers. More efforts were made to visit existing dealers in person as well as approach potential dealers. This was, however, not formalized into a job function and therefore not done on a regular basis.

An individual with a strong, sales background was hired in the mid-1990's to focus on sales and marketing. In the last half of the 1990's, the company still was achieving some success in recruiting new dealers, especially in the eastern part of the province. At the same time, the number of customers who purchased directly from Hannas Seeds was increasing although not as rapidly as dealer sales. In 2000, direct sales declined for the first time in many years.

Forage Seed Business
Forage crops were mainly used by farmers to produce hay and pasture for feed to livestock. The most common forage crops were alfalfa, clover, bromegrass, fescue, ryegrass, and timothy. Most of these crops were perennials which meant that, once seeded, they would grow year after year. Even though this was the case, farmers usually reseeded every three or four years because after this period of time the forage crops started to loose vigor and production declined. Although Patricia was not sure how many pounds of forage seed were sold in Alberta each year, her best guess was approximately 8,500,000 pounds, and that this had remained relatively stable for many years. The industry was hoping that the Canadian Seed Trade Association would start to collect and publish this type of information.

Although some seed companies developed their own proprietary lines of forage seeds, most accessed products from either public or private seed breeding organizations. Public seed breeders included universities and government agencies. The University of Alberta, for example, had an active forage seed breeding program. When they developed a new forage variety, they provided information about this variety to a number of seed companies and solicited bids from these companies. The company with the winning bid was then allowed to grow and distribute the variety and paid the developing organization a royalty. In addition to public institutions, there were a number of private seed breeders who developed varieties and provided them to seed companies on a similar royalty basis.

Most seed companies did not own seed production facilities. Instead, they contracted with farmers (seed growers) to produce seed on their behalf. The seed companies supplied seed growers with a small amount of the seed they want produced and then the growers multiplied this seed for the seed company under a contract. After the seed had been multiplied, it was transported to the seed company for cleaning and packaging under the company's brand name. In cases where more than one company had access to the same variety, seed companies often "traded" with each other. For example, if Hannas Seed had an excess supply of Alsike clover, they might sell some of this to a competitor who was short this variety.

There were a number of seed companies in the Alberta forage market. The most active were:

Agricore, formerly the Alberta Wheat Pool, distributed forage seeds in all regions of Alberta through their system of grain elevators and local farm supply outlets located in most communities in the province. Agricore was estimated to have a market share of approximately 10%.

Western Seeds out of Manitoba operated in central and Southern Alberta, mainly through a dealer organization. Western Seeds had one sales rep in Alberta who spent most of his time managing the existing dealer organization and obtaining new dealers. The company experienced some growth in recent years by increasing their number of dealers. Hannas

Seed recently lost some dealer accounts to Western Seeds. Western Seeds was thought to have a 15% share of the forage market in Alberta.

Peace Seeds was located in the Peace River region on Alberta and had its head office in Grande Prairie. Although primarily an exporter of creeping red fescue, Peace Seed's had a small dealer organization in northwestern Alberta and northeastern British Columbia. They did not have sales reps on the road, relying instead on telephone contact with their dealers. Their current share was thought to be about 5%.

International Seeds was a Saskatchewan seed company that had developed some business in eastern Alberta. They were a division of a very large European seed breeding organization. Recently they created a division called Performance Seeds to set up a dealer organization in Alberta. Their estimated share of the market was 10%, but many thought it was likely to grow in future.

North American Seeds was an eastern Canadian based business with a division in Alberta. The Alberta division had a number of dealers, but also four sales reps who did a lot of direct business with larger farmers. They were probably the largest forage seed company in the province with an estimated share of 20%.

Alberta Seed Company out of Edmonton sold in central Alberta. They sold only through a dealer organization and had approximately 10% of the market.

Canada West Seed was owned by Continental Grain of Manitoba. They sold through independent dealers as well as through their comprehensive network of grain elevators in many Alberta communities. In addition, they had five sales reps selling a complete line of seeds directly to large farm accounts. They currently had a market share of about 15%.

Current Operations
By the end of the 1990's, three distinct divisions made up the operations of Hannas Seeds: the garden center, international forage seed sales and domestic forage seed sales.

The garden center provided a wide assortment of competitively priced gardening products and accessories to Lacombe and area gardeners. Products included vegetable and garden seed, lawn grass seed, bird feed, horticultural supplies, ornamental concrete products, bedding plants and nursery stock in an 1,800 ft^2 retail store and a 1,000 ft^2 greenhouse situated in downtown Lacombe. The garden center accounted for approximately 5% of total company sales in fiscal year 1999-2000.

The international forage seed division exported high quality creeping red fescue seed to the United States, Japan, and eastern and western Europe. This division accounted for approximately 65% of total sales in fiscal year 1999-2000.

The domestic forage seed operation provided a wide selection of competitively priced, high yielding seeds to western Canadian farmers for use in the production of annual and perennial legumes and grasses. Although these products were sold throughout western

Canada, the primary market was central Alberta. Domestic forage seed sales accounted for approximately 30% of total company sales in fiscal year 1999-2000. Exhibit 1 provides a list of all products sold by Hannas Seeds in the domestic market and their prices as of March 2000.[1] Patricia felt the real growth opportunities for Hannas Seeds were in this area of the business. Although the size of the forage seed market in Alberta was not growing, Patricia felt the company could increase its current 15% share of the market.

All the forage seed products sold by Hannas Seeds were non-proprietary varieties of annual and perennial legumes and grasses. These varieties were developed in public institutions such as agricultural universities and provincial and federal government research departments. Hannas Seeds acquired the rights to sell these products and contracted with Alberta seed growers to produce certain quantities of seeds which were cleaned and shipped to Hannas facilities for packaging and distribution.

Marketing and sales were under the direction of Warren Stowkoski. Warren had been with the company for six years but had extensive prior experience as a sales rep for BMW Canada. Although Warren's responsibilities were to manage both the company's direct and dealer sales of domestic forage seeds, time pressures meant that he spent most of his time working in the direct sales area of the company. Warren also attended a number of trade shows in Western Canada as well as industry meetings in both Canada and the United States. Patricia managed the company's modest advertising program which averaged 2% of sales, and was mainly spent on local newspaper and Yellow Page ads.

Exhibit 2 shows the operating statement for the domestic forage division for the fiscal year ending July 31, 2000.

Direct Distribution

Hannas Seeds had been involved in direct distribution of forage seeds in the Alberta market since its inception. At first, distribution was through the retail store in Lacombe. Local farmers visited the store to purchase forage seeds, usually prior to or during the spring, summer or fall planting seasons. This was an excellent method of reaching local farmers, but as Hannas Seeds wanted to expand outside the local area, other activities became necessary. In the early 1980's, the company started to advertise in community newspapers in areas up to 200 kilometers from Lacombe. The ads included a 1-800 phone number that prospective customers could use to obtain more information and place orders. Hannas Seeds also obtained a number of farmer lists they used for direct mail.

In 1989, the company purchase a custom designed display booth for use in various farm, turf, seed industry and horticultural trade shows. Most competing seed companies had been attending such shows for years and it was felt that it was time for Hannas Seeds to establish its own presence at these shows and reach more prospective customers.

In 1990 an annual Customer Appreciation Day was created where customers and prospects on the mailing list were invited to Lacombe for a one day event where they could purchase

---

[1] The average retail price of a pound of forage seed was approximately $2.00. Direct costs of producing and processing the seed were about $1.25 per pound.

forage seeds at a 10% discount. The day, usually scheduled for mid-March, also featured live entertainment, product seminars and a great meal. Attendance at this event grew every year reaching a peak of 250 in 2000. Company records indicated that approximately 33% of direct sales were made on this day. The event took a lot of staff time to organize and cost Hannas approximately $15,000 in out-of-pocket costs.

All of these efforts allowed Hannas Seeds to develop a direct marketing list of approximately 6,000 customers and prospects by the year 2000. This list was used extensively: in 2000 they spent approximately $60,000 on direct marketing activities, mainly direct mail. The direct distribution activities were carried out by Warren with the assistance of three ladies in the office who were all capable of assisting forage seed customers in person or on the phone.[2] These women would pass a "difficult" customer on to Warren when that customer required more technical information, had a complaint or specifically asked to talk to "a man." Hannas Seed also had a production manager who was responsible for all shipping and receiving. The office staff was responsible for maintaining the customer and prospect database. Warren enjoyed this part of his job, especially the customer contact.

Once an order was obtained, Hannas Seeds shipped the product to the customer. Because of the small volume purchased by each customer, shipping costs were relatively high at $0.10 per pound. Hannas Seeds paid the full cost of distribution to all direct customers except those who purchased and took delivery at a Customer Appreciation Day.

Direct sales of forage seeds in 1999-2000 were approximately 840,000 pounds. This was down about 50,000 pounds from the previous year.

Dealer Distribution

In the early 1980's, Hannas Seeds began to dabble in dealer distribution as well as direct distribution. Patricia felt this was an important step for the company to achieve significant sales growth.

There were four types of dealers available for seed distribution in Western Canada: independent farm supply dealers, branches of large distribution companies, co-ops and farmer dealers. Farm supply dealers varied in the type of product lines they carried. Some dealers carried a very narrow line such as fertilizer, seed or feed whereas others carried a broad product line including most of the items a farmers would need to purchase for his farm. Seed cleaning plants often carried branded forage seeds to supplement their main business of cleaning grain for local farmers. In addition to the agricultural dealers, there were a few highly specialized dealers serving the oilfield and land reclamation markets.

Independent dealers were locally owned businesses that normally had one or two retail outlets. Although the number of independent dealers had been declining in Alberta, it was estimated that there were approximately 100 businesses in this category.

---

[2] Each of the office staff was paid $30,000 in salary and benefits. Warren's salary and benefits totaled $75,000 in 2000.

A growing percentage of farm supplies were sold by branches of large distribution companies such as Agricore, Continental Grain and United Farmers of Alberta. With the exception of United Farmers of Alberta, the other large distribution companies had their own lines of forage seeds making it difficult, but not impossible, for a company like Hannas to establish distribution in this channel. Each of the three major distribution companies in Alberta had approximately 50 retail outlets serving the province. Most of their retail outlets carried a full line of farm supplies.

Co-ops were farmer owned retail outlets that operated much like independent dealers. Most co-ops had one or two retail outlets serving local farmers. Patricia and Warren felt there were probably 50 co-ops in their market area.

In an attempt to develop new sources of income, some farmers would become dealers for seed companies. Although some farmer dealers were very active in attempting to develop business, most were fairly passive, waiting for customers to contact them.

All forage seed dealers performed similar activities. They ordered supplies of forage seeds based on their sales forecast. Once received, these supplies were put in a warehouse for storage until purchased. This usually was done in the winter months as dealers prepared for the busy spring selling season. To the extent possible, they trained their inside and outside sales people on forage seeds so they were able to advise customers on which varieties to purchase. If seed companies supplied them with point-of-purchase material, this was normally displayed in the retail store. With the exception of specialized seed dealers, most retailers did not make a special effort to push forage seeds; they simply attempted to answer questions and took orders.

Patricia took major responsibility for recruiting new dealers for the company and then Warren worked with the dealers once they were established. To date, Patricia had set up 37 dealers that carried Hannas Seeds products. Exhibit 3 shows a listing of all Hannas dealers. Exhibit 4 shows the sales of these dealers over the past four years. Based on this information, Patricia was able to estimate the average size of different types of dealers in pounds sold per year. The average sizes were:

Type of Dealer	Pounds/year
Farmer dealers	45,500
Feed dealers	14,500
Fertilizer dealers	50,000
General farm supply dealers	37,000
Oilfield supply dealers	91,000
Reclamation supply dealers	98,500
Seed cleaning plants	31,000
Seed dealers	116,000

Contact with dealers was minimal and irregular. Warren made it a point to personally visit each dealer at least once a year, and supplemented this with phone calls, letters, faxes and emails. Most competing companies had sales reps that would call on dealers on a much more frequent basis.

Hannas dealers were allowed the industry standard 15% margin on all seed products they sold. So, for example, if a dealer purchased 1,000 lbs of Climax Timothy, which had a retail price of $1.75 per/lb, they would be invoiced for $1,487.50[3]. Hannas Seed paid all freight on dealer sales except in cases where dealers would place an order for a couple of bags they needed in a hurry. This was usually shipped via courier and paid for by the dealer. If a dealer wanted to pick up an order from the Hannas warehouse, the invoice would deduct the cost of shipping. Because of larger volumes, shipping costs to dealers averaged only $0.02 per pound. All accounts were expected to be settled in 30 days. In the case of a few very large dealers, Hannas would rent a large truck trailer, load it with seed and drop the truck off at their yard. At the end of the season, Hannas would pick up the truck trailer and invoice them for what was sold.

Other than margin, payment terms and shipping, Hannas had not developed any dealer policies in areas such as sales incentives, training, exclusivity or territory protection. Although Patricia was pleased with the growth of dealer sales over the last ten years, she was sure this aspect of the business could be improved by expanding the number of dealers and by getting existing dealers to increase sales.

Many of the current Hannas dealers had been recruited in the early 1990's when this was a priority task for Patricia. Lately, growth in dealer numbers had declined because Patricia was not able to devote as much time to this activity. In fact, recruiting dealers was a very time consuming process. The first step was to identify prospects and then it was necessary to contact these businesses and sell them on the benefits of carrying Hannas products. If a prospect did not carry forage seeds, it was much easier for Patricia to sell them on the idea of adding this product line than it was to sell a dealer currently carrying forage seeds on changing brands or adding a second brand. Patricia had no idea how many potential Alberta farm supply dealers currently did not carry any forage seed products, but estimated it might be twenty percent. The data in Exhibit 3 shows Patricia's estimate of the number of competing brands of forage seed carried by existing Hannas dealers.

In addition to recruiting new dealers, Patricia felt there was a lot of opportunity in working with existing dealers to help them increase sales of Hannas products. In reviewing sales by dealer (Exhibit 4) she noted that there was a lot of variability from dealer to dealer and, for any dealer, from year to year. Only a few dealers had shown a steady increase in sales over the past five year. She was not sure why this was the case, but speculated that it might be due to dealers starting to carry more than one line of forage seeds or dealer dissatisfaction or apathy. In an effort to understand the perspectives of dealers more fully, Patricia interviewed a number of dealers on a fairly wide range of topics. These interviews revealed a number of issues:

- Some dealers were unhappy with the fact that Hannas sold seed direct as well as through a dealer system. They felt that some customers would come to their

---

[3] The difference between the retail value of $1,750.00 and the purchase price of $1,487.50 is the margin the retailer earns.

dealership to obtain information on forage seeds and then go to the Hannas Customer Appreciation Day to purchase their needs at a 10% discount.

- Other dealers expressed some concern over the fact that Hannas had established two or more dealers in close proximity to each other leading to some local competition for sales. In a few cases these dealers said there was occasional price cutting at the local level to secure sales.

- There was fairly general concern over the fact that Hannas did not provide sales support for their dealers. Although Hannas did provide brochures listing their products and some technical information on each product, this was the only thing they did.

- A number of dealers mentioned that the financial rewards for carrying Hannas products were not adequate.

- Some dealers mentioned that they could not afford the time and expense to aggressively sell forage seeds. This line represented such a small portion of their business that it was not worth it to devote much effort to selling it. If farmers asked for a forage seed, they would take the order and fill it, but that was the extent of their involvement.

- A few dealers expressed concern over occasional delays in receiving orders.

Future Direction

Patricia and Warren were at odds in terms of how to expand sales of forage seeds in the Alberta market. Warren was strongly in favor of gradually phasing out dealer sales and putting major effort into direct sales. He felt it would not be possible to get a consistently strong effort from dealers to provide the sales growth Hannas Seeds required to meet company objectives. In his mind, using the margin currently allowed dealers to fund other marketing efforts would have greater payoff. Some of the activities he had in mind included the use of company sales people to call on large accounts, greater use of advertising and direct mail, the possibility of having Customer Appreciation Days at other locations in Alberta and the use of the Internet. He also noted that a substantial increase in direct sales would require hiring at least one more person in the office since the three current employees were operating a maximum capacity at the present time.

Patricia, on the other hand, had serious concerns about direct distribution. She felt that some face-to-face contact with customers was required to sell forage seeds and that it would simply be too costly for Hannas to do this themselves. Having dealers allowed for this face-to-face contact at a reasonable cost. She was, however, concerned about the ability of the company to attract good new dealers and motivate existing dealers to sell larger volumes of seed. She realized the company needed to review its distribution policies, particularly those policies related to compensating and motivating dealers. She also wondered whether it was possible to operate a system of direct distribution along with dealer sales.

Exhibit 1: HANNAS SEEDS RETAIL PRICE LIST – MARCH 1, 2000

ALFALFAS	$/lb	WILD RYE	$/lb
Alfalfa, Common No.1	**1.70**	**Altai wild rye, Common No.1**	**6.75**
AC Blue J	2.75	Altai wild rye, Prairieland	7.75
Algonquin	1.95	Dahurian wild rye, Common No.1	2.15
Beaver	1.95	Dahurian wild rye, James	2.25
Hannas High Tech Brand	**2.25**	**Russian wild rye, Common No.1**	**2.50**
Proleaf	2.50	Russian wild rye, Swift	ask
Rambler	2.20		
Rangelander	2.20		

WHEATGRASS

Crested wheat, Common No.1	2.25		

CLOVERS		Crested wheat, Fairway	2.75
Alsike clover, Common No.1	3.10	Crested wheat, Kirk	2.75
Red clover, Common No.1	0.90	Intermediate wheat, Common No.1	1.90
Red clover, double cut	1.95	Intermediate wheat, Chief	1.95
Sweet clover, Common No.1	0.70	Northern wheat, Common No.1	17.95
Sweet clover, Norgold	1.25	Pubescent wheat, Greenleaf	2.50
White clover, Common No.1	2.50	Slender wheat, Common No.1	2.10
		Slender wheat, Revenue	2.25

SPECIAL LEGUMES			
Streambank wheat, Common No.1	11.00		
Birdsfoot Trefoil, Common No.1	2.50	Streambank wheat, Sodar	11.50
Birdsfoot Trefoil, Leo	2.75	Tall wheatgrass	2.75
Cicer Milk Vetch, Common No.1	2.40	Western wheat, Common No.1	8.95
Cicer Milk Vetch, Oxley	2.45	Western wheat, Rosanna	9.95

BROMEGRASS		SPECIAL GRASSES	
Meadow brome, Common No.1	3.25	Canada bluegrass, Common No.1	2.95
Meadow brome, Fleet	3.95	Creeping foxtail, Common No.1	2.70
Smooth brome, Common No.1	0.90	Kentucky bluegrass, Common No.1	1.95
Smooth brome, Carlton	1.30	Meadow foxtail, Common No.1	2.70
Smooth brome, Manchar	1.95	Orchardgrass, Common No.1	1.20
		Orchardgrass, Potomac	1.35
FESCUE		Reed canargrass, Common No.1	3.50

Creeping red fescue, Common No.1	**1.70**	**Reed canarygrass, Palaton**	**3.75**
Creeping red fescue, Boreal	*1.75*	*Reed canarygrass, Rival*	*3.80*
Hard fescue, Common No.	*1.95*		
Sheeps fescue, Common No.1	*4.25*		

TIMOTHY

Tall fescue, Common No.1	**1.25**	**Timothy, Common No.1**	**1.25**
		Timothy, Basho	*1.75*
RYEGRASS		*Timothy, Carola*	*1.75*
Annual ryegrass, Common No.1	*0.60*	*Timothy, Champ*	*1.75*
Italian ryegrass, Common No.1	*1.10*	*Timothy, Climax*	*1.75*
Perennial ryegrass, Common No.1	*1.25*		

SPECIAL SEED

* Prices subject to change without notice *

Fall rye, Prima		*0.22*
Field peas	*0.19*	

HANNAS SEEDS
*5039-49 St * Lacombe, Alberta * T4L 1Y2

**Exhibit 2: Domestic Forage Seed Division Operating Statement
For the Period Ending July 31, 2000**

Gross sales	$2,462,000
Less: Discounts	$55,440
Net sales	$2,406,560
Less: Cost of Goods	$1,625,000
Less: Delivery	$65,480
Gross Margin	$716,080
Expenses	
Marketing manager	$75,000
Office staff	$90,000
Bad debts	$13,000
Advertising and promotion	$52,000
Direct marketing	$60,000
Customer Appreciation Day	$15.000
Travel	$30,000
Division overhead	$200,000
Division Profit	$181,080

Exhibit 3: Hannas Seeds Dealers

Name	Product Line	Ownership	Other Brands Carried	Years a Dealer
Agri Farm Supplies	General farm supplies	Independent	0	5 to 9
Alberta Agro Services	Fertilizer dealer	Independent	2	Less than 5
Alberta Ranch & Farm	General farm supplies	Independent	2	Less than 5
Alberta Seed Cleaning	Seed cleaning plant	Independent	2	10 or more
Aylmer UFA	Feed dealer	Branch	0	Less than 5
Bruce Seeds	Seed dealer	Independent	2	5 to 9
Cedarview Co-op	General farm supplies	Co-op	1	10 or more
Clarence Seed Cleaning	Seed cleaning plant	Independent	1	10 or more
Dartmouth Supplies	General farm supplies	Independent	0	10 or more
Drumbo Co-op	General farm supplies	Co-op	1	Less than 5
Eccles Co-op	General farm supplies	Co-op	2	10 or more
Eyckville Fertilizer	Fertilizer dealer	Independent	0	10 or more
Fowler Farm & Ranch	General farm supplies	Independent	0	10 or more
Francesville Agri Supplies	General farm supplies	Independent	1	Less than 5
Grimsby UFA	General farm supplies	Branch	1	Less than 5
Harry Krabbe	Farmer	Independent	0	Less than 5
Harvard Fertilizer	Fertilizer dealer	Independent	1	10 or more
Hi Tech Agro	Fertilizer dealer	Independent	1	10 or more
John Krug	Farmer	Independent	0	5 to 9
Laroche County Supply	General farm supplies	Independent	1	5 to 9
Lawrence Seed Cleaning	Seed cleaning plant	Independent	1	10 or more
Len's Feed Store	Feed dealer	Independent	0	10 or more
Lloyd's Seed Cleaning	Seed cleaning plant	Independent	1	5 to 9
Muller Feed Mill	Feed dealer	Independent	0	10 or more

Parkview Fertilizer	Fertilizer dealer	Independent	0	5 to 9
Philip Reynolds	Farmer	Independent	0	5 to 9
Purvis Seeds	Seed dealer	Independent	1	Less than 5
Richardson Supplies	Oilfield supplies	Independent	0	5 to 9
Riverside Supplies	General farm supplies	Independent	1	5 to 9
Sagamore Livestock Supplies	Feed dealer	Independent	0	5 to 9
Smith Feeds	Feed dealer	Independent	0	5 to 9
Smithville Co-op	General farm supplies	Co-op	2	5 to 9
Sunshine Seeds	Seed dealer	Independent	2	5 to 9
Valley UFA	General farm supplies	Branch	2	Less than 5
Western Farm Supplies	General farm supplies	Co-op	1	Less than 5
Western Forest Supplies	Reclamation supplies	Independent	0	5 to 9
William Torsten	Farmer	Independent	0	5 to 9

Exhibit 4: Hannas Seeds Dealer Sales

Name	Lbs Sold 96-97	Lbs Sold 97-98	Lbs Sold 98-99	Lbs Sold 99-00	Total
Agri Farm Supplies	4,460	3,430	4,230	7,735	19,855
Alberta Agro Services	0	950	750	9,060	10,760
Alberta Ranch & Farm	0	0	265	0	265
Alberta Seed Cleaning	9,655	165	1,895	165	11,880
Aylmer UFA	0	0	280	1,795	2,075
Bruce Seeds	5,150	14,467	9,290	22,055	50,962
Cedarview Co-op	8,712	9,870	18,604	165	37,351
Clarence Seed Cleaning	1,495	16,150	19,625	10,965	48,235
Dartmouth Supplies	47,370	36,525	42,663	34,305	160,863
Drumbo Co-op	0	3,525	15,497	11,256	30,278
Eccles Co-op	31,969	33,985	45,192	23,050	134,196
Eyckville Fertilizer	8,430	11,905	13,710	1,660	35,705
Fowler Farm & Ranch	12,930	29,335	12,139	18,515	72,919
Francesville Agri Supplies	3,765	0	0	535	4,300
Grimsby UFA	0	200	1,924	2,635	4,759
Harry Krabbe	0	875	1,750	55	2,680
Harvard Fertilizer	15,684	11,265	13,657	1,485	42,091
Hi Tech Agro	8,870	0	11,350	14,640	34,860
John Krug	29,060	36,265	25,370	33,545	124,240
Laroche County Supply	975	2,900	2,860	2,575	9,310
Lawrence Seed Cleaning	18,787	17,295	13,615	1,000	50,697
Len's Feed Store	2,098	1,510	2,885	1,500	7,993
Lloyd's Seed Cleaning	705	2,360	4,960	4,870	12,895
Muller Feed Mill	0	100	50	0	150
Parkview Fertilizer	12,898	17,475	46,261	50,674	127,308
Philip Reynolds	3,190	2,275	6,517	14,085	26,067
Purvis Seeds	51,533	81,010	61,808	49,465	243,816
Richardson Supplies	13,701	22,335	7,455	47,515	91,006
Riverside Supplies	2,745	2,695	630	2,355	8,425
Sagamore Livestock Supplies	15,385	10,770	15,288	9,341	50,784
Smith Feeds	350	1,760	5,655	3,715	11,480
Smithville Co-op	4,165	0	100	0	4,265
Sunshine Seeds	2,550	10,135	25,691	14,978	53,354
Valley UFA	0	1,200	6,710	5,250	13,160
Western Farm Supplies	0	700	6,111	11,745	18,556
Western Forest Supplies	26,850	19,085	15,218	37,395	98,548
William Torsten	10,640	6,045	2,868	9,245	28,798
	354,122	408,562	462,873	459,329	

This case was prepared by Tom Funk of the University of Guelph and Patricia Hannas of Hannas Seeds. It is intended as a basis for classroom discussion and is not designed to illustrate either effective of ineffective handling of administrative problems. Some of the information in the case has been disguised to protect confidentiality. Copyright 2001 by Dr. Tom Funk

42   INCREASING PERSONAL FLOTATION DEVICE (PFD) WEAR RATES

Introduction

Sharon Sellars walked along Water Street in St. John's, on a rare hot spring day. The sun reflected on the water of the harbor, and she wished that she could spend the afternoon out on her boat. However, she had a more urgent priority.

This morning she received, by e-mail, the final report on a series of focus groups, which were recently conducted, on personal flotation devices (PFDs) by Canadian boaters. These focus groups were conducted with respondents who seldom or never wear lifejackets/PFDs when on the water. Groups were held in Toronto, Quebec City and Halifax.

The objective of the research was to obtain qualitative data about boaters' attitudes and perceptions about PFD wear. This was the first time that the Office of Boating Safety (OBS) undertook a study of this nature. The OBS, part of the Canadian Coast Guard, is mandated with the task of making recreational boating safer by initiating marketing programs to educate boaters about safe boating practices and about changes in boating regulations so that compliance rates will increase resulting in fewer deaths, accidents and expensive search and rescue missions.

Background

Recreational boating is a popular, growing activity. It is estimated that more than 8 million Canadians use 2.7 million recreational vessels of various types annually. There are no reliable estimates of activity by type of craft or the number of person boating hours per boating season. However, as the level of income increases and shorter workweeks become more common, the number of boats, boaters and frequency of use are expected to increase.

Unfortunately, every year, about 200 Canadians die in boating related accidents. About 90 percent of the people who drowned in recreational boating accidents were not wearing a lifejacket or PFD. Almost all of the these deaths would not have occurred if the victims wore a lifejacket that would have kept an unconscious person face up in the water until help arrived.

Another reason to improve recreational boating practices is that, according to Canadian Coast Guard statistics, recreational boaters are responsible for more than 50 percent of search and rescue incidents, placing a great strain on the limited Coast Guard resources.

There are some similarities between boating safety and road safety. In both cases, high speed and alcohol are frequent causes of accidents and deaths. Similarly, the most likely age to be involved in an incident is the under 35-year-old category. Males predominate (and the high-risk segment is often referred to as the testosterone group), but over time a growing number of females in this age category exhibit these risky behaviors.

Automobile travel is usually at higher speeds and in heavier traffic than boating. Therefore, many people perceive that boating is much less dangerous than car travel.

Lifejackets (PFDs) are part of a family of safety devices that includes seat belts for cars and helmets for motorcyclists and bike riders. Historically, attempts to encourage voluntary use of these safety devices have been unsuccessful. Legislation mandating use of seat belts and helmets was not popular and required regular, active enforcement, including fines and demerit points. Several jurisdictions announced plans to table legislation to make the wearing of helmets compulsory for bike riders. These plans, because of strong opposition, were never turned into laws. The State of Florida actually reversed itself and watered down an existing law that required motorcycle riders to wear helmets.

The history of seat belt use is interesting. When seat belts were introduced to Canada they were an option. Few people elected to pay for this safety option. Then the law stated that every car sold in Canada must be equipped with seat belts. Wear levels remained very low. Only when the law was changed to require people to wear seatbelts and provide sanctions (fines and demerit points against driving permits) did wear rates improve significantly. It is now estimated that more than 90 percent of people in cars regularly buckle up.

Another example of implementing the use of safety devices is how the National Hockey League (NHL) decided to make the use of helmets compulsory. There was strong resistance from the players who were already in the NHL to the proposed regulations. These players have played hockey all their lives and felt that the safety equipment would interfere with their ability to play hockey. In addition, they have learned, for the most part, to accept the dangers of the game. The NHL and the junior hockey leagues made the decision that all children born after a certain date would be required to wear a helmet when they first started to play organized pee wee hockey. Over a number of years, these people reached the NHL and were obligated to continue to wear the safety equipment. Now all players in all leagues use the safety device.

Several American states passed laws requiring children under a certain age (from 12 to 16 years, depending on the state) to wear a lifejacket/PFD when on the water. The rationale was that these young people would develop good wear habits and would continue to wear lifejackets/PFDs even when no longer legally required. In practice, the vast majority, when legally allowed, stopped wearing a lifejacket/PFD on a regular basis.

The Office of Boating Safety
Since it was established, the OBS has undertaken a number of important initiatives:

1. In order to increase comfort and acceptance, the OBS instituted changes to the standards of PFDs to allow for a greater range of approved colours (in addition to the traditional colours of red, orange or yellow) and for the use of inflatable personal floatation devices for certain water activities.

2. The OBS was instrumental in forming a Steering Committee to deal with issues surrounding the use of PFDs and lifejackets. The creation of this committee was an important milestone, in that it brought together a number of organizations that have an

interest in water safety but who, up to this time, had worked independently – sometimes duplicating each other's activities.

The committee is composed of a wide cross-section of stakeholders including: the Canadian Red Cross, the Lifesaving Society, coroners from Ontario and Quebec, the RCMP, Transport Canada, manufacturers of PFDs and the U.S. Coast Guard. The American participation is important because residents of both countries frequently boat in the other country's waters. In addition, Canadians watch American TV and are exposed to the U.S. water safety messages.

3. The OBS was responsible for recommending the new boating regulations and making Canadians aware of the significantly expanded requirements.

4. Now that the OBS has put in place the safety framework, emphasis is being concentrated on education campaigns to improve compliance with the boating regulations and to reduce avoidable boating fatalities. As part of this initiative, the OBS conducted a literature search, which produced large quantities of drowning and other water statistics but no information on attitudes or behaviors concerning lifejacket/PFD use. An observational study, which recorded the number of people who wore a PFD while on the water, concluded that only about 20 percent of boaters wore a PFD.

Focus Group Findings
Because of the small number of participants and because the respondents were not selected at random, the findings that follow must be viewed as directional rather than conclusive.

Most respondents consider lifejackets and PFDs to be synonymous. Of those who said there are differences between the two, very few knew that the term PFD included a wide range of flotation devices that a person could wear. Lifejackets (a form of PFD) are designed to be worn; if the wearer is in the water, the lifejacket will keep an unconscious person floating face-up until help arrives. The other PFDs do not have this capability. Examples of other PFDs include floater jackets and pants, kayak vests, or other inflatables.

According to the focus group participants, small craft operators almost always have PFDs on board because:

▪ the law requires that there be a PFD of appropriate size for every person on board

▪ they are comfortable to sit on or to kneel on

▪ they should be kept in case they are needed. (There is widespread belief that, if needed, people could quickly put on their PFD or at least grab a floating PFD once you fall into the water.)

It appears that recreational boaters know the law and carry the required number of PFDs, but few boaters wear them regularly

The respondents provided a number of reasons why they tend not to wear a lifejacket/PFD when on a small craft including:

▪ The physical discomfort of wearing a lifejacket/PFD is perceived to far outweigh the potential benefits for the boater. Included in this category are bulkiness, restriction of movement, sweaty in hot weather, clammy when wet, and the tendency to "ride up" on the wearer. Other reported negatives include finding one that fits reasonably well, the stains and odors of old ones and the awkwardness of being able to do it up properly.

▪ Most respondents think that under usual boating conditions, the risk of a boating accident or of being harmed (except getting wet) is so small that many people do not consciously assess the risk.

▪ The use of lifejackets/PFDs is associated with childhood, imposed rules, and being nervous around the water. Wearing a lifejacket/PFD is "uncool" and unflattering. According to respondents, not wearing a lifejacket/PFD is associated with maturity, self-confidence, individual responsibility, freedom and fun.

When asked if there were benefits to wearing lifejackets/PFDs, the respondents were not as quick to present their comments .The main benefit (perceived by those few people who had a previous bad experience) was the feeling of security. That is, if you fall into the water, you would definitely float (face-up, it was assumed). Other benefits (each noted by only a few respondents) include setting an example for kids, allaying the fears of nervous family members on shore, and the security in certain risky water activities such as water-skiing and riding a PWC/Seadoo.

There is only limited awareness of new styles of lifejackets/PFDs that may be more comfortable, less restrictive in movement, more attractive and stain and mould resistant. Respondents thought that these improved lifejackets/PFDs would be expensive.

For some small craft boaters, especially but not limited to young men, there is virtually no decision making concerning the wearing of lifejackets/PFDs. They dislike wearing them and avoid doing so except in the direst circumstances, usually a drastic shift in weather and/or water conditions.

Respondents identified a number of factors that may be considered in the decision to wear a lifejacket/PFD or not. This composite list appears in Appendix 2.

The decision-making process is also influenced by the frequency of doing a boating activity. The greater the frequency of an activity (or experience with a specific watercraft), the less likely it is that the person will wear a lifejacket/PFD for the activity.

Attitudes toward lifejacket/PFD wear start to form when boaters are young and persist into adult life. There are a least two different attitudes that can be traced back to the impressionable age of childhood:

1. Many participants grew up around water (at home or at the cottage) and have used boats and observed others using boats for most of their lives. As children, they were expected to wear lifejackets/ PFDs when on the water. This expectation generally ceased as soon as they were able to prove to their parents that they were competent swimmers and that they were able to handle the boat (Often around the age of 10 or 12). Since their elders seldom wore a lifejacket/ PFD, not wearing one became a symbol of maturity, trust, individual responsibility and freedom. Wearing one is associated with childhood, lack of confidence and being a wimp.

2. Boaters have learned from their elders and from their own experiences that recreational boating is fun and safe, if you know what you are doing (They generally feel that they know what they are doing.). They are also confident that they can recognize the circumstances where one has to be cautious and wear a lifejacket/ PFD (see Appendix 2). Although these boaters may consider a number of factors in their decision to wear or not to wear a lifejacket/ PFD, they will not wear one if they think that they can manage the risk.

In conclusion, the habits and attitudes formed in childhood persist to this day. There is a time and place (and an age) for lifejackets/ PFDs, but consistent wear under any and all circumstances is not only unnecessary for knowledgeable, responsible adults like them but is a bit silly. The habit of wearing a lifejacket/ PFD regardless of the situation has never been formed.

Advise Sharon Sellars on what should be done by the Office of Boating Safety to increase PFD wear rates in Canada. Support your recommendations.

Appendix A: Selected Respondent Verbatim Comments

- ➤ "I've heard the term (PFD) but I really don't know what the difference is."
- ➤ "PFD is probably just a fancy name for lifejacket. It is in the league of calling a garbage collector a sanitary engineer."
- ➤ "I think that there are differences between lifejackets and PFDs, but I do not know what they are."
- ➤ "I don't feel a need for it (lifejacket) and I am not scared…we never get close to nothing."
- ➤ "I can't foresee anything happening to make me wear one all the time."
- ➤ "You should always wear a lifejacket if the conditions are dangerous."
- ➤ "If you drive sensibly, you don't have to worry about getting knocked out of the boat and you do not need a lifejacket."
- ➤ "You don't need it all the time. …There are many times that it doesn't make sense to be wearing a lifejacket, e.g., it is calm and the risk isn't high."
- ➤ "I think you have 'way more of a chance of getting into a car accident than getting hit out on the water."

- ➤ "I feel a lot safer in my boat on my lake than in my car on the highway; fewer boats, less speed and you are not restricted to a lane."

- ➤ "I don't go out if there is wind or rain, so I don't need a lifejacket."

- ➤ "Never wear a lifejacket unless I am skiing or the weather is really bad."

- ➤ "It is a small lake. I stay close to shore. I am confident of my swimming. No need to wear."

- ➤ "If I go out far enough from shore, nobody is going to get me. Why prolong the agony? Seriously."

- ➤ "On a nice sunny day, you do not think anything will happen."

- ➤ "In early spring and fall it (lifejacket) provides warmth and the water is choppy and cold."

- ➤ "Look at the geek. He has to wear a lifejacket because he cannot swim well."

- ➤ "Who wears a lifejacket all the time? People who are nervous – they are afraid of getting hit by a car every time they walk down the street."

- ➤ "There is a stigma. No guys my age (middle age) are going around in 18-foot boats, with like jackets on. It is not cool."

- ➤ "I never grew up wearing one …I think that is the big difference."

- ➤ "I never wear it; and I don't intend to."

- ➤ "If I am meant to die, I am meant to die."

- ➤ "I know that experienced boaters don't wear their lifejackets."

- ➤ "I've been boating without a lifejacket for 30 years .You won't change my mind. You might make a difference with the young people coming up."

- ➤ "Lifejackets are in the boat, to sit on – but no one wears one."

- ➤ "You always take it (lifejacket) with you and it is not just to sit on … I feel much safer with the lifejacket along in the boat."

- ➤ "In the canoe, I'm sitting on it or it is close at hand so if it does tip, I can reach it."

- ➤ "I don't wear one at all unless danger is close; then it quickly comes off the floor …on a nice sunny day you do not think anything will happen."

- ➤ "I will wear one if the water is cold."

- ➤ "I only wear one in certain conditions."

- ➤ "We pick the nicer days."

- ➤ "We do not go out if the conditions are not ideal."

- ➤ "I wear a lifejacket to set an example, if there are kids in the boat."

- ➤ "You can't put a lifejacket on and fish. You get tangled up everywhere."

- ➤ "It pushes your bust up to your neck. …They're designed for men."

> "It is hard to look attractive on the water with them on."

> "They smell when they get wet – musty, mildewy."

Appendix B: The Many Factors Affecting Decisions About Actually Wearing Lifejackets/PFDs

> the type of craft and its perceived stability

> the operator's experience and familiarity with that type of craft and with the particular boat

> the body of water, i.e., its size, exposure to elements, combined with the operator's experience in it

> the distance from shore and the speed on the water

> the temperature of the water, particularly in spring or fall

> the law (the main reason jet skiers wear lifejackets)

> the number of people in the craft, or whether the operator is alone

> the ages of the passengers, particularly whether there are kids on board

> the operator's personal comfort around water and confidence in his/her swimming ability

> the nature of the operator's prior experience with boating or water mishaps

> the amount and speed of traffic on the water, particularly motorized craft

> the purpose of the outing, i.e., whether for a sport, sightseeing, partying or transportation to/from a cottage or larger boat

> whether liquor is being (or was recently) consumed

> the time of day or night

43   RISK PERCEPTION VERSUS UTILITY: A MINI-STUDY OF CELLULAR TELEPHONE USERS

Abstract:
A study of business people from western Canada and Washington state, USA, reveals a nominal acknowledgement of risk in regard to radiation, and its acceptance, as a trade-off for the utility and convenience provided by cellular telephones. An increased awareness of risk potentiality does little to deter expected behaviour, even when the risk factors are presented in some detail. What occurs is a shift in attitude toward acceptance of new technology as a risk modifier.

Introduction

The increased usage of cellular phones in the business and personal life of North Americans has prompted some concern about the potential effects, if any, from radiation emitted through radio transmissions. According to the Cellular Telecommunications Industry Association (CTIA), there are currently over 110 million wireless telephone users in the United States. This number is increasing at a rate of about 46,000 new subscribers per day. Experts estimate that by 2005 there will be over 1.26 billion wireless telephone users worldwide. (Source: National Cancer Institute, 2002) The almost exponential growth in the number of cellular phones and the associated human exposure to radio frequency (RF) fields raises a certain concern as to the possibilities of health risk and other consequences.

In a report on the use of wireless technology, the American Office of Technology Assessment[1] reviewed the available data and made the observation that "Research to date has found no conclusive evidence that low power microwave radio communications signals adversely effect human health. However, currently available scientific information is insufficient to conclude that there are no long term adverse effects - either from hand held devices or from towers."

The absence of a definitive statement in regard to electromagnetic field radiation (EMF) and other RF sources has encouraged great deal of discussion and rhetoric. It is expected the controversy will continue for some time to come up with little resolution either way. Articles will continue to emerge from those that claim a hazard, those that recommend "prudent avoidance" of heavy cellular use, and those that deny any possibility of health risk. For the most part, until there has been assembled a cohesive, consistent and appropriately supported research result or conclusion, the notion of radiation from cellular phones will continue to present an element of risk to the user.

Consumer Research

Two research studies were carried out as part of a program to evaluate the degree of need that might be associated with a new technology for cellulars; an improved RF directional antenna. The first study was a random sample of 40 retail outlets in two market areas. Managers or sales personnel were interviewed about their own and their customers'

---

[1] Chapter 11, "Wireless Technologies and the National Information Infrastructure," Office of Technology Assessment, Congress of the United States, July 1995. pp 239-249

perception of risk in association with cell phone use. The method for this study was a structured questionnaire that obtained detailed answers regarding types of phones, demographics, behaviour and risk.

The second study was a focus group study carried out in Seattle, Washington. The focus group was comprised of Canadian and American business people who were heavy users of cell phones. The procedure followed a progression in three stages. The first was the behavioral aspect of using cellulars; frequency, duration, years of use etc. The second stage introduced the concept of risk from radiation, and the possible effects that such risk could have on purchases of cell phones. The third stage introduced a summary of organizational arguments for and against the existence of a hazard, as well as a summary of 7 health research studies, some of which resulted in correlations between EMF radiation and adverse effects on the health of rodent subjects. After hearing the summary of arguments, the respondents were offered a presumed solution to the risk in the form of new technology, the improved RF directional antenna.

The principle objective of these studies was to determine the degree to which individuals perceived risk in the use of cellular phones, and their response to a product that presumably would reduce that risk. If risk perception is high, then the need motivation to reduce risk is assumed to attach to the new technology and encourage its development.

Results of the First Study: Survey of Retailer Perceptions
In appealing to new customers, retailers are expected to field many questions regarding the costs, functions and effects of using a cell phone. Most consumer concerns center on commercial questions; price, durability, warranty and so on. As to concern for risk from RF hazard, most shoppers are only mildly concerned.

Figure 1   STORES REPORTING RADIATION CONCERNS

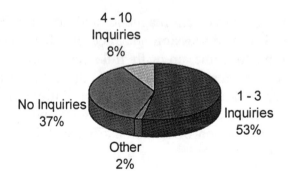

A majority of stores (53%) may have 1 - 3 customers out of 100 raise the issue of potential hazard from RF radiation. Only a small number (8%) have more clients...as many as one out of ten raise the point. In almost all instances the concerns are easily dismissed and the question has no further effect on the decision to employ the phone. Overall, less than 1.5%

of consumers voluntarily raise any question as to the potential risk in using cellulars. Even so, the level of concern is so low that it is easily eliminated by the sales person.

Nor are retailers themselves convinced there is a hazard.

Table 1   Retailer Perception About Radiation Hazard

Not Sure of Hazard	21%
Do Not Think it is a Hazard	42%
NA	11%
	100%

A minority (26%), when confronted with the question agrees there is a hazard. However some care must be given to this interpretation since there is the likelihood of demand bias entering into the response. It may well be the case that many who acknowledge a hazard are not really convinced as to the harm, an observation corroborated by the following table.

Table 2   Degree to Which Retailer Acknowledges Hazard *

Does not bother her/him	40%
It is thought provoking	32%
Would look into it further	21%
Could be a problem	16%
Other	40%

* After being shown a newspaper article on radiation

Here it seems retailers are still not convinced even after reading an article that claimed there was a radiation hazard from cellulars. Only 16% expressed the view that the "evidence" could pose a problem. The free response of the 40% of retailers with another point of view, "Other," indicates a variety of observations, but none really expressing alarm or implying change to behaviour.

A final question addressed the expectation of consumer response based on exposure to negative information about cellulars. What would consumers do if they were advised of the presumed hazardous nature of cell phone usage? Here, retailers were responding to the newspaper article. Their response was cast on behalf of two groups; customers whose primary use for the cell phone was family-oriented and customers whose primary use for the cell phone was business oriented.

Figure 2

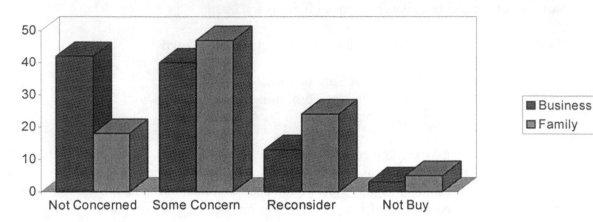

Likely Effect on Cellular Purchase

The retailer would expect that even with information from a "credible" source, in this case a newspaper article, few people would reject the purchase of a cellular telephone.

In a final prompt, retailers were shown the effects of potential hazard from radiation, in a technical brochure. The resulting perception of risk forced a shift in attitude toward acceptance of the technology as a methodology that would permit continued use of the product. The perception of the retailer is that those purchasing for business purposes would not be as persuaded by the technology (25% indicating the antenna as a sales aid) as would the family type purchase where over 40% indicated the technology would help.

Figure 3

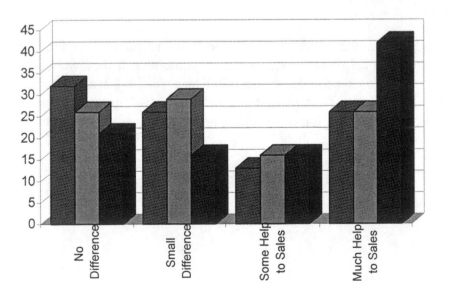

Likely Effect as Sales Aid for Cellulars

Results Of The Second Study: Focus Group

The perceptions of business people were recorded during a three-hour session on the usage, risk perception and consumer implications for a new technology. The session included eight business people, ranging from a founding CEO in the telecommunications industry, to a well traveled marketing executive, as well as an organization administrator who employed two phones, one for business, the other for personal use.

The session followed a conventional procedure in four steps: (a) Warm-up session discussing the function and roles of focus groups, (b) An examination of personal cellular phone usage, behaviour, attitudes, choice, etc., (c) Introduction to risks presumably associated with cellular telephone usage and (d) Documentation of hazard and the group's response.

Perception of Risk

Heavy users very much depend on their cellulars to give them what they want; the ability to communicate reliably any time. Most regard the instrument as a "right arm" in conducting their affairs. They leave it on all the time, (occasionally taking delight in having the "off" button} and regard it as an indispensable tool.

When exposed to a newspaper article that stated cellulars may cause cancer, as quoted by a British scientist, the group responded by agreeing to risk potential, but mildly rejecting the veracity of the news item. There was some discussion regarding lawsuits but for the most part there was a general expectation, perhaps an implicit trust, that the industry was providing an acceptable product and/or that phones would become safer in the future.

Risk was seen as a condition of life. It was noted to exist in a number of everyday occurrence; including food, drinking water, TV screens, high-tension lines and plastics. The conclusion was that whatever the hazard, the utility of cell phones more than compensates for the perceived risk. And should there seemingly be a problem, now or in the future, the concept of moderation ameliorated the imagery of harm and, barring any real compelling evidence to the contrary, none would really modify behaviour.

Response to Hazard Perception

The group was given a summary of organizational arguments and health research studies. Questions were asked about the specifics of some of the findings, but since there was no other input given to the group either way, the issues were dealt with in a cautious, uncertain manner. Those who employed the phones more in a personal, family related fashion were more inclined to press for more information, while those who were more business oriented, were interested in options such as "hands-free" sets, use of payphones and so on. In effect, there was a reluctance to modify behaviour.

Introduction of the improved antenna with its re-directed radiation pattern apparently brought a certain relief. The subjects confirmed an *a priori* confidence in technology finding the answer that would permit continued usage and current patterns of behaviour.

Discussion and Conclusion

The study very much confirms the view that people are reluctant to change. It was not the intent to persuade the consumer groups studied that there was or was not a hazard. While there was a desire to understand the arguments and evidence to date, the objective was to evaluate human response to a potential hazard and the perception of risk. Hence the study developed a body of material that could be examined and upon which to render some judgment. Notwithstanding the evidence, pro and con, most individuals are prepared to accept the risk in exchange for the utility and convenience provided by the cellular telephone. Even when exposed to material suggesting grievous harm, people are inclined to offset any personal effect that might occur by the option of modified behaviour and the expectancy of product safety from the manufacturer. In effect the culture inherent with cellular telephone usage is such that hazard is ignored and risk accepted. As observed by one discussant, "I need my phone. I'll take my chances."

By Ken Blawatt

44   Provel

Dr. Bob McManus, newly appointed Manager of Provel, was in the process of preparing a marketing plan for his first product, Micotil, a very effective single injection therapy for the treatment of Bovine Respiratory Disease (BRD). The product had just received registration for use in all non-dairy cattle in Canada. Bob knew this was a large market and the potential for Provel could be substantial. He also knew that the marketing decisions he made for this product would have long run implications for his new company. With these thoughts in mind, Bob started to think seriously about the development of his first year's plan.

Provel

Provel, located in London, Ontario, is the new Veterinary Products division of Eli Lilly Canada Inc. The company was established to provide pharmaceutical products and technical services exclusively to veterinarians. Prior to the establishment of Provel, Elanco, another division of Eli Lilly Canada, acted as the distributor of all Lilly products to both the over-the-counter and ethical markets. The over-the-counter market consists of selling to farmers through a variety of retail outlets such as feed and farm supply dealers. The ethical market, on the other hand, involves reaching end users through veterinarians. Provel was established because of the increasingly important role veterinarians play in the use of products for animal agriculture. Currently, the veterinarian market for pharmaceutical products in Canada is estimated at $60 million and expected to grow rapidly in the future. The company focuses exclusively on products for large animal, commercial agriculture, particularly beef, dairy, and swine. Its goal is to have ten products in its line by the end of the first five years. Although Provel itself is a new company, both Lilly and Elanco are well-established organizations with outstanding reputations for quality products and services.

Micotil

The first major product available to Provel from Eli Lilly is Micotil, a very effective single injection therapy for the treatment of Bovine Respiratory Disease. Bovine Respiratory Disease is a term used to describe certain types of pneumonia in cattle. The North American practice of calving in the Spring and weaning in the Fall contributes to this problem. Calves are protected against this disease while they are nursing because their mother's milk contains protective antibodies. At the time of weaning, they lose this protection. Unfortunately, at six months of age the calves' own immune system is not fully functional. This, combined with the stress involved in moving to a feedlot, predisposes young cattle to BRD. BRD is the most significant disease occurring in cattle that enter a feedlot. Experience has shown that approximately 35% of all calves entering a feedlot may be affected by BRD, and therefore require treatment. Mortality associated with BRD can range from 5% to 10%. In addition, cattle with BRD experience slow growth and poor feed conversion. As a result, the economic value of these loses to a feedlot operator can be substantial.

Although there are a number of markets that appear attractive for Micotil, the two largest are the veal market and the feedlot market. Veal production in Canada is concentrated in Ontario and Quebec, and is estimated to consist of approximately 400,000 animals annually. There are approximately 7,500 veal producers in Canada. Most veal operations fall in the 50 to 100 animal range.

Feedlot operations are found in all regions of Canada, but are especially important in Western Canada. There are approximately 2.5 million calves entering feedlots each year of which 1.5 million are in the West. Although the average feedlot in the country produces approximately 60 steers, there is a tremendous range in annual production. For example, there are over 2,000 feedlots that have annual capacity in excess of 500 steers.

There are three types of products currently on the market for use in treating BRD. The key products, together with their manufacturers and approximate market shares, are shown in Exhibit 1. Exhibit 2 summarizes key characteristics of BRD products. Withdrawal period refers to the length of time required for all traces of the antibiotic to be gone from the animal. Treated animals cannot be slaughtered until the withdrawal period is complete. Shorter withdrawal periods, therefore, give producers more flexibility in marketing their cattle.

Exhibit 1: Competitive Products

Product	Manufacturer	Market Share
Trivetrin	Hoechst Coopers	30%
Liquamycin	PVU Inc. Rogar/STB	67%
Excenel	Upjohn	3%

Exhibit 2: Key Product Characteristics

Characteristic	Trivetrin	Liquamycin	Excenel	Micotil
Treatment or preventative	Treatment	Treatment	Treatment	Treatment
Withdrawal Period	10 days	28 days	No withdrawal period	28 days
Method of Injection	Intramuscular	Intramuscular	Intramuscular	Subcutaneous
Average Number of injections	3.5	1.4	3.5	1.0
Single Dose for a 500 lb animal	16.5 ml per injection	25.0 ml per injection	6.5 ml per injection	7.5 ml per injection
Bottle sizes	100 ml 250 ml 500 ml	100 ml 250 ml 500 ml	80 ml 20 ml	100 ml
Requires mixing	No	No	Yes	No

Stored at room temperature	Yes	Yes	Must be refrigerated once it is mixed	Yes
Key Product Advantages	Broad spectrum control of many bacteria	Inexpensive	New product. No withdrawal	New product. Single Injection. Very effective on BRD.
Key Product Disadvantages	Some bacteria becoming resistant	Large volume per injection requires more time. Some bacteria becoming resistant	Must be mixed then refrigerated	Narrow spectrum of control.
Length of Time on Market	Many years	Many years	One year	Not yet on market

Veterinary Market in Canada

There are two channels of distribution from pharmaceutical manufacturers to end users: the over-the-counter market and the ethical market. The ethical market consist of selling through veterinarians to farmers. Use of this channel has been increasing in recent years as pharmaceutical products become more complex to use, and the advice of a veterinarian becomes more important. In fact, at the present time in Quebec, provincial law dictates that all pharmaceutical products for use in or on animals must be prescribed by a veterinarian. Most other provinces were actively considering similar legislation.

Veterinarians play a key role in commercial agriculture in Canada. Most livestock farmers have a veterinarian they deal with much the same as most families have a doctor. The relationship between a farmer and his veterinarian can vary a great deal. Some farmers simply call their veterinarian when they think they have a problem, have the veterinarian inspect the animals and, if required, prescribe some treatment. In other cases, veterinarians may work on a retainer basis with farmers and manage their entire herd health program. Regardless of the exact relationship between a farmer and his veterinarian, it is obvious that the recommendations of the veterinarian are of utmost importance in deciding which pharmaceutical products to use. Although, in some cases, veterinarians actually administer products like Micotil, usually this is done by the farmer using products recommended and/or sold by the veterinarian.

At the present time, there are in excess of 600 large animal veterinary practices in Canada employing nearly 1,200 veterinarians. These practices vary greatly in size and the amount of pharmaceutical products they purchase. Exhibit 3 presents a geographical and size breakdown of large animal veterinary clinics in Canada. The average large animal veterinarian represents approximately $150,000 of billings per year of which roughly one-third is accounted for by pharmaceutical products. The typical margin earned by a veterinarian on pharmaceutical products is 30%.

Exhibit 3: Size and Geographical Distribution of Large Animal Veterinarians in Canada

		Number of Veterinarians Per Clinic				
Province	Number of Clinics	1	2	3	4 to 5	More than 5
P.E.I.	3	0	0	1	2	0
Nova Scotia	14	2	4	4	3	1
New Brunswick	12	6	3	1	1	1
Newfoundland	4	3	1	0	0	0
Quebec	193	113	25	15	20	20
Ontario	147	69	35	20	20	3
Manitoba	42	26	10	5	1	0
Saskatchewan	56	43	8	3	1	1
Alberta	100	66	19	8	6	1
B.C.	51	32	12	5	2	0
Total	**622**	**360**	**117**	**62**	**56**	**27**

A number of animal health distribution organizations have emerged across Canada to act as purchasing agents for veterinarians. In some cases they are private companies, and in other cases they are cooperative organizations owned by the veterinarians they serve. The five main animal health distributors serving Canadian large animal veterinarians are:

Name of Center	Type of Business	Location
Steere Enterprises	Private	B.C. and Saskatchewan
Associated Vet Purchasing	Cooperative	British Columbia
Western Drug Distribution Centre	Cooperative	Alberta and Saskatchewan
Manitoba Veterinary Drug Centre	Government	Manitoba
St Mary's Vet Purchasing	Cooperative	Ontario
C.D.M.V.	Government	Quebec and Maritimes

None of the drug distribution centres have sales people that call on veterinarians. They serve mainly a logistics function by purchasing products from pharmaceutical companies to fill orders received from veterinarians. For most products these organizations operate on a 12% markup on their selling price.

The buying process of a veterinarian can range from a relatively simple rebuy situation to a fairly complicated evaluation of a new product. A recent study conducted at Cornell University in New York outlined some key factors in the decision-making process of a veterinarian in purchasing new pharmaceutical products. Results of this study indicate that most veterinarians have a core set of drugs they know well and are happy with. Because these products have worked well for them in the past, they are very reluctant to make changes. There are, however, many new products coming on the market every year which may offer improvements over existing products. Veterinarians hear of these through a variety of sources such as: other veterinarians, researchers, manufacturers, sales representatives, veterinary journals, seminars, and conferences. After becoming aware of a new product, the veterinarian may make comparisons with products or procedures currently being used. At this time, veterinarians require considerable information on such factors as efficacy, spectrum of control, product safety, mode of action, method of administration, ease of use, and withdrawal times. This type of information usually comes from trials conducted by the manufacturer or universities. Product price also becomes an important factor at this point because the veterinarian needs to assess the cost/benefit relationship for his customers. Products which are assessed to offer better results at a similar price, or a better price with similar results, may be tried by the veterinarian.

Marketing Plan

Being a veterinarian himself, Bob was quite familiar with the overall nature of the ethical market. With this as background, he began preparation of the first year's marketing plan for Micotil.

Target Market

Micotil had been given label registration for the treatment of pneumonia in cattle. Because the product cannot be used in lactating dairy cows, the main applications are for veal and feedlot cattle. Although the feedlot market is considerably larger than the veal market, Bob thought he could approach both markets in the first year. This would mean, of course, that his target would be large animal veterinarians that had at least a significant portion of their business in one of these two areas. Available statistics indicated that approximately 80% of all large animal veterinarians met this requirement. In addition, he felt he should also target the veal producers and feedlot operators themselves to create awareness and interest in the product. Finally, he thought he should also include key influencers such as university scientists, government extension people and feed company nutritionists in his target.

Product

Micotil has been under development and testing by Eli Lilly scientists for a number of years. The product itself is a preconstituted solution of the antibiotic Tilmicosin. Tilmicosin is a member of the macrolide class of antibiotics. Although these antibiotics are extremely effective in controlling BRD, they are painful when injected and can cause minor irritation. Veterinarians that have tried the product report that "it is always as good, and sometimes better than what is currently on the market."

Provel planned to sell Micotil initially only in 100 ml bottles. This is because, given the low dosage required, the cost per bottle of Micotil compared with most other products is very high. Selling only in the smaller bottle size may reduce the impact of what Bob calls "sticker shock." All product for Canada will be imported from the United States. Provel's cost is $41.00 per 100 ml.

Although Micotil has many strengths, its key feature is single injection. All other competing products require administration more than once, some as often as four or five times. Single injection has benefits to both the farmer and his animals. It means a substantial reduction in the labor required for treatment and the stress level in treated cattle. The reduction in labor can be significant, especially in larger feedlots where many animals require treatment. To identify and treat one animal can take two men as long as ten minutes. Reducing stress in the cattle is also important because it translates into more rapid and efficient weight gain.

Although Bob definitely was going to feature the single injection characteristic of Micotil, he had not yet developed a complete positioning strategy for the product.

Price

Pricing a new product is always a difficult task. If the introductory price is set too high, this may discourage a lot of potential users of the product; if the introductory price is set too low, the company may be limiting its profitability. Establishing an introductory price for Micotil is particularly difficult because there is such a wide range in prices of competing products. Current retail prices of key competitors are shown in Exhibit 4.

Exhibit 4: Current Retail Prices of BRD Products

Products	Small Bottles	Medium Bottles	Large Bottles
Trivetrin	$22.31 per 100 ml	$49.90 per 250 ml	$84.23 per 500 ml
Liquamycin	$14.25 per 100 ml	$28.49 per 250 ml	$47.50 per 500 ml
Excenel	$38.64 per 80 ml		

Although Bob was not sure at all what retail price he should suggest for Micotil, he felt it would have to be in the range of $100 to $200 per 100 ml bottle.

Distribution

Distribution of Micotil, and all Provel products for that matter, has been restricted to the ethical veterinary market. As outlined earlier, this means that the product will be sold to veterinarians through veterinary product distributors across Canada. These organizations supply a broad range of products to veterinarians and operate on a 12% margin. They carry a minimum level of inventory of most products and, therefore, place frequent orders with manufacturers. Most pharmaceutical companies have their sales representatives make monthly calls on the distributors to check on inventory levels, introduce new products and obtain orders.

Promotion

The biggest problem facing Bob was in the area of promotion. He knew he had several issues to deal with in creating demand for Micotil now, and other Provel products in the future. Foremost among these issues was the question of how he should reach target veterinarians with adequate information to get them to try Micotil. There appeared to be several options available.

Sales Force

The first option is to hire salespeople to make personal calls on target veterinarians with the objective of introducing Micotil and explaining its potential benefits. In consultation with others in sales management, Bob estimated that a typical salesperson could make 3 to 4 calls on large animal veterinarians a day. On average, a sales person would have approximately 200 days a year for active selling. This means that one salesperson could make approximately 700 sales calls a year.

It would take a well-trained person to do this type of work. Ideally, the person should have a background in animal agriculture and several years of selling experience. Bob felt it would cost somewhere in the neighborhood of $90,000 per year to attract and retain this type of individual. This figure includes a salary of approximately $65,000 and car, travel and general expenses of $25,000.

The job of a sales person for Provel would involve establishing new customers as well as working with existing customers. In establishing a new customer, the salesperson would make an initial contact with the veterinarian, arrange an appointment and then visit the veterinarian to introduce himself, Provel, and Micotil. It probably would take one hour with the veterinarian to accomplish these objectives. Although it was hoped that, at minimum, this call would result in a trial order of Micotil, Bob's experience suggested that not all veterinarians would be willing to even place a trial order. This was especially true for products with lots of well-established competitors. Follow-up calls would be required in cases where veterinarians were not prepared to make a purchase on the first call.

Once a veterinarian became a customer, sales calls would still be required at regular intervals. The purpose of these calls would be to check on customer satisfaction, deal with any product or service problems, and encourage increased usage of Micotil and other Provel products. Any orders generated by Provel sales people would by channeled through the appropriate distributor.

Some competing pharmaceutical companies with extensive product lines use sales reps in the ethical market. The more aggressive firms call on vets at least once a month. Other competitors with less extensive product lines find it difficult to justify the expense of a sales force.

A few pharmaceutical companies used sales reps to contact feedlots. Only the very largest feedlots are considered of sufficient size to justify this type of activity. Bob wondered if he should consider this approach as part of his overall communication plan?

Telemarketing

A second approach Bob was considering involved direct marketing. Under this option, all contact with veterinarians would be made by telephone instead of in person. This approach had a lot of appeal to Bob because it solved the real problem of distance. Large animal veterinary practices in Canada are located in rural communities across the country As a consequence, travel time and cost can be a significant factor using traditional face-to-face selling. To a large extent, telemarketing can overcome this problem.

Bob felt that a telemarketing rep should have essentially the same qualifications as a personal sales representative so salaries would need to be identical. Based on the experiences of other companies with telemarketing, he figured that a rep should be able to make a minimum of 15 contacts a day. Over a 200 day year this would be 3,000 calls.

The main direct cost of telemarketing is long distance tolls. Cost data from Bell Canada revealed that a typical ten minute call would cost approximately $6. Of course, calls within Ontario would be less while calls to distant locations would be substantially more.

Telemarketing was new to Eli Lilly in Canada so they decided to do a short survey of veterinarians to determine how they felt about this approach. Key results of this survey are shown in Appendix 1. In addition, Bob attended a seminar sponsored by the Canadian Direct Marketing Association to learn more about this method. While at this meeting he heard a presentation given by the marketing manager of the Business Products Division of Control Data Canada. Control Data had recently set up a telemarketing operation to sell computer accessories such as disks, tapes and forms to small business across the country. The Control Data marketing manager mentioned that they were successful in making a sale in approximately one call in four. This success rate was about half the comparable rate in face-to-face selling. Bob wondered if he could achieve similar results with veterinarians.

In addition to using telemarketing with veterinary clinics, Bob wondered if there might be an opportunity to use the approach with some feedlots. As far as he knew, although one or two competitors were using telemarketing on a limited basis with vets, no competing firms were using this approach with feedlots.

Direct Mail

A third approach Bob was considering involved the use of direct mail. Under this option, the number of sales calls would be minimal, while the use of high quality direct mail would be extensive. Based on input from Provel's advertising agency, Bob estimated that the cost per contact using high quality direct mail was approximately $12.00. This included the cost of preparing and printing the direct mail piece, as well as the cost of postage and handling. Direct mail was widely used in this industry. Most competitors had extensive direct mail programs with veterinarians, and some used direct mail with larger feedlots and veal producers.

Media Advertising

A final option would be to concentrate promotional expenditures on media advertising. The strategy here would be to communicate the benefits of Micotil to both veterinarians and farmers through print advertising in veterinarian journals and farm publications. Exhibit 5 shows advertising rates for various publications that could be used to reach veterinarians, while Exhibit 6 shows similar rates for farm publications.

Exhibit 5: Advertising Rates for Selected Veterinary Publications

Publication	Frequency	Four Color Rates	Circulation
Veterinarian Magazine	6 times/year	$2,950 Full Page $3,500 Back Cover	4,426
Canadian Vet Supplies	6 times/year	$3,300 Full Page $3,890 Back Cover	4,536
Canadian Veterinary Journal	3 times/year	$2,235 Full Page $2,900 Back Cover	Not Available
LeMedicin Veterinarian	3 times/year	$1,585 Full Page $2,365 Back Cover	Not Available
Compendium on Continuing Education for the Practicing Vet	12 times/year	$1,775 Back Cover	2,212

Exhibit 6: Advertising Rates for Selected Beef and Dairy Publications

Publication	Frequency	Four Color Rates	Circulation
Cattlemen's Corner (Grainews)	17 times/year	$7,213 Full Page $8,655 Back Cover	60,484
Cattlemen	11 times/year	$4,428 Full Page $5,313 Back Cover	33,985
Alberta Beef	12 times/year	$1,860 Full Page $2,220 Back Cover	13,849
Ontario Milk Producer	12 times/year	$2,215 Full Page $2,565 Back Cover	13,288
Le Producteur Lait Quebec	12 times/year	$2,770 Full page $3,230 Back Cover	16,623

In addition to ads, publications could be used to distribute inserts. An insert is a brochure that normally is four pages in length and contain a significant amount of information. A single four page insert in *Compendium on Continuing Education for the Practicing Vet* costs $6,300. The cost of inserts in other publications are similar on a per reader basis.

Decision

Although it was unrealistic to expect Provel to break even in the first year with just one product, Bob was excited about the long term prospects for the company. He knew, however, that the launch of Micotil was critical to the success of the entire concept.

Reaching target veterinarians with proper information was the main issue facing Bob. Although he felt that sales representatives could give the product the most push, he was concerned about the high cost of this approach. Media advertising, direct mail and telemarketing were less costly approaches, but would they give Provel the right image in the marketplace, and would they generate sufficient volume? What is a realistic promotional budget for Micotil? At what level should prices be established? These were key questions Bob would have to answer prior to the launch in a few months.

Appendix 1: Market Research Results

1. Nearly 40% of veterinarians felt that telemarketing gives a company a negative image, an additional 40% felt it has no effect on a company's image, and only 20% felt it gives a company a positive image.

2. Key factors associated with a negative image were:

    *   Need personal contact to relay information and to build relationships

    *   Telemarketing conjures up an image of a cheap, "fly-by-night" operation.

    *   Telemarketing is a waste of a veterinarian's time.

    *   Telemarketing provides a difficult atmosphere in which to promote products.

3. Key factor associated with a positive image were:

    *   Telemarketing provides more information at the convenience of the veterinarian.

4. When asked to rank three selling approaches, the response of veterinarians was that personal selling is first, direct mail is second, and telemarketing is third.

5. A similar ranking was found when veterinarians were asked to rank the three methods in terms of best use of their time and which method gives the most product information.

6. A small percentage of the veterinarians indicated that they had been serviced by another animal health company using telemarketing. In general, this amounted to 15% to 20% of the veterinarians.

7. Where telemarketing has been used in the animal health industry, it has been used for order taking, inquiry follow-up, and informing veterinarians of specials and promotions.

8. Almost all veterinarians believe that the use of telemarketing to veterinarians will increase in the future.

9. Although direct mail is seen as the second best approach to personal selling, it is not widely read by veterinarians. It is estimated that only about 40% of all direct mail received in a veterinary clinic is ever read by a veterinarian. In many cases, direct mail is opened by a secretary or animal health technician who screens this and selects what to pass on to the veterinarian.

10. The main reason given by veterinarians for not reading direct mail is because it is seen to be too long and would take too much time to read.

This case was prepared by Tom Funk and Stephan Fleming of the Ontario Agricultural College at the University of Guelph, Guelph, Ontario, Canada. It is intended as a basis for classroom discussion and is not designed to present either correct or incorrect handling of administrative problems. Some of the data in the case has been disguised to protect confidentiality. Copyright 1998 by Thomas Funk

45   Improper Use of Medication by Seniors

Pierre and Johanna were meeting at Health Canada to review a suggestion from a senior manager for a new program to develop a campaign to reduce the inappropriate use of medication by patients, especially seniors. The Marketing and Partnerships Division, Health Canada is mandated to promote healthy lifestyle choices and the avoidance of risk related behaviors by Canadians. By disseminating useful information, Health Canada, encourages people to increase control over and improve their health. Although well known for its high profile campaigns against the use of tobacco and alcohol and other drugs, the Division is active in many areas of health promotion including, for example, the promotion of breast feeding, child safety, nutrition and active living, promotion of safe sun exposure, and education about sudden infant death syndrome. The suggestion for a new campaign is of interest because Canadians should only use medication that is clinically indicated for a specific condition. "Improper use of medication" includes:

> ➢ Inappropriate dose modification - that is taking doses too early or too late, taking too many or too few doses or perhaps taking smaller or larger doses than indicated
> ➢ Taking someone else's medication
> ➢ Taking a drug other than for accepted therapeutic reasons.

The improper use of medication may produce many undesirable results for the patient including:

> ➢ Adverse reactions
> ➢ Inadequate therapy - the patient does not get better or does so at a very slow rate
> ➢ Injuries
> ➢ and the possibly of fatality

In addition to the possible hardships for the patient there are financial implications for governments. In many provinces, medication for seniors is either free or significantly subsidized and the cost of treating patients who inappropriately use drugs is higher than necessary. Similarly there is a significant increase in hospitalization costs because of improper use of prescribed drugs.

The potential for incorrectly using medication exists for all Canadians. However extensive marketing research identified the senior population as being of the greatest risk. This segment is especially important for several reasons:

> ➢ It is a quickly growing segment and will expand even more as the baby boom ages
> ➢ As people age they are more likely to require medication for one, or, frequently, for multiple illnesses
> ➢ People are now living longer than before
> ➢ Modern treatment plans have identified that it is better for the patient and less expensive for society if patients remain at home rather than be hospitalized or placed in an institution
> ➢ The older population is generally less educated than today's average Canadian
> ➢ The older generation is more likely to hold the doctor in awe and is less likely to question a doctor's instructions
> ➢ Older people may react differently to drugs and may require different prescriptions

The senior segment represents 11 percent of the population (people over 65 years of age) but is estimated to use between 25 to 30 percent of all prescription medication. They are also the largest users of over the counter (OTC) drugs.

The senior population may be subdivided in a number of ways including:

a) Highly intelligent people who inappropriately use medication. They tend to think that because they are so intelligent, that they can modify the instructions of health care providers. Intelligence does not compensate for their lack of medical training and these seniors do not recognize the potential problems and dangers associated with their risky actions.

b) Gender. As the population ages, males tend to die at a younger age than females. Therefore the proportion of the senior population that is female constantly increases. Elderly women tend to use both prescription and non-prescription drugs more often than men.

c) Support and supervision. Some senior citizens still live with their mates in traditional home settings. However demographics indicate that increasing number of seniors live on their own either because of divorce or the death of a mate. Some seniors live in a supervised environment (eg. Chronic care facility, old age home or hospital).

Inappropriate medication use in the senior population is multidimensional and includes:

1. Over prescribing by physicians (either by the primary physician or by various specialists in combination)
2. Lack of monitoring by pharmacists
3. Non compliance of patients, did not understand instructions
   a. Print too small
   b. Container difficult to open
4. Inadequate follow up and poor communication between health professionals and their patients. Patients are not told to watch for side effects and do not report them.

Patient understanding of the appropriate use of medication is a critical element of the health care process. Many seniors are very competent and deal with their medication without problems. However, it is estimated that 40 percent of seniors do not use their medication appropriately. Because of the seriousness of possible dangers and the large, growing market segment there have been many initiatives by provincial, regional and local health departments as well the pharmacists association and the pharmaceutical manufacturers.

These initiatives fall into two categories:

Mechanics such as:
- Bigger print on labels
- Replacing "take as directed" with more detailed instructions
- Easy to use containers
- Dispensers that assist in proper timing of consumption

Better Communications such as:
- Health providers, through education, are encouraged to ask questions to obtain full disclosure of the patient's history and current use of medication and to take

the time to clearly explain the medication plan and to check that the patient fully understands.

- Seniors are encouraged to ask health care providers to repeat instructions until the patient completely understands what is needed. The patients are also encouraged to ask and obtain satisfactory answers to why the medication is being prescribed, what are the potential side effects and what to do if the side effects develop.

These initiatives, which have produced improved levels of appropriate use of drugs among some seniors, are based on the premise that the patient is willing and able to participate in the communication process and accurate two-way information exchange is possible and exists.

However stress, fatigue, medication, illness and advanced age interfere with accurate communication and learning. Experts estimate that up to 40 percent of seniors, in varying degrees, suffer from these impediments to communication. Some seniors recognize that they are not functioning at their full capacity and seek assistance; many others do not recognize that they have a problem. In fact marketing research consistently indicates that older people think that they are younger than they really are. They do not want to admit to their age and possible reduction in physical and mental capabilities.

Health Canada management identified this un-addressed problem and suggested the development of a social marketing strategy to correct the situation. It was thought that a public education program should be developed to do two things. First, to educate the children and grandchildren of seniors about the possible problems associated with the use of medication. Secondly, for them to take an active role in the use of medication by their parents and grandparents, including, if indicated, direct communication with the senior's health providers. There is evidence from other programs that support of family and friends encourages and reinforces healthy behavior. For example positive family support leads to higher success rates in prolonged breast-feeding and in smoking cessation.

Although experts see the problem of seniors' drug abuse as real and important there are a number of questions which must be addressed before Health Canada will commit resources to the proposed strategy to deal with the problem:

- Will the younger people agree that the problem exists?
- Will they make the effort to be involved?
- Will they risk damaging family relationships in order to safeguard the health of a senior family member? How great is the risk?
- Should campaigns be addressed to young family members in general or more specifically the young women relatives who may relate better to senior women?
- How receptive will seniors be to the "interference" by younger members of the family?
- Should the program be directed to all seniors or should separate campaigns be developed for each sex?

What type of marketing research study should be used to address each of the concerns listed above. If appropriate some topics may be combined and covered in one study rather than in separate studies.

Appendix I: Research facts

➢ Multiple drug use increases with age among senior women but decline with age among senior men.

➢ Approximately twice the number of prescription and OTC drugs are used by senior females as senior males.

➢ Women account for twice as many drug related emergency room visits as men.

➢ Single people consume fewer medications than married people. Divorced or widowed people consume more medications than either married or single individuals.

➢ At least two thirds of seniors habitually consume prescription drugs and report using from 3.1 to 7.9 medications (prescription and non prescription) at one time.

➢ Studies report that more than 35 percent of senior women take five or more prescription drugs.

➢ It is estimated that inappropriate medication use accounts for 40 percent of medication related hospital admissions and 19 percent of all acute care admissions for persons over age 50.

➢ Research indicates that in most cases the use of excess medication is usually inadvertent and is due to the lack of information and understanding of proper drug use.

by Maurice Borts

46   PharmHealth Inc.

Dr. Janet Ripley, Director of Marketing for PharmHealth, gazed out her 11th floor office window at the snow-capped mountains in the distance. She thought of the ski season that was about to begin at Lake Louise and wished she was skiing on the hills instead of sitting in her Calgary office worrying about the dismal sales projections for 1995. Her major concern was PharmHealth's best selling large animal product, Wheez-Ease, a bovine injectable antibiotic that many in the company felt would face stiff generic competition within the next year. Several of Janet's colleagues at PharmHealth had been more than eager to share their particular strategies on how to deal with the expected generic threat to Wheez-Ease. Janet had three main options to choose from, but as yet, she had not decided which was best. Her president, Les Richards, would be calling within the hour and would be expecting her recommendation.

The Canadian Animal Health Market

The Canadian livestock industry was hit by the recent recession. This dreary trend was expected to continue far into 1995. During the last five years, rising input costs and stagnant prices had reduced margins further and made beef producers more sceptical of returns and profitability. Recently, there had been a vast exit of unprofitable livestock producers, leaving fewer, better managers with cost cutting plans in place. A reduction of costly routine medication programs had been a high priority.

The Canadian animal health industry is comprised of three major product categories: feed additives, pharmaceuticals and biologicals. Feed additives are medications that are mixed into the feed at a local mill and fed orally to animals on a low-dose daily basis. A prescription from a veterinarian is not required. For example, a pneumonia outbreak in a swine herd may be treated by feeding a low dose of penicillin mixed with soybean meal and added to the regular feed ration.

Pharmaceutical products are medicinal drugs, usually available through professionals such as veterinarians and dispensed on a "prescription only" basis. Pharmaceuticals classified under veterinarian use can include many diverse products such as antibiotics, anti-inflammatory preparations, dietary products, hormone substitutes and insecticides.
Biologicals are vaccines produced from live antigens to inoculate an animal against major viral and secondary bacterial diseases. The use of biologicals as a preventative measure is well established in the pet market with the use of vaccination programs against rabies for dogs and cats.

Competition in the animal health industry had become more aggressive in recent years. Companies were well-prepared to roll back prices and offer deals to maintain unit sales and market shares. As a result of current pressures on the industry, and the acute need for reduced input costs on the farm, a ripe opportunity had been created for relatively low cost generic animal health products to enter the marketplace.

Generic products are relatively new entrants in the animal health industry. Companies that make generic products, copy the formulation of well-established branded products when patent protection expires. Generic companies have not had to incur the up-front costs involved in research and development. As a result, they have not experienced the substantial product development costs that begin in the laboratory and end with a satisfied customer in the marketplace. Many generic products command significant market share as they enter the market priced 20% to 30% below the average selling price of branded products.

Animal Health Industry Sales

The Canadian animal health market had been sluggish over the past few years. Average annual growth rates of this industry were low, but steady at 4 to 6%. Unfortunately, expert projections for 1995 and 1996 were not much better. The pharmaceutical sector was expected to be the poorest performing, with a growth rate of 4% to 5%. Growth rates of biologicals were projected at a strong 12% to 14% for 1995. (Table 1)

Table 1: Canadian Sales of Animal Health Products

	1993 ($'000's)	1994 ($'000's)	Growth Rate (%)
Pharmaceuticals	$123.3	$128.8	4.5%
Feed Additives	$57.4	$60.7	5.7%
Biologicals	$30.0	$33.0	10.0%
Total	**$210.7**	**$222.5**	

The entire animal health industry was also feeling the pressure from free trade. Significantly lower-priced U.S. products were now crossing the border and competing with Canadian products in all segments of the market. Tough economic times had severely affected product loyalty with veterinarians and producers. Current users of animal health products appeared to be more price sensitive than a few years ago.

Canadian Livestock Sector

Industry livestock numbers were static or decreasing, depending on the species. Dairy cattle and swine numbers were decreasing at 5% and 2% per year respectively. The beef sector was experiencing a slight recovery as beef cattle numbers were expected to increase 3% in 1995 and 1% in both 1996 and 1997, due to the large number of feeder cattle being exported to the U.S. (Table 2).

Table 2: Canadian Livestock Inventory, July 1994

	Beef	Dairy	Swine
Newfoundland	661	4,825	15,625
P.E.I.	12,977	18,318	106,728
Nova Scotia	27,629	28,913	133,640
New Brunswick	22,627	23,330	76,093
Quebec	187,498	514,542	2,909,251
Ontario	389,659	442,996	2,924,936
Manitoba	411,131	56,106	1,287,196
Saskatchewan	898,339	45,324	808,968
Alberta	1,635,727	105,905	1,729,870
British Columbia	242,742	74,919	223,776
Total Canada	**3,828,630**	**1,315,178**	**10,216,083**

The Company

Established in 1955, PharmHealth originated as a leader in beef herd health. Since that time, it had grown to employ 90 staff and expanded its product line to include all farm and companion animal species. Despite industry-wide pressures, PharmHealth was able to hold its own in sales and earnings over the last few years. With 29 companies competing in a small marketplace of $222.5 million, PharmHealth was fortunate to still rank in the top 5 with 1994 sales of $28.3 million. Tables 3 and 4 provide the firm's 1994 balance sheet and income statement.

Table 3: PharmHealth Balance Sheet
October 31, 1994

Assets		*Liabilities*	
Current Assets		**Current Liabilities**	
Cash	$1,134,200	Short Term Debt	$2,370,000
Accounts Receivable	$2,031,080	Accounts Payable	$1,317,680
Inventory	$2,370,800	Taxes Payable	$900,000
Work In-Process	$1,290,400	**Long Term Debt**	
Fixed Assets		Mortgages Payable	$2,687,410
Plant & Equipment	$10,752,700	Other	$1,790,590
Goodwill	$1,567,300	**Shareholder Equity**	
Less: Acc Dep	$3,690,000	Common Stock	$2,960,000
		Retained Earnings	$3,430,800
Total Assets	**$15,456,480**	**Total Liabilities**	**$15,456,480**

Table 4: PharmHealth Income Statement
October 31, 1994

Total Revenue		$28,285,000
Cost of Goods Sold		$11,166,917
Gross Profit		$17,118,083
Operating Expenses		
Research & Development	$1,599,011	
Selling	$7,212,221	
Administration	$1,847,844	$10,660,076
Gross Operating Income		$6,458,007
Depreciation		$1,643,988
Net Operating Income		$4,814,019
Other Expenses		
Mortgage Interest	$537,360	
Debenture Interest	$300,000	$837,360
Net Income Before Taxes		$3,976,659
Income Taxes (50%)		$1,988,330
Net Income		$1,988,329

In the last 5 years, feed additives and biologicals were added to complement PharmHealth's solid pharmaceutical line. Feed additives were the most profitable products sold by PharmHealth, with an average gross profit margin of 76%, followed closely by companion animal products with a 65% margin. (Table 5)

Unfortunately, producers were now using less feed additives on a routine basis as a means of cutting their input costs. As a consequence, sales of PharmHealth's feed additives had been steadily declining. (Table 6)

Table 5: 1994 Sales By Product Group

Product	Sales	Gross Profit ($)	Gross Profit (%)
Feed Additives	$10,465,450	$7,953,742	76%
Pharmaceuticals			
Large Animal	$12,728,250	$6,109,560	48%
Small Animal	$4,242,750	$2,757,788	65%
Biologicals	$848,550	$296,993	35%
Total	$28,285,000	$17,118,083	60%

Table 6: Product Group as a Percentage of Sales

Product	1989 % of Sales	1994 % of Sales
Feed Additives	42%	37%
Pharmaceuticals		
Large Animal	49%	45%
Small Animal	9%	15%
Biologicals	0%	3%

Sales and Marketing

PharmHealth recently experienced a frustrating plateau in sales and did not achieve its projected sales goals for the last two quarters. The company had an image with its customer base as a conservative, premium-priced organization that "rests on its research laurels." PharmHealth was not known for its flexible pricing or lucrative discounting policies.

PharmHealth did very little media advertising with only quarterly corporate ads placed in the *Canadian Veterinarian Journal*. Most market communication focused on the "science" of the products, rather than the features and benefits to different customer segments. This marketing approach resulted from the fact that the majority of PharmHealth's senior managers received their formal training in veterinary medicine, with limited expertise in business and/or marketing. It was, however, for this very reason, that the company had a solid reputation for research and very effective products.

PharmHealth had a strong commitment to personal/value added selling, with one of the largest salaried sales forces in the industry. PharmHealth had 22 sales representatives compared to their next closest competitor who had a sales staff of 14. Most companies in the industry put their promotional efforts into advertising and direct mail campaigns, while PharmHealth still preferred to sell face-to-face with their many different customer groups. PharmHealth's sales staff were the best equipped in the industry, as they were provided with laptop computers, the most advanced territory management software and cellular phones.

The majority of animal health companies in Canada used specialized, commissioned sales representatives that focused on clients of a specific type. For example, a sales representative may only see veterinarians who specialize in dairy herd health management. PharmHealth followed a geographic protocol in their sales approach. Sales territories for PharmHealth reps included vets, industry specialists, producers, feed mills, as well as distributors. As a result, many sales reps felt over-burdened with territory management and unclear of their selling objectives and priorities. (Table 7)

Typical sales activities for PharmHealth sales representatives included calls on small and large animal veterinarians to promote the top pharmaceutical products. Representatives also visited the feed mills in their territory to discuss the volume and movement of their feed additive products with mill managers. Depending on the season, reps also called on their larger beef, dairy and swine producers to emphasize the benefits of PharmHealth products and address any concerns. At the end of each week, sales reps were required to take half a day for administration and fill out sales call activity and gross profit reports for their territories.

Table 7: Sales Force

Province	Sales Reps	Customer Base	$ Sales
British Columbia	1	A,D,F	$2,048,000
	1	B,E	$652,000
Alberta	4	A,D,E,F	$6,689,000
Saskatchewan	1	C,D,E,F	$4,103,000
Manitoba	1	C,C,E,F	$2,804,000
Ontario	5	C,D,E,F	$3,066,000
	1	B	$1,834,000
Quebec	4	A,D,E,F	$2,536,000
	1	B	$764,000
Maritimes	3	C,D,E,F	$3,789,000
Total	**22**		**$28,285,000**

A = large animal vets
B = small animal vets
C = large & small animal vets
D = feed mills & feed sales reps
E = vet product distribution centers
F = large producers

Product Line

PharmHealth had over 100 products. The extent of this product line was not typical of other animal health companies. A large portion of the products were old or rapidly ageing, and targeted towards therapeutic markets in beef, swine and dairy. A large portion of the products had marginal sales and contributed very little to the overall profit of PharmHealth. The top 15 products represented nearly 80% of the firm's total sales. (Table 8) The company also had a very limited range of products to adequately meet small animal and equine health needs.

Table 8: Top Fifteen Products in 1994

Category	Product	Factory Sales
Large Animal	Wheez-Ease	$2,290,216
	Topazone	$1,970,380
	Udder Gel	$1,659,040
	Parabanum	$1,360,790
	Epilog	$1,030,980
	Synavet	$978,630
	Pig-Kem	$728,249
Small Animal	M.P.G.	$1,147,390
	Vita-Tablets	$967,414
	Faxix	$505,264
	Pred-D	$486,506
	Sibrin	$416,157
Feed Additives	Ampromed	$3,756,842
	Sur-Gro	$2,920,170
	Premiere	$2,187,439
Total		**$22,405,467**

Wheez-Ease

PharmHealth's biggest selling large animal product was "Wheez-Ease" a bovine injectable antibiotic used to treat respiratory disease (bacterial pneumonia) in cattle. This product had been on the Canadian market for fourteen years. Bovine respiratory disease is the leading cause of death among immune suppressed calves, and a financial menace to producers. Typically, producers are forced to treat calves when they are most vulnerable, between 150 to 200 kilograms in size. On average, it is estimated that 40% to 50% of Canadian beef cattle are affected by the disease. During an especially wet season, the pneumonia incidence rate can reach as high as 80% in some herds.

Wheez-Ease competed at the premium end of the antibiotic market for beef cattle in Canada. This indicated that the product was recognized for it's overall effectiveness when compared to lower priced antibiotics such a penicillin. Producers fighting a disease outbreak, were more than willing to pay for a premium antibiotic, as cattle often became resistant to penicillin products used in high doses. In Canada, the bovine premium injectable antibiotic market was estimated to be slightly less than $10 million in 1994, with very little growth expected in the future. Presently, there were four dominant players in the market. (Table 9)

Table 9: Bovine Injectable Antibiotic Market

Company	Product	Market Share
Koopers	Tetrabovine	26%
PharmHealth	Wheez-Ease	32%
Speering	Bovocillin	20%
Techford	Oxysteer	22%

Wheez-Ease was a broad spectrum antibiotic prescribed by veterinarians in a moderate treatment dose of 1 mg per 10 kg live weight, once a day for 3 days. Wheez-Ease's main competitor was Tetrabovine, which was a one-shot antibiotic with a required dosage of 5 mg per 10 kg live weight. Veterinarians found Tetrabovine very convenient, but not always as effective. Speering manufactured Bovocillan, widely considered the cheapest antibiotic available, but required a large volume dose, which was difficult for producers to administer safely. Oxysteer had experienced moderate sales success in the last few years, although the long withdrawal period was a significant disadvantage. (Table 10)

Wheez-Ease was very beneficial to the producer as the product had a "zero hour" withdrawal period. Typically, a producer must not send an animal to slaughter until a certain amount of time had elapsed since the last medication, for example, 72 hours post treatment. However, with Wheez-Ease, cattle could go directly to slaughter. This could significantly reduce feed costs and labor time for the producer which could give Wheez-Ease a distinct advantage. The fact that the product did not carry any meat residue at all was a very important potential feature because of rising food safety concerns. To date, this food safety advantage had not been fully explored by management.

Table 10: Key Product Features of Main Competitors

Features	Wheez-Ease (PharmHealth)	Tetrabovine (Koopers)	Bovocillin (Speering)	Oxysteer (Techford)
Withdrawal	None	10 days	10 days	22 days
Injection	Intra -muscular	Intra -muscular	Intra - muscular	Intra -muscular
Dosage	1 mg/10 kg 1 x 3 days	5 mg/10 kg for 1 day	4 mg/10 kg 1 x 4 days	1 mg/10 kg 1 x 3 days
Expense	Most expensive	Moderate	Least expensive	Moderate
Packaging	6 g vial 2 g vial	6 g vial	10 g vial 6 g vial	4 g vial 2 g vial
Advantages	Broad spectrum No residue	Single injection	Inexpensive	Very effective
Drawbacks	Bacterial resistance	Narrow spectrum	Large volume/injection	Long withdrawal
Time on Market	14 years	6 years	20 years	12 years

1 gram = 100 mg
The product was available in a 2 gram and a 6 gram vial package size, which retailed for $22.15 and $64.20 respectively. Of the total Wheez-Ease sales in 1994, 60% was derived

from the sale of the 6 gram size.[1]   Although veterinarians felt that Wheez-Ease was an effective product, some felt it was over-priced for the average to smaller producer.

Biological Products

With the advent of better skilled producers striving for minimal disease herds, the new biological (vaccine) market was becoming very popular in the 90's. PharmHealth was at the forefront of developing a new vaccine for respiratory disease in cattle, which would meet the needs of producers more interested in prevention than treatment. The new vaccine was expected to be approved and registered by Agriculture Canada for distribution in late 1997. There were plans for the biological line to eventually include vaccines for swine, canine and feline health needs.

Using new bioengineering techniques, it was possible to produce a new vaccine in two years. The cost of this process was approximately $650,000. It could take another 12-18 months for Agriculture Canada to test and approve a new product.

Veterinary Product Distribution

PharmHealth's veterinary product distribution practices followed the industry norm. Seven regional buying groups across Canada purchased products directly from manufacturers The buying groups then sold to veterinarians who, in turn, distributed to producers. A common practice was for veterinarians to purchase a membership in the closest distribution centre, share in buying group discounts, and capitalize on volume order prices. Such a co-operative system gave an advantage to all veterinary clinics, as they were not forced to stock large quantities of required products at their own expense. However, this approach created a semi-controlled pricing structure for animal health companies, as it was difficult to give special deals and rebates to targeted areas and clinics. There were also strict regulations governing the advertising and promotion of veterinary products, for example tactics such as "buy one and receive the second one free" was strictly prohibited.

Buying groups operated on a 12% margin, while veterinarians normally receive a 20% margin on prescription products such as Wheez-Ease.

PharmHealth's Dilemma

Marketing decisions in the animal health industry were affected by many factors such as livestock prices, consumer trends and the overall agricultural economy. Aggressive competition from numerous companies was also an imposing factor. All these elements, and others, were currently pressuring PharmHealth into making some critical decisions for the near future. Compounding the complexity of the situation, was the fact that the senior managers of the company suggested vastly different solutions to the stagnant sales performance and impending generic invasion. (Exhibits A to C).

After contemplating all the facts before her, Janet knew that something had to be done before it was too late. PharmHealth was currently operating in an unusually difficult environment. In the past, the company had made short-term decisions with relative ease. Today, however, not even her own colleagues were able to provide a unified direction.

---

[1] This results in a weighted average retail price of $10.85 per gram.

Janet was deep in thought when the ringing of the phone snapped her back to reality and she suddenly realized an hour had passed.

Exhibit A: INTER-OFFICE MEMO

PharmHealth
Calgary, Alberta

TO: Dr. Janet Ripley, Director of Marketing

FROM: Hugh Whitehall, Director of Operations

DATE: November 14, 1994

SUBJECT: Under-Utilized Manufacturing Capacity

As you are aware, our manufacturing plant, which has a capacity of making 500 lots of Wheeze-Ease annually, is currently operating at only 60% of its capacity. I believe this under-utilization presents PharmHealth with a great opportunity to decrease our production costs and increase our sales volume by manufacturing our own unlabelled form of Wheez-Ease. I have a tentative commitment from another animal health company to buy up to 150 lots of unlabelled Wheez-Ease at $5.75 per gram during 1995.

My colleagues and I are convinced that the likely introduction of a generic form of Wheez-Ease by a competitor in the near future will result in the loss of market share and units sold. Using our manufacturing capacity as I've suggested will ensure that we increase our through-put and alleviate the need to reduce production staff. This strategy will also allow us to bring in additional revenue from manufacturing, while placing no additional burden on our sales force.

Attached are current production costs for Wheez-Ease. For many valid reasons, I'm sure you'll agree this manufacturing opportunity deserves your utmost consideration.

Hugh

Wheez-Ease Production Costs At Current Volumes

	Quantity	Unit Cost	Total Cost
Direct Costs			
Raw Materials			
Tetracline	630	$2.35	$1,480.50
Methylparaben	280	$1.97	$551.60
Propylparaben	110	$1.30	$143.00
Total	1,020		$2,175.10
Packaging Materials			
Bags	1,020	$0.14	$142.80
Back labels	1,020	$0.05	$51.00
Shippers	50	$1.00	$50.00
Total			$243.80
Labour (hours)			
Manufacturing	8	$35.00	$280.00
Quality Control	3	$44.00	$132.00
Packaging	5	$30.00	$150.00
Total			$562.00
Total Direct Costs			$2980.90
Indirect Costs			
Depreciation			$30,000.00
Administration			$100,500.00
Quality Control			$81,000.00
Engineering			$61,800.00
Total Indirect Costs			$273,300.00
Indirect Costs per Lot			$911.00
Direct and Indirect Costs per Lot			$3,891.90
Cost per Gram			$3.89

Unit = 1 gram vial

Lot size = 1,000 units

Yield - 98%

Exhibit B: INTER-OFFICE MEMO

PharmHealth
Calgary, Alberta

TO:	Dr. Janet Ripley, Director of Marketing
FROM:	Penny Gosling, Corporate Business Development
DATE:	November 14, 1994

SUBJECT: Sell Generic Form of Wheez-Ease

Intensifying threats from generic competitors should be encouraging us to consider the manufacture of our own generic bovine injectable antibiotic.

As you are well aware, the 15 year patent on Wheez-Ease expires in 1995. Rumblings in the industry suggest that Global Pharmaceuticals will produce a generic Wheez-Ease and aggressively market it within the next 12 months. Since we will be competing with generics anyway, I see no reason why PharmHealth should not introduce our own generic form of Wheez-Ease. This strategy will make better use of our currently under-utilized manufacturing plant, and will increase our sales volume (which as you know has been slightly under budget for 6 months now). Generics are typically priced 20% to 30% below branded products. The lower contribution of the generic will be more than offset by the increase in sales volume.

I have been in contact with a firm that is interested in distributing our product for a 12% commission. The company has 8 sales reps who currently sell various animal health products throughout the country . I believe they could do an excellent job for us. Or better yet, we could use our own sales force for distribution, and cut down on the additional costs that would be required with third party distribution. I strongly believe we could do this without jeopardizing our relationship with current customers or sales staff.

After extensive research for this proposal, I have taken the liberty of providing a three year sales forecast for selling our own generic bovine antibiotic. As I'm sure you will see, the future could look very rosy.

I would be interested in hearing your thoughts.

Penny

Four Year Sales Projection
Generic Wheez-Ease

Year	2 gram	6 gram	Total Grams
1995	33,070	17,850	173,240
1996	40,530	23,210	220,320
1997	42,050	26,880	245,300

Exhibit C: INTER-OFFICE MEMO

<u>PharmHealth</u>
Calgary, Alberta

TO: Dr. Janet Ripley, Director of Marketing

FROM: Joey Turkstra, National Sales Manager

DATE: November 14, 1994

SUBJECT: Our Sales Slump is Short Term

I am concerned that senior management is about to make a strategic decision that will be detrimental to our long-term viability and sales force motivation and effectiveness. I do not believe that production of our own generic Wheez-Ease product or private labelling for a competitor, are desirable actions to pursue at this time.

I am convinced that the poor sales performance we are currently experiencing is due to the agricultural recession and the limited resources we have allocated to our sales and marketing efforts. Pursuing other drastic actions at this premature stage is completely unnecessary and, in time, may prove to be very harmful to our sales figures. The only approach we need to take at this time, is to implement an innovative sales plan that provides better selling tools and financial incentives for our sales staff.

PharmHealth should begin an aggressive promotional program that demonstrates the unique features and benefits of Wheez-Ease. If we do encounter any future competition from generics, now is the time to heavily promote the "value added" concept of a branded product. This campaign should include a focus on customer needs and meet those requirements with better service and flexibility in our pricing policies.

I have outlined a promotional budget that includes marketing and selling activities that are essential to not only maintaining, but increasing our Wheez-Ease sales figures. My proposal includes increasing our marketing expenditures as a percentage of sales from 2.5% to 15% for Wheez-Ease. I am confident that this strategy will give us the revenue we require, at a minimal outlay of resources.

Joey

Increased Marketing & Sales Costs

Marketing Cost

Catalog/Trade Publications	$30,000
Journal Advertising	$25,000
Direct Mail	$5,000
Displays	$18,000
Detail Materials	$8,000
Special Promotions (Discounts)	$50,000
Symposiums/Speakers	$20,000
Conferences	$20,000
Translation Costs	$4,000
Total Marketing Costs	$180,000

Sales Activity

Samples	$40,000
Trade Shows	$14,000
Incentive Bonus	$45,000
Sales Training	$75,000
Clinic Seminars	$15,000
Total Sales Costs	$189,000
Total Increased Marketing & Sales Costs	$369,000

This case was prepared by Carmel Augustyn, Katy Kuzminski and Thomas Funk of the Ontario Agricultural College at the University of Guelph, Guelph, Ontario, Canada. It is intended as a basis for classroom discussion and is not designed to present either correct or incorrect handling of administrative problems. Some data in the case have been disguised to protect confidentiality. Copyright 1996 by Thomas Funk

47   UNIVERSAL WIRELESS ANTENNA INC.

Paul Bransom rolled the pencil sized cell phone antenna between his thumb and forefinger. He had just received notification from the International Patents Office in Geneva that his invention, a radiation – reduced antenna, was accepted for world patents rights application. He was still not sure the antenna was perfect for the marketplace. It really needed more R & D. In the last five years he had raised and spent millions of dollars on research and in traveling North America to develop the concept and gauge the market potential. Now he had less than $400,000 in reserve and wondered what to do. Should he implement a marketing campaign to sell product. If so what marketing strategy should he use? Or should he continue to lock-in the intellectual property for his device by doing more research and filing patents?

COMPANY HISTORY

Universal Wireless Antenna Inc, (UWAI) started out in 1993 producing and selling a simple shield that slipped over a cellular phone to protect the user from potentially harmful radiation. Most cell phones at the time emitted a comparatively strong EMR, or electro-magnetic radiation, from the base of the antenna during broadcast. The antenna in fact usually comes into play as a radio wave receiving device. On the other hand the transmitting signal is emitted from the base of antenna, very proximate to the users' head where, by some accounts, the effect was similar to exposure to a microwave. Bransom often told his potential investors and suppliers, "You are putting your head in a micro-wave oven every time you use the cellular phone."

The UWAI story began in 1993 when Paul's wife purchased a cell phone for their daughter who was attending the University of British Columbia. Shortly thereafter Bransom read an article that alarmed him. The family of an automobile car salesman was suing Motorola for having caused his brain tumor. The lawsuit contended that cell phone radiation had induced a growth in his brain, which ultimately proved fatal. Using his experience as an x-ray technician at Columbia Hospital in New Westminster BC, Bransom devised and applied for a patent for a shield that wrapped around the cell phone and was held in place with Velcro.

By 1994 he raised almost one million dollars from family, friends and people in the medical profession and started to produce and sell shields. The company issued a Confidential Offering Memorandum. He hired a distributor out of Los Angeles to market his product in the US and handled the Canadian market himself from the company's new location in Burnaby. The shield was produced in Taiwan where the authorities were not so concerned for the lead by-products that were produced in manufacturing the plastic-lead shields. At the end of the company's first fiscal year UWAI had broken even. More exciting was the finding of a technician he had hired to conduct research in the company's testing laboratory. Located in its office-warehouse in Burnaby. Peter Bellows, a highly skilled junior engineer had modified an antenna wave booster concept called a "parasite" which moved the energy developed during transmission toward the top end of the antenna, away from the user's head.

Bransom immediately recognized the potential for the antenna and filed for patents on the concept and the new design. He knew he would require a good deal of money to develop the antenna and produce it. Following on the success of his 1994 funding Bransom decided to put the company on the NASDAQ. He hired a knowledgeable Reno patent attorney, acquired a relatively clean company shell, one that had previously been de-listed on the NASDAQ, and in 1995 raised $2.45 million from the new company's initial public offering.

By 1997 the company's share value had reached $2.00 US and would reach $7.50 in 1998 on the strength of the company's world patent rights. In 1996 the company's sales had dropped to less than one million dollars and current sales levels were nominal. The company had pretty much abandoned sales of the protective shields. Bransom anticipated an expansion into the antenna market.

THE WIRELESS INDUSTRY
The global picture at the time showed an industry with almost exponential growth in its previous few years. What had begun as essentially an expensive mobile telephone had rapidly turned into the fastest growing part of the telecommunications market. From the 1980's with only a few thousand cellular phones in use, the industry had grown to over 200 million subscribers. Consumers on a worldwide scale were drawn to these devices because of their mobility and the ability to communicate at will with home or office in a rapid, timely, efficient manner at a comparatively low cost.

The case is disguised and written by Dr. Ken Blawatt, Visiting Professor at the University of the West Indies and formerly Adjunct Professor at Simon Fraser University.

48   The Search for A Family Physician

Helen, our gracious hostess, had just finished clearing the dining room table and we were waiting for her excellent homemade dessert, and coffee. During a lull in the conversation about the day's news, I decided to change the topic.

"My wife and I have been in Ottawa for eight years and we have found it difficult to find doctors with whom we are really satisfied. Although we both have Ottawa based doctors, we could not find a dentist that we like and trust, so we still have our dental work done in Montréal. However, unlike dentistry, occasionally medical issues must be treated immediately and we need to have a local doctor. Does anyone have any suggestions?"

My request was met with sympathy and interest. Seven of the eight people seated at the table were not native to Ottawa. We had moved, at different stages of our lives to Ottawa and had been residents of the region for various lengths of time.

Anne was one of the first to comment. "You know, I experienced the same difficulties when I moved to Ottawa and I tried several different approaches to find a physician with whom I would be happy. One strategy was to find out who was the chief of the department at the local hospitals. After doing this, and making appointments to see these physicians, I quickly came to realize that the skills and interests that make somebody a department head, were not the same strengths that I wanted in a physician. I tried another approach; I asked specialists that I knew to recommend other doctors. That didn't work out either. In my opinion, the doctors making the recommendation referred me to their friends and colleagues not necessarily to top practitioners. Finally I got the bright idea that I would ask my doctor friends for the names of their own personal physicians. Guess what? They don't have any. It is a case of the shoemaker's children not having any shoes."

"Billy, you are a cardiac surgeon, do you have a physician that you see for your own health," I enquired?

Billy, slightly embarrassed, agreed with Anne's comment. He admitted that he does not have a physician that follows his health.

At that point, Helen came into the dining room carrying a platter of assorted cakes and cookies. "I was listening to the conversation while I was in the kitchen," said Helen. "I have a really good doctor who I would recommend."

Immediately my wife responded with, "Helen, how do you know that your doctor is good?"

"Well," replied Helen, "She is friendly, a good listener and she never rushes me out of her office. I like her and would gladly refer my family and friends to her."

"Helen," said my wife, "That is the problem with trying to find a good doctor. You told me that you like her, and of course that is very important, but it says nothing about her skills as a physician. You hear horror stories all the time of doctors misdiagnosing illness or prescribing improper treatment plans causing death or having serious long-term negative impacts on the patient's quality of life or long-term health. Unfortunately, as medically uneducated people we have great difficulty in determining the skill levels of prospective doctors."

My wife went on, "Remember the old riddle, what do you call the person in medical school with the lowest graduating grades? The answer for those who do not know is, Doctor. In addition, I recently read that many practicing doctors are unable to, or do not even try to stay up to date on the latest advances and a large percentage of great practitioners for example were misdiagnosing asthma. I have read extensively in newspapers, magazines, and the Internet, about my illness and health in general. More often than I would like, I find I know about new studies and results that my doctor has not yet heard about. This does not encourage confidence in my primary health provider.

For example, one family physician that I saw suggested that swimming is an excellent exercise for people with osteoporosis. I immediately decided that this physician was not for me. Swimming is an excellent exercise especially for the cardiovascular system but it is not a weight bearing exercise. Weight bearing exercises are essential in arresting the progress of osteoporosis. In fact many treatment plans include periodic increases in the weights carried. She had made a mistake on a basic piece of knowledge, how could I trust her for more serious things?

The personality of a doctor is also very important to me. If he or she is always in a rush, won't listen to me, does not explain the disease and the implications of the possible treatment plans or treats me like a piece of machinery, I will quickly find another doctor."

"You are right, respect is very important." Myra interjected. "I want to make it clear, that I am not really down on all doctors. Sometimes when I have asked a doctor a question, they have responded with, 'I don't know the answer.' However, I found one doctor, who said he didn't know but that he would find out. He not only found the answer, he faxed it to me. He is a doctor who cares and respects me as a person not just as an interesting case of an illness or as another Medicare card to process."

Meyer, a university professor who approaches challenges in a systematic, objective manner joined the conversation by asking, "You have basically said what you don't want in a family physician, but what do you really want and how will you know if your doctor possesses these characteristics or not?"

In order to respond to Meyer, I stopped eating my third piece of chocolate cake (not a healthy behavior). "Meyer, you in fact have summarized the problem into one question. It is easy for me to determine: If I like the personality of the doctor, and if he or she will listen to me. By asking, it is easy to find out if the doctor lectures part time at the local medical school or if they do research and has published papers. To me, (and it may be right or wrong), these activities would be a reflection of level of expertise, at least on the topic of research and staying up to date on the newest developments in medicine. However I will never know, based on my own educational background, if the doctor is highly competent, an average physician, or one who is more than likely to make technical mistakes or to exhibit poor judgment."

While I was listening to other people talk and continuing to enjoy the chocolate cake I did some thinking.

When buying a tangible product, I usually take some time to inspect it before making the purchase, and it becomes apparent on inspection, if the product will do what I want it to.

After using some services, I will know if I made the right decision or not. For example, going to the barber, having the house painted, or playing a round of golf. However for other services where I do not have the technical expertise to evaluate the skills of the services provider and I must trust the person to not only deliver the desired results but to select the safest, most efficient approach. Sometimes when somebody says, "trust me" the results are more than satisfactory, other times the reverse is true and the results are poor. If the service is important to me, I cannot take a chance, I must be confident that the service provider will perform as needed.

Although we have been talking about health professionals, the same problems exist in selecting professionals in many other fields such as law, and accounting where we as consumers lack the technical expertise to evaluate the skills and performance of the service provider.

Based on our discussion, I am no closer to finding an Ottawa based family physician or dentist. In fact I have found this whole discussion stressful and I am ready for a snifter of Remy Martin to accompany another cup of coffee.

49   Zeneca Ag Products

"We may be behind some other companies in biotechnology, but our new precision agriculture technology should be a huge help to us in selling our more traditional products. In addition, it should be a profitable product in itself." So thought Colin Steen, Manager of Pulse and Oilseed Products for Zeneca Ag Products (Zeneca), as he began thinking about his upcoming presentation to management on the introduction of some exciting new precision agriculture technology Zeneca had developed for disease detection in Saskatchewan lentils (peas).

Agriculture in Western Canada and the world had undergone a significant shift over the past five years. The crop protection industry that once relied on traditional chemistry as a source for sales and profits, now used biotechnology to develop crops that contained traits never before seen. A good example of this was herbicide tolerance as exemplified by Monsanto's Roundup Ready technology. Using genetic engineering, Monsanto was able to develop new crop varieties that were resistant to Roundup, their popular non-selective herbicide. After planting these varieties, farmers could spray a field with Roundup and kill all vegetation except the crop they wanted to produce. This industry shift occurred very quickly, and left Zeneca trying to catch up to other companies leading the biotechnology movement. Though Zeneca was investing significant research dollars in biotechnology, the company was at least five years behind the industry in this area. Colin was sure that the new precision agriculture approaches would help Zeneca maintain the perception of technological leadership until other, new high tech products were developed.

Zeneca Ag Products
Zeneca, created from a demerger of ICI, the large British chemical manufacturer, was a leading global supplier of crop protection products. The company's products included herbicides, insecticides and fungicides for a broad range of crops. In Canada, Zeneca was a major supplier of crop protection products.

Zeneca had substantial strength in fungicides which were chemical products designed to control disease problems in plants. Zeneca brands in this category included Bravo, Quadris, Amistar, Heritage, and Abound. According to market research, Zeneca was the world leader in fungicide sales in 1999 with products registered for use in over 43 crops in 46 countries. Key crops requiring fungicides were potatoes, rice, and turf in the United States, and canola and lentils in Canada. The fungicide portfolio was among the fastest growing line of products manufactured by Zeneca, and sustaining this growth was very important to the future of the company.

Precision Agriculture Technology
Zeneca Ag Products had invested significant resources in developing a broad range of precision agriculture technology over the last five years. To date, the most promising technology was photo imagery that allowed farmers to identify disease symptoms that may not be present to the naked eye. Using high resolution images from orbiting satellites or fixed wing aircraft, Zeneca could determine the presence of disease symptoms long before visible symptoms occurred. Based on the premise that unhealthy plants reflect a different

band of color than healthy plants, this technology had the potential to save farmers thousands of dollars in lost yields due to disease pressure. Zeneca also felt it could boost fungicide sales and be a profitable service they could provide customers.

Zeneca had some initial success with this technology in tomato and turf crops in the United States, identifying disease in advance of symptoms and preventing yield and profit reductions. By being able to identify diseased plants before visual symptoms occurred, farmers would be able to apply a fungicide to control the disease and, therefore, avoid the economic losses associated with the disease. In addition, this break-through technology had the potential of giving Zeneca the perception of technological leadership, even in the absence of a line of biotech crops and products.

Zeneca expected that when the process was in operation, they could provide reports to farmer within 24 hours of an initial request. The report generated for the farmer consisted of a series of field maps that outlined the relative health of crops. An example of a field map is shown in Exhibit 1.

Initial estimates placed the cost of providing a photo at approximately $2.50 per acre.

Lentil Production in Western Canada

Lentil production in Western Canada was very important to the success of Zeneca. Acreage in Saskatchewan had increased dramatically over the past five years, reaching 1.6 million acres in 2000. The lentil acreage was divided into three markets: large seeded green, small seeded green and red lentil. The Crop Development Center, based at the University of Saskatchewan, had been responsible for the influx of lentil varieties well suited to the Saskatchewan climate. Exhibit 2 illustrates the growth in lentil acres in Saskatchewan since 1978.

Lentil growers in Saskatchewan faced plant diseases that potentially could affect yield and quality. Depending on when the farmer detected the disease, the financial impact could vary from minimal to severe. The main diseases that affected lentil production were ascochyta and anthracnose.

Ascochyta (*ascochyta lentis*), was a stubble and seed borne disease primarily affecting seed quality, and in severe cases, also affecting yield. Primarily spread by rainsplash throughout the growing season, ascochyta was prevalent in most areas of Saskatchewan. An application of Bravo at 0.8 liters/acre, which cost a farmer approximately $10.25/acre, stopped the spread of infectious spores in the crop by preventing new infection from forming. A second application of Bravo was sometimes necessary if weather conditions continued to be moist. The lesions that developed from ascochyta were cream colored with a tan margin and black spores in the center. Under severe disease conditions, ascochyta blight seeds became partly or wholly brownish in color, resulting in economic losses due to poor quality. The losses from poor quality lentils due to ascochyta could range from 5% to 70% of the value of the lentil. Ascochyta also could reduce the yield of lentil in cases of severe infection in a range of 10% to 50%.

Severe **Anthracnose** (*Colletotrichum truncatum*) resulted in significant impacts on yield. Anthracnose lesions developed on the leaves and stem, causing plants to turn golden brown when they coalesced, resulting in plant death. Anthracnose was primarily stubble borne, and spread from leaf to leaf via rainsplash throughout the growing season. Bravo was the only product registered for the prevention and control of this disease. An application of Bravo at 0.8 l/acre prevented the formation of new lesions on what was already a healthy crop. A second application was sometimes necessary later in the growing season to protect new crop growth from lesion development. As anthracnose attacked the lower part of the stem, it was important to apply Bravo early in the growth stage, preferably just before flowering. Bravo served only as a protectant, and did not cure disease already present. This underscored the importance of early detection of lentil disease.

Farmers were limited in the ways they could deal with disease problems in lentils. The most satisfactory method was to use Bravo. Zeneca estimated that 40% of lentil acres in 2000 were treated with this fungicide. Some farmers felt they could not justify the use of a fungicide based on likely economic returns. Other farmers felt that once they saw visible signs of disease it was too late for a fungicide to do any good.

Over the past several years, researchers at the University of Saskatchewan had developed several varieties that were resistant to lentil diseases. Although resistant to disease, most of these varieties had a ten to fifteen percent lower yield potential than non-resistant varieties.[4] This made them less attractive to farmers resulting in relatively low adoption. In 2000, disease resistant varieties were seeded on less than 20% of lentil acres in Saskatchewan.

In addition to Bravo, Zeneca also offered three other products for lentil production - Touchdown (glyphosate), Venture (grass herbicide) and Reglone (desiccant). This broad product line, and the visibility of Zeneca among growers, made lentils a very important crop to the success of Zeneca in Saskatchewan.

Marketing the Imagery Technology

Although Colin was excited about the new imagery technology, and the impact it could have on Bravo sales, he had little idea how farmers might react to the product. To gain additional insight he decided to retain the services of Agri Studies, a Calgary based marketing research firm, to determine farmer reaction to the new technology. Appendix A contains a summary of the key results of this research.

Colin felt the research supported the introduction of the new technology. Even at the highest price level tested, the research showed a high proportion of farmers that said they would try the imagery. Colin knew, however, that to say they would try it in a research study, and to actually try it, were two different things. He also knew that trying the technology was only half the battle; the other half was making sure they were satisfied with the results and would use it again in subsequent years. To achieve a high level of trial and repeat buying required a solid marketing plan behind the product.

---

[4] Many scientists believed that the "yield drag" associated with disease resistant varieties would become smaller as additional plant breeding work was undertaken.

In developing the marketing plan, Colin first considered the target market. Obviously, the broad target was the 5,000 lentil growers in Saskatchewan. Colin wondered whether there were smaller groups that would be better prospects for the new product?

The product itself was very simple – a color satellite photo of a field with an accompanying legend indicating the degree of disease infestation. Colin felt he should stop short of including a recommendation for Bravo use, although he was not sure of this. He also wondered how he should position the new technology. Should it be positioned as a tool that would help farmers better manage fungicide use? Or a tool that could help farmers maximize returns per acre from lentils? Or was there some other positioning that should be used?

The price of the service was also something that was not determined. In the marketing research, three price levels were tested - $6 per acre, $8 per acre and $10 per acre. Although the $6 per acre would undoubtedly promote faster adoption of the technology, higher prices would increase the contribution margin on the imagery product significantly.

Distribution was a real dilemma because there were different ways to approach this. The first was to distribute the images through the same dealers that sold Bravo. Under this plan, farmers would place orders for an image with a chemical dealer. The dealer would forward the request to Zeneca who would then arrange to have the photo taken and couriered or sent electronically to the dealer. The dealer would then deliver this to the farmer. Under this system the dealer would receive a margin on the sale. Colin was not sure what margin was appropriate but felt something in the range of 20% (the same margin they received on the sale of Bravo) was reasonable.

In Saskatchewan, there were approximately 100 dealers that sold fungicides for use on lentils. Of these dealers, 25 sold approximately 75% of the total fungicide used. Colin felt there might be some merit in restricting distribution to the top dealers.

A second distribution approach was for Zeneca to sell the product directly to farmers. Colin thought this could be done by sending the farmers information on the imagery product and having farmers order by calling a 1-800 number or on the Zeneca website. The photos would be delivered by courier or electronically if the farmer had the appropriate computer technology to receive them in this manner.

The final area Colin needed to address was promotion. Here, of course, there were many options available. Some of the main options were:

- Farmer meeting where groups of 25 to 50 farmers could be assembled and introduced to the technology. These meetings usually featured an information session followed by a meal. To do a session in the right way would probably cost approximately $20 per farmer.
- Advertising in publications specifically oriented to lentil growers. The most obvious choice here was the magazine "Lentils in Canada" which was published quarterly. A full page color ad in this publication costs $6,500.

- Direct mail targeted at all lentil growers. To produce and distribute a high quality direct mail piece would cost about $20 per farmer.
- Personal sales calls could also be used. Since the time of the existing Zeneca rep was fully committed with current activities, any personal selling would have to be done through part time reps hired specifically for this purpose. Colin felt that summer students might be a great choice. The total cost for a personal sales call was estimated to be $50.

A final area Colin wondered about was the possibility of bundling the imagery technology with sales of Bravo[5]. He was not sure if this was a good idea or how to put together such a program. One possibility was to offer a discount on Bravo purchases if a farmer had already purchased images.

Colin wondered what impact the imagery technology might have on Bravo sales. On the one hand, he felt it could boost Bravo sales because more farmers would be aware of disease problems and want to use Bravo to solve these problems. On the other hand, some farmers who, in the past had sprayed Bravo to prevent disease, might now discover that they did not have a problem at all, or only a problem in certain parts of fields that might be dealt with using a spot treatment.

The Decision
As Colin pondered his decision, he was very aware of the fact that the imagery technology was new, and seemed to meet a real farmer need, He was almost sure it would have a positive impact on the brand image of Bravo both in lentils and other crops. The likely introduction of competitive products into the fungicide category made the establishment of a strong brand position all the more important.

Zeneca management felt the introduction of the imagery technology in lentils should cover additional overhead costs of $200,000 a year. They expected the new product might lose $100,000 in the first year, earn a contribution of $500,000 in the second year and earn a contribution of $1,000,000 in the third year.[6] They would view the imagery product in a much more favorable light if it resulted in higher Bravo sales in lentils.

---

[5] The contribution margin on Bravo w)proximately 60%.
[6] These contribution values include gains or losses from changes in Bravo sales.

Exhibit 1: Example of Field Map

The following is an example of a map that measures relative crop vigor. The lighter areas are healthy crop while the darker areas are unhealthy crops. Moving from NW to the SE, the crop worsens and disease pressure increases.

Areas of crop drowned out
from excess rain

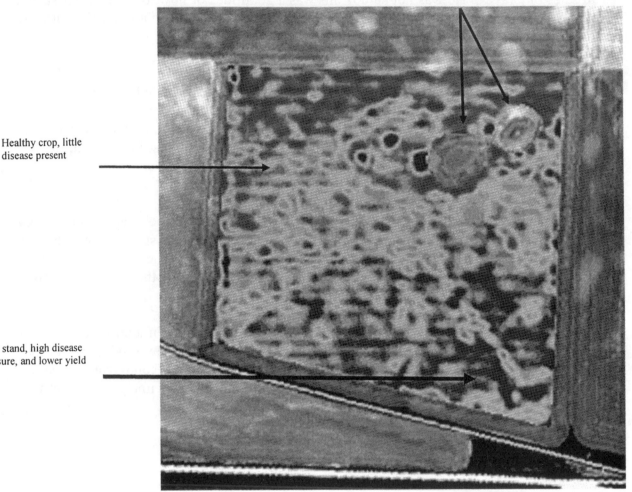

Healthy crop, little
disease present

Thin stand, high disease
pressure, and lower yield

Exhibit 2: Lentil Production in Saskatchewan 1980 to 2000

Year	'000 Acres
1980	50,000
1982	100,000
1984	100,000
1986	100,000
1988	400,000
1990	300,000
1992	400,000
1994	700,000
1996	1,000,000
1998	1,300,000
2000	1,600,000

Appendix 1: Results of Marketing Research

In order to assess the potential of the new imagery technology, Zeneca carried out some marketing research in the Summer of 1999 with a random sample of 100 Saskatchewan lentil producers. The sample was selected from a database maintained by Zeneca. Data was collected using personal interviews. Personal interviews were used because it was necessary to show farmers images of their own fields and explain the technology prior to asking questions. A brief summary of research findings follows:

After explaining the technology, each farmer was asked to indicate what he/she saw as the primary benefits of this approach. The most frequently mentioned benefits were:
- Save money on fungicides – don't need to spray if the results show no disease is present.
- Facilitate spot treatment of a fungicide – only treat areas of a field where there is evidence of disease.
- Monitor disease susceptible varieties of lentils – allows for better selection of disease resistant varieties in future.

Respondents were also asked to indicate potential concerns with the technology. The most frequently mentioned concerns were:
- Accuracy of the imagery.
- Possible misinterpretation of fertility problems for disease problems.
- Amount of time it might take to get images.
- Cost of the technology.

Three price points were tested in the research - $6/acre, $8/acre and $10/acre. One-third of the sample was asked their willingness to try the new technology at each of these prices. Results are shown below:

	$6	$8	$10
Definitely would try it	26%	14%	11%
Probably would try it	56%	36%	23%
May or may not try it	18%	44%	45%
Probably would not try it	0%	4%	11%
Definitely would not try it	0%	0%	0%

Regardless of the price, respondents who indicated they would try the technology indicated they would use it on 20% of their lentil acres in year 1 and, if successful, they would use it on 50% of their lentil acres in year 2 and 100% of their lentil acres in year 3.

When asked how they currently used fungicides, the following responses were given
- 20% said they used a disease resistant variety so they didn't need to worry about spraying.
- 40% said they used a fungicide if disease was detected in a field after carefully examining the crop.
- 20% said they always used a fungicide as a preventative measure.
- 10% said they used a fungicide when weather conditions appeared to favor a disease problem.
- 10% said they would only use a fungicide if they saw a neighbor using one.

Lentil growers indicated varying degrees of disease problems in the past
- 30% indicated they had past disease problems, but the associated economic losses have been small.
- 50% indicated they had past disease problems that resulted in significant economic losses.
- 20% indicated they had past disease problems that resulted in severe economic losses.

50   Nature Plus Limited – US Expansion?

On August 1, 1998, Brian Reis, President of Nature-Plus Canadian Operations, located in Toronto, Ontario, faced the following problem. The number of new distributors that were joining the company each month had been steadily declining. After reviewing a proposal to expand Canadian operations into the U.S., Brian wondered what action he should take next.

INDUSTRY OVERVIEW

The Direct Selling Association estimated that 1996 United States (U.S.) and Canadian retail sales by direct selling sources amounted to $US 20.84 billion. The percentage of sales by major product groups was as follows: home and family care products (cleaning, cookware, and cutlery etc.) 33.6%; personal care products (cosmetics, jewelry, and skin care, etc.) 29.2%; services and miscellaneous, etc. 18.3%; wellness products (weight loss, vitamins and nutritional supplements, etc.) 13.1%; and leisure items (books, toys and games, etc.) 5.8%.

The total North American market for wellness products was highly fragmented and rapidly growing. For the U.S. market, 1996 sales were U.S.$6.5 billion compared to U.S.$5.0 billion in 1994. This rapid growth was due to a number of factors, including increased interest in healthier lifestyles, the publication of research findings supporting the positive effects of certain nutritional supplements, and the aging of the "baby boom" generation combined with the tendency of consumers to purchase more wellness products as they age.

NATURE-PLUS: GENERAL COMPANY BACKGROUND

Nature-Plus was a network marketing company that was established in June 1995 by Brian Reis and his wife, to pursue the expanding market for wellness products in North America and internationally. Mr. Reis directed his talents towards examining the nutritional requirements of the human body and to developing products that would help improve the health and quality of life for individuals. The products that Nature-Plus developed, packaged, and marketed, included nutritional supplements, antioxidants, and weight management products. The company was a privately held organization incorporated under the laws of the Province of Ontario, Canada. The registered office of the company was located in Toronto, Ontario, Canada.

CANADIAN AND U.S. OPERATIONS

Nature-Plus had an established Canadian network of distributors who actively marketed and sold the company's products to individuals across ten provinces. (Company sales presence throughout Canada can be found in Exhibit 1.)

The company only recently expanded activities into the U.S. In order to do this, Brian recruited Alex Harkins as Nature-Plus National Sales Manager to startup a network marketing organization in the U.S., with a small office and distribution warehouse in Southern California. Additionally, Canadian distributors saw the U.S. market as a golden opportunity for new business. Consequently, many Canadian distributors had began developing their own down-line sales organizations into the U.S.

PRODUCTS AND NEW PRODUCT DEVELOPMENT

Existing Products
The line of Nature-Plus products consisted primarily of consumable products that were designed to target the growing consumer demand for natural health alternatives for nutrition and wellness. In developing its product line, the company had emphasized quality, purity, potency, and safety.

Nature-Plus created a simple four-step system for better health: Step 1 - Cleanse and Detoxify; Step 2 - Restore and Protect; Step 3 - Nourish; and Step 4 - Balance. Included within this system was: Revive™, a product that helped the body maintain normal regularity and rid itself of accumulated digestive waste, that had been found to contribute to fatigue and sickness; Renew™, a product that helped the body eliminate unwanted parasites, that had been found to cause symptoms including stress, fatigue, and general poor health; Repel™, a product that helped protect the body from free radicals, that had been shown to cause cancer, stroke, Alzheimer's and Parkinson's disease; Exfat™, a product that helped the body control body fat by breaking down existing fat, reducing the formation of new fat, and reducing food cravings; and Essentials Plus™, a natural vitamin and mineral dietary supplement.

New Product Development
Nature-Plus expanded its product line through the development of new products. New product ideas were derived from a number of sources including trade publications, scientific and health journals, the company's management and consultants, and outside partners. Nature-Plus did not maintain its own product research and development staff but relied upon independent research, vendor research, research consultants, and others for such services. When the company, one of its consultants, or another party identified a new product or concept or when an existing product had to be reformulated for another market, the product or concept was generally submitted to one of the company's suppliers for development. The company did, however, own the proprietary rights to most of the product formulations.

MANUFACTURING AND RAW MATERIALS

Nature-Plus purchased its vitamins, nutritional supplements, and all of its other products from third parties that manufactured these products to the company's specifications and standards. Nature-Plus did not have any long-term supply agreements with any single vendor. The company believed that it could establish alternate sources for most of its products and that any delay in locating and establishing relationships with alternative sources would not result in significant product shortages and back orders.

Raw materials were purchased from reliable sources and back-up sources were available. Most of the raw material suppliers were large, well established North American companies. Raw materials represented approximately 50% of the cost of goods sold for the company.

The company sought the highest quality ingredients from competitive sources. These products were encapsulated and packaged by licensed pharmaceutical companies. All nutritional supplements, raw materials, and final products were subject to sample testing, weight testing, and purity testing by independent laboratories.

COMPANY STRUCTURE

General Workforce
As of December 31, 1997, the company employed six people. There were no collective bargaining agreements in effect at that time. The company enjoyed good ongoing relations with employees. Employees received competitive benefit and compensation packages.

General Management
Nature-Plus was managed by Brian Reis - President, Christine Cook - Vice-President, Marketing, and Alex Harkins - National Sales Manager.

Brian Reis - President
Brian Reis had been with Nature-Plus as a co-founder since its inception. His primary responsibilities included the regular administration of the company's operations, oversight and negotiation of sales and purchasing for the company, and the development of the company's business. Mr. Reis had over 11 years of related industry experience and had run several large network marketing organizations including the Canadian operations for Body Wise from 1991-1994. He was a director of the Multi-level Marketing International Association and a member of the Direct Sales Association's Strategic Committee that dealt directly with Health Canada. Mr. Reis had received his Honors Business Administration Degree from the University of Western Ontario in 1986.

Christine Cook - Vice-President, Marketing
As co-founder of Nature-Plus , Ms. Cook had over eight years of network marketing experience on two continents. From 1989-1993 she was the marketing manager for Vita-Max Inc. of Carlsbad, California where she oversaw the advertising and marketing activities for this international nutrition company. Her duties included the co-ordination of advertising efforts on behalf of the company, the development of advertising strategies, consumer research, managing the advertising budget, and acting as liaison with divisions in China, the United Kingdom, and Canada. Ms. Cook received her Honors Bachelor of Science degree from the University of Loughborough in England in 1989.

Alex Harkins - National Sales Manager
Prior to his appointment at Nature-Plus , Mr. Harkins had been an independent marketing and advertising consultant responsible for projects that included marketing director for Endless Health Products Inc., where his responsibilities included the design and creation of advertising materials and direct response programs, the development of special training programs, and the creation of product sales efforts for Links Golf Company. From 1994-1996 Mr. Harkins was the Director of Marketing for Nu-Ideas In Travel of Irvine, California. From 1993-1994 he was the National Marketing Director for Mega-Merger Bancorp, a financial services company in Irvine, California. Mr. Harkins received his Bachelor of Arts Degree from the University of California, Irvine, in 1983.

Company Advisory Council
In order to assist in the implementation of its marketing strategy, Nature-Plus created a six-person Advisory Council. Members of the Advisory Council were available to provide the company with ongoing support with their views on new products, potential development plans, and trends within the

industry. Members of the Advisory Council were selected according to their knowledge of and experience within the nutrition industry.

SALES AND MARKETING

Nature-Plus established three primary marketing objectives for its company:

(1)   To produce a strong distribution network for the sale of its products.
(2)   To develop a comprehensive and regular customer base.
(3)   To establish an expanding network of distributors across North America.

Distribution

The company's products were distributed through a network marketing system consisting of approximately 5,000 distributors who serviced about 20,000 customers. Distributors were independent contractors who purchased products directly from the company for their own use and resale to retail consumers.

Nature-Plus created an environment that valued people first, that brought health and opportunity to all people through a network marketing system that enabled distributors to become involved on a part-or full-time basis. Nature-Plus concentrated its efforts on encouraging individuals to develop their own business, at their own pace, without the costly expense inherent in franchise operations or other start-up enterprises. Network marketing gave individuals the opportunity to go into business without significant risk, yet offered them significant upside potential, albeit wholly dependent upon their own efforts.

Network marketing used word-of-mouth advertising to grow and capture market shares. It was people talking to other people, sharing something they believed in. In addition, network marketing allowed an individual to leverage his or her time, talent and energy to earn commissions from sales to all the people that were introduced to the business.

There were three major marketing plans that were common to network distribution organizations: (1) stair step, (2) uni-level / matrix, and (3) binary system. Management believed, that because the binary system, which was employed at Nature-Plus, provided greater contact between the company and the consumer, this system would dominate the network marketing industry in the future.

The development of these marketing networks was most commonly achieved through word-of-mouth. Classified advertising was also used. Most of the distribution occurred through home-based distributors. These organization methods had proven to be a simple and effective distribution model.

The compensation plan developed at Nature-Plus for its distributors provided several opportunities for distributors to earn money. Each distributor was required to purchase and sell products in order to earn any compensation. Therefore, the distributor could not simply develop a downline sales organization or receive payment based upon the recruitment of new distributors.

The first method of earning a commission was through retail mark-up on product sales. Distributors purchased product from the company and resold the product at retail prices to consumers. The difference between the price paid by the distributor and the retail price was a distributor's profit or compensation.

The second method of earning money through the distribution of the company's products was by receiving commissions on sales volumes generated by the distributor's sales organization, which consisted of as few as two additional distributors introduced to the company by the distributor, and by meeting certain personal sales volumes.

The company's ability to increase sales was significantly dependent on its ability to attract, motivate, and retain distributors. The company utilized a marketing program which it believed was superior to programs offered by other network marketing companies. The program provided financial incentives, distributor training and support, a low-priced starter kit, no inventory requirements, and low monthly purchase requirements. Management attempted to reach new distributors through various advertising initiatives, the company's World Wide Web site, teleconferencing, and regional sales meetings.

In an effort to continue to motivate distributors, Nature-Plus developed several programs. Some of these programs included: The Car Advantage Program, which made car payments of up to $3,000 per month for qualifying distributors; The Personal Recruiting and Sales Campaigns, which were developed to assist distributors in developing their downline distribution networks and increasing sales; 24-Hour Teleconference and Voicemail, that provided access to a weekly recorded teleconference call to its distributors including interviews with successful distributors, up-to-date product information, announcements, and current product specials offered by the company; Health and Wealth Trends and Living Well Magazines, that provided information on network marketing and the company. The magazines were developed to recruit new distributors by answering the questions most commonly asked by potential new distributors; Product Literature, that was produced for its distributors including comprehensive and attractive catalogues and brochures that displayed and described the company's products; and Toll Free Access, for the placement of orders, customer service assistance, and faxing of orders and inquiries.

Competition

Nature-Plus competed with many companies marketing products similar to those sold and marketed by the company. It also competed directly with other network marketing companies in the recruitment of distributors.

Not all competitors sold all the types of products marketed by Nature-Plus. Some competitors marketed products and services in addition to those offered by Nature-Plus. For example, some competitors were known for and were identified with sales of herbal formulations, others with household cleaning and personal care products, while others were known for and identified with sales of nutritional and dietary supplements.

Another source of competition in the sale and distribution of health and nutrition products was from direct retail establishments such as large retailers, independents, and non-category stores (e.g., drug stores). The most prominent retailer was the General Nutrition Center (GNC) which had a number of retail stores located both in the U.S. and in Canada.

There were also many network marketing companies with which the company competed for distributors. Some of the largest of these were Amway, Herbalife International Inc., Rexall Sundown Inc., Market America Inc., and Relive International Inc. These companies were substantially larger than Nature-Plus and had access to far greater resources. The company competed for these distributors through its marketing program that included its commission structure, training and support services, and other benefits.

MANAGEMENT INFORMATION SYSTEMS

The company maintained a computerized system for processing distributors' orders and calculating commissions and bonus payments that enabled it to remit such payments promptly to distributors. The company believed that prompt remittance of commissions and bonuses to distributors was critical to maintaining a motivated network of distributors.

The company's computer system made available to the company's distributors a detailed monthly accounting of sales and recruiting activity. These statements eliminated the need for substantial record keeping on behalf of the distributor. The computer system was also integrated with the company's reporting system that generated monthly reports, invoices, and payroll.

The company's objective was to handle service inquiries made by distributors and customers immediately. However, only about 50% of all telephone inquiries were being handled in this manner. The current system was reaching capacity limits and would require upgrading as sales from business increased. Brian estimated that these upgrades would cost approximately CDN$50,000 for additional hardware and software. An effective information system impacted directly on the profitability of the company. Communication between the company and its distributors was central to the growth and development of the company's business.

COMPANY FINANCIALS

Overview
The financial performance of the company showed steady improvement despite its short history, and a significant increase in net income from 1995 to 1997. (Comparative financial statements for 1995 to 1997 can be found in Exhibit 2.)

Inflation
Inflation could affect the cost of raw materials, and goods and services purchased by the company. The competitive environment limited the extent to which the company could raise prices to recover costs. Generally, overall product prices had been stable and the company expected to recover increased costs through improved productivity and cost containment programs. The company had not been subject to material price increases by its suppliers and inflation was not expected to have a significant effect on operations in the next twelve months.

FUTURE OUTLOOK
The company believed that its success to date was due to its reputation and commitment to provide a wide range of premium quality, innovative health and nutritional products, and an appealing business opportunity for persons interested in establishing a direct sales business.

The company's primary objective for the future was to capitalize on its operating strengths in order to become a leading distributor of consumer products in each of its markets. The company intended to do this by introducing new products, opening new markets, attracting new distributors, and increasing brand awareness and loyalty.

SITUATION

New Distributors

During the last six months, the number of new distributors joining the firm each month had been declining. This indicated that business in Canada was slowing down. Because the network marketing industry was essentially a cash business, where money was received when product was sold, as the number of new distributors declined, so did the cash flow for the business. New distributors and renewed distributors were critical to the success of any network marketing operation. This was a key indicator of the overall health of a network marketing company. Essentially, if distributor growth declined or levelled off, something had to be done.

Payments to Suppliers

As a result of this decline and subsequent slowdown in cash flow, Brian found himself behind on some of his payables. Suppliers had been expressing concern over the timing of late payments and Brian knew that if this continued, they could ultimately cut off his supply of products. This would have very serious implications, and could result in the cessation of the business. Brian owed suppliers approximately CDN$100,000 in past due payables.

U.S. EXPANSION

Rationale for Expansion

Brian felt that the U.S. would provide access to the new distributors needed to sustain his business for the long term. Expansion into the U.S. seemed to represent a logical progression since the company had successfully demonstrated its viability and the quality of its products in the Canadian market. The company believed that it had refined its marketing strategies and procedures to be able to capture a profitable portion of the U.S. market. Past experience within the market had achieved some success and, therefore, indicated the possibility for greater opportunity. (Financial forecasts for 1998 to 2000 for the U.S. and Canada can be found in Exhibit 3.)

Strategic Plan

Management developed a strategic plan, whereby the company intended to establish an effective distribution network for the sale of its products in the U.S. As a result, the company would be concentrating on marketing all of its products, and developing and expanding its market penetration in these markets.

The expansion plan also encompassed a comprehensive training and educational program designed to teach distributors the specific methods and procedures for the marketing and distribution of its product line.

The company intended to expand its distribution network through the use of increased distributors. Southern California was selected as the base of American operations for several reasons. This area represented one of the largest markets for health and nutritional products. Network marketing systems were generally more accepted in California. In addition, the company believed that a number of positive marketing features for distributors were inherent to southern California, such as rallies, seminars, and incentive plans, all of which could be administered through the company's U.S. office.

Additional Resources Required

At this point, the company had leased approximately 1200 square feet of office and warehouse space. However, Brian believed that he would need an additional 1800 square feet of space if he was to commit to the U.S. expansion. Brian had estimated that this additional space would cost Nature-Plus an additional U.S.$1,000 per month.

Management also anticipated that its facility in the U.S. would require a contemporary and attractive design and décor. The company was contemplating retaining an interior design consultant to assist in the layout of these offices which would include a well appointed reception area. This feature was essential since this area would convey the first impression to prospective distributors. Two meeting rooms would also be included. Remodelling costs were estimated between U.S.$30,000 and $40,000.

Existing information systems in Canada would be insufficient to meet the needs of the U.S. market. In order to develop an integrated operation, the U.S. would require computer upgrades in hardware to link the company's offices and their operations. These hardware costs were estimated at U.S.$25,000.

In addition to hardware upgrades, Brian would have to purchase additional software to effectively handle the dramatic increase in business that was expected. This software would cost approximately U.S.$100,000.

In order to run the U.S. operations effectively, additional personnel would be required. Similar to the Canadian Operations, two administrative staff, and a U.S. Sales Manager would be required. The cost for these additional personnel would be approximately U.S.$40,000, and U.S.$50,000, respectively. These costs would include base pay and basic benefits but not performance bonuses. Brian was not sure if he could manage both the Canadian and U.S. operations at the same time. He estimated that a General Manager for the U.S. would cost approximately U.S.$60,000.

To effectively launch Nature-Plus products and attract new distributors to the company, Brian had estimated that he would need approximately U.S.$100,000 as an annual budget for advertising and promotion in the U.S.

Opportunities For Fund Raising

In order to meet anticipated funding requirements for expansion into the U.S., Brian identified six sources for funds:

1. Brian had calculated that for a CDN$2,000,000 public offering, he would be able to raise approximately CDN$1,700,000 net of fees and charges. In order to complete the public offering, Brian would have to undergo an extensive audit going back three years. This audit would cost approximately CDN$20,000. He would also have to prepare a detailed business plan for potential investors, and arrange for an investment banker.

It could take anywhere from six to twelve months to complete the offering. The offering would require Brian to give up 49 percent ownership of his company. Also, there was no guarantee that the offering would be successfully completed since it ultimately depended on the public's interest in the company as a viable investment. However, taking the company public could raise the credibility and public's awareness of the company, thereby stimulating more growth in new distributors.

2. Brian could also raise funds through a private offering. Similar to the public offering, he would have to undergo an extensive audit, develop a business plan, and arrange for an investment banker to handle the private offering. Brian would offer potential investors a 50 percent discount on the share price identified for the public offering. Brian believed that he could raise approximately CDN$150,000 to $200,000 this way. The offering could take anywhere from one to six months to complete, depending on investor interest.

3. Brian could go to the Canadian Business Development Bank (CBDB) where he would get a CDN$250,000 secured (against company and Brian's personal assets) loan at 15% interest. This loan would be repayable over a five-year period. It would take approximately one to two months to secure the loan from the CBDB.

4. In one to two weeks' time, Brian could obtain a personal bank loan for CDN$50,000 at 12% interest over five years.

5. Various members of Brian's family had offered to invest CDN$75,000 into Nature-Plus. They would have the money for him in two to three weeks. However, he was not sure what they would expect as a return on their investment, or when they would expect repayment.

6. As a last resort, Brian believed that in about one week he could come up with CDN$50,000 of his own money. This represented the bulk of Brian's net worth, and he was not really sure that he wanted to risk the investment.

U.S. Regulation

Although the company confined its activities to marketing and distribution, the manufacturing, processing, formulation, packaging, labelling, and advertising of the company's products in the U.S. were subject to regulation by federal agencies. The company's network marketing system was subject to governmental laws and regulations generally directed at ensuring that product sales were made to consumers of the products and that compensation and advancement within the organization were based upon sales of the products rather than investment in the organization by distributors.

However, the company did not believe that these laws or regulations would have a material effect on its products or operations. Nutritional and dietary supplements such as those sold by Nature-Plus, for which no therapeutic claim was made, were not subject to Federal Drug Administration approval prior to sale. Also, the company did not anticipate developing any new products that would fall under this regulation in the future.

DECISION

Having gathered the key information that he felt relevant, Brian wondered what action he should take next.

Exhibit 1: Company Sales Force Presence in Canada

Province	Approximate Number of Distributors	Approximate Percentage of Overall Revenue
Maritimes	500	8
Quebec	200	5
Ontario	3,000	55
Manitoba	500	10
Saskatchewan	250	10
Alberta	250	5
British Columbia	300	7

Source: Internal Company Documents

Exhibit 2: Comparative Financial Results from 1995 to 1997

(Canadian Dollars)	Year Ended 1997	Year Ended 1996	Year Ended 1995
Income Statement			
Sales	$1,559,055	$1,207,462	$173,539
Less Cost of Sales	993,728	775,911	111,817
Gross Margin	565,327	431,551	61,722
Gross Margin %	36.2%	35.6%	35.5%
Less Expenses	455,211	408,314	103,373
Net Income/(Loss) before tax	$110,116	$23,237	($41,651)
Balance Sheet			
Total Assets	$240,839	$194,794	$113,887
Working Capital	59,698	(44,171)	(69,270)
Shareholder's Equity	105,371	(18,288)	(41,524)

Source: Internal Company Documents

Exhibit 3: Company Sales Forecasts for the U.S. and Canada from 1998 to 2000

Canadian Dollars	Year Ended 1998	Year Ended 1999	Year Ended 2000
Income Statement			
Sales			
Existing Products	$1,700,000	$4,900,000	$16,000,000
New Products	300,000	5,100,000	4,000,000
Product Literature	80,000	400,000	800,000
Other Income (net)*	48,000	249,000	480,000
Less Cost of Sales			
Products and Literature	314,000	1,568,000	3,140,000
Commissions & Other	910,000	4,660,000	9,320,000
Gross Margin	**$904,000**	**$4,421,000**	**$8,820,000**
Less Expenses			
Operating (net wages)	483,000	1,636,000	2,283,000
Wages	220,000	1,425,000	2,000,000
Net Income/(Loss) before tax	**$201,000**	**$1,360,000**	**$4,537,000**

* Other Income (net) includes freight and miscellaneous less returns.

Assumptions
1. Gross Margin was expected to improve because of larger production runs and greater cost savings due to volume purchasing.
2. Commissions for 1998 were expected to be lower than 1997 because of adjustments to the compensation plan.
3. The geographical breakdown for revenues was estimated to be 70/30 between Canada and the U.S. in 1998 and 40/60 for 1999-2000.

Source: Internal Company Documents

Joseph J. Schiele prepared this case for the Direct Selling Education Foundation of Canada, solely to provide material for class discussion. The author did not intend to illustrate either effective or ineffective handling of a managerial situation. The author may have disguised certain names and other identifying information to protect confidentiality.

51   Amway of Canada, Ltd.

On January 30, 1995, Tom Whytall, newly appointed Manager of Distribution for Amway's Canadian Operations, located in London, Ontario, faced the following problem. Amway had been struggling with the problem of dealing with the pressure that increasing sales were placing on the company's distribution system. As well, distributor preferences were beginning to affect the way Amway might be required to do business. After gathering the key information he felt was relevant, Tom wondered what action he should take next.

AMWAY CORPORATION: GENERAL COMPANY BACKGROUND
Amway Corporation was one of the world's largest direct selling companies with 1994 estimated retail sales of approximately six billion dollars U.S.. More than two and a half million people in 45 countries had embraced the Amway business opportunity. Amway was founded in 1959 by friends, Jay Van Andel and Rich DeVos, in the basements of their homes in Grand Rapids, Michigan, U.S.A.. Amway's very first product was L.O.C.® (Liquid Organic Cleaner), an all-purpose cleaning solution containing biodegradable surfactants.

AMWAY CORPORATION: OWNERSHIP AND MANAGEMENT
Amway Corporation was privately held by the DeVos and Van Andel families and was governed by the Amway Policy Board (which functioned as the corporation's board of directors), composed of both co-founders and eight second-generation members of the DeVos and Van Andel families. Amway management was led by Chairman Steve Van Andel and President Dick DeVos, who shared management responsibility for world-wide business and who led a global management team of seasoned Amway executives. Tom Whytall served as Manager of Distribution for Amway of Canada, Ltd..

COMPANY VISION, MISSION, AND VALUES
The founding families believed that it was vital for everyone at Amway to understand the philosophy upon which the business operated and the strategic direction by which it would move forward. This was outlined in the following vision, mission, and values statements.

Vision
To be the best business opportunity in the world.

Mission
Through the partnering of distributors, employees, and the founding families, and the support of quality products and services, Amway set out to offer all people the chance to achieve their goals through the Amway business opportunity.

Values
Amway identified the following six fundamental values as the essential and enduring standards, not to be compromised, by which it operated:

Partnership
Amway was built on the concept of partnership, beginning with the partnership between the founders. The partnership that existed among the founding families, distributors, and employees was their most

prized possession. They always tried to do what was in the best interests of their partners, in a manner which increased trust and confidence. Amway would reward all who contributed to its success.

Integrity

Integrity was essential to Amway's business success. It tried to do what was right, not just whatever "worked." Amway's success was measured not only in economic terms, but by the respect, trust, and credibility it earned.

Personal Worth

Amway acknowledged the uniqueness created in each individual. Every person was worthy of respect, and deserved fair treatment and the opportunity to succeed to the fullest extent of his or her potential.

Achievement

Amway founders, distributors, and employees were builders and encouragers. They strove for excellence in all that they did. Their focus was on continued improvement, progress, and achievement of individual and group goals. They anticipated change, responded swiftly to it, took action to get the job done, and gained from their experiences. They encouraged creativity and innovation.

Personal Responsibility

Each individual at Amway was responsible and accountable for achieving personal goals, as well as for giving 100 percent effort in helping to achieve corporate or team goals. By helping people help themselves, the company furthered the potential for individual and shared success. Amway also had a responsibility to be a good citizen within the communities where its people lived and worked.

Free Enterprise

Amway was a proud advocate of freedom and free enterprise. Human economic advancement was clearly proven to be best achieved in a free market economy.

Taken as a whole, the above points constituted the foundation upon which Amway felt it could achieve its vision: to be the best business opportunity in the world.

AMWAY CORPORATION: SISTER COMPANIES

Amway Japan Limited was the exclusive distribution company for Amway Corporation in Japan. Amway Asia Pacific Limited was the exclusive distribution company for Amway Corporation in Australia, Brunei, New Zealand, Thailand, Taiwan, Malaysia, Macau, Hong Kong, and the People's Republic of China. Certain trusts, foundations, and other entities that were established by or for the benefit of the founders were the majority shareholders of each company. A minority of each company was publicly traded. Both companies were listed on the New York stock exchange: Amway Japan Limited as AJL and Amway Pacific Limited as AAP.

AMWAY CORPORATION: FACILITIES

Amway of Canada was based in London, Ontario. Manufacturing occurred at the Ada, Michigan, world headquarters; Amway's Nutrilite facilities were in Lakeview and Buena Park, California; and there were facilities in South Korea and China. Amway's ARTISTRY® Cosmetics and Skin Care products were manufactured at the corporation's state of the art manufacturing facility in Ada,

Michigan, for distribution on six continents. Products were delivered to Amway distributors in the United States and Canada through ten Amway Service Centers. Amway had 46 affiliate operations world-wide serving 80 countries and territories. Approximately 70 per cent of Amway's business occurred outside of North America. Amway and its affiliates employed more than 14,000 people world-wide.

AMWAY CORPORATION: CANADIAN OPERATIONS

Amway Corporation's Canadian operations were started as Amway's first foreign affiliate in October 1962, with a 600-square foot facility on Hyman Street in London, Ontario. In 1964, Amway moved to its present location on Exeter Road, into a 4,000-square foot facility that was ultimately expanded to 170,000 square feet.

The Canadian headquarters, with approximately 365 employees, provided distribution of Amway's products and services to Amway's 76,000 Canadian distributors across the nation. The number of new distributors joining the company in Canada had increased 9.5 percent annually over the past five years.

Amway of Canada's revenues at estimated retail for the fiscal year ended August 31, 1994 were approximately $203 million, up from $170 million the previous year. The average annual growth in Canada over the previous five years was 18 per-cent.

During 1994, Amway of Canada processed an average of 41,000 orders per month. These products were supposed to be shipped out within 24 hours of ordering, to various locations across Canada.

AMWAY CORPORATION: PRODUCTS AND SERVICES

Over time, Amway products and services had expanded to include more than 450 personal care, nutrition and wellness, home care, home tech, and commercial products, developed and manufactured by Amway, plus a variety of products and services carrying the Amway name. Based on 1994 sales, Amway was one of the world's largest manufacturers of branded vitamin and mineral supplements in tablet and capsule form.

Amway also offered goods and services from a variety of major companies, including the Amway Food Storage System created exclusively for Amway by Rubbermaid. Other products included thousands of brand name items in Amway of Canada's PERSONAL SHOPPERS® Catalogue and other specialty catalogues, available in both English and French. These products included a wide range of food products, clothing, furniture, jewelry, appliances, televisions and other home entertainment products, plus many other personal and commercial use items.

Amway of Canada Ltd. also marketed a variety of services, including AT&T Canada Long Distance Telephone Service, Cantel cellular phone service, the Franklin Covey Day Planner System, and the Amway Auto Club, administered by the Dominion Automobile Association.

AMWAY CORPORATION: SALES AND MARKETING

As of 1994, a core force of more than two million distributors world-wide, including more than 64,000 Canadians, represented the primary distribution network for Amway products and services. These distributors were independent business owners, not Amway employees. They were sponsored and trained by active distributors, and they operated their businesses using the Amway Sales and Marketing Plan.

New distributors began by buying a Business Kit, valued at approximately CDN$133, which contained 13 of Amway's most popular products, as well as information on Amway products and programs. The kit was returnable if a distributor chose not to continue.

There were two ways in which an Amway distributor earned income. First, Amway distributors earned income from the mark-up of products and services they sold directly to consumers. Typically this mark-up was 25 to 30 percent of the wholesale price, but distributors were entitled to determine independently the prices at which they sold products. In most cases, distributors sold to consumers in their homes; you could not buy Amway- branded products off store shelves.

The second method an Amway distributor could earn income was from bonuses earned from the down-line sales of distributors that they sponsored. A distributor would receive bonuses not only from his or her direct sales but also from the sales of those within their respective down-line sales organizations.

Although these distributors were independent entrepreneurs, distributors were not alone in building their business. New distributors were trained by a sponsor to ensure that they knew best how to build their business. The Business Kit came with the Amway Sales and Marketing Plan that provided information on business principles. Ethical values were outlined in the Amway Code of Ethics, and rules of conduct were also provided to distributors before they were allowed to set out on their own.

COMPETITION
Amway competed with many companies marketing similar products. Few competitors in the direct marketing industry marketed the number of products and services offered by Amway. Another source of competition in the sale and distribution of products was from direct retail establishments such as large retailers, independents and non-category stores (e.g., drug stores).

Amway also competed directly with other network marketing companies in the recruitment of distributors. Some of the largest of these were Avon, Mary Kay Cosmetics, Tupperware, and NuSkin. The company competed for these distributors through its marketing program that included its commission or bonus structure, training and support services, and other benefits.

TOM WHYTALL, MANAGER OF DISTRIBUTION, CANADIAN OPERATIONS
Tom Whytall, Manager of Distribution for Amway's Canadian operations, had recently joined the company in early January 1995. Prior to joining Amway, Tom had spent nearly 25 years in the distribution and logistics field with Baxter Corporation, Simplex, and Wicor. His background included experience with designing and building facilities, and with private trucking and transportation in Canada. Tom was described as a seasoned professional with a demonstrated assertive, decisive and participative management style. His proven track record in the distribution and logistics field was further enhanced by his finely honed leadership, communication, and managerial strengths.

Tom's responsibilities at Amway included the development and implementation of cost-effective, nation-wide distribution strategies, to better service Amway's rapidly growing distributor network.

Included in his duties were the direction and co-ordination of Amway's catalogue and warehouse operations, including stock picking, shipping, receiving, warehousing, maintenance, carrier negotiations and liaison, as well as related activities in a non-unionized environment.

SITUATION

Changes in the Competitive Business Environment

Several changes were occurring within the competitive business environment. First, many other network marketing companies were increasing the level of service to their customers. Distributors were gaining more flexibility with the options they had for both ordering and receiving products. Traditionally, Amway distributors had to order case lots of products even though they might not need the entire case lot. This meant an increased level of investment for the distributor as well as other associated complexities such as storage and additional handling of material. As a result, distributors were requesting that they have the option to order products on an individual basis, rather than in case lots. Other companies within the market were already providing this service.

Second, up to now, Amway distributors had to purchase the products for their own group of distributors, to be delivered to a single destination. This meant that orders from individual distributors had to go first to their respective group leader (distributor); then on a weekly basis the group leader would place an order to Amway, and when that order was received by the group leader, he or she would then distribute products to the other distributors. This process was seen by some distributors as inefficient and time-consuming. Not all distributors were conveniently located near the group leader. Other companies were allowing individual orders to be placed not only by individual distributors but also by individual customers, whereby ordered products would be delivered directly to the person ordering.

Sales Growth

The Canadian business volume between 1986/87 and 1993/94 had more than tripled. Despite this growth, the material handling system and catalogue pick[7] to order methods had remained fundamentally unchanged since they were installed in 1979/80.

The increased volume demands on the London facility had presented several serious operational challenges:

(1) Facility Space. There was an insufficient number of truck docks for both shipping and receiving. As well, there was inadequate space for palletizing and staging loads for shipment, and for other operations including order rework, back order filling, and soft goods receiving.

(2) Pick Capacity. Current pick capacity was severely limited. Increased orders had resulted in several inefficiencies including increased time required for order picking and incorrect picks.

(3) Conveyer Capacity. The conveyer system used to move goods from receiving, to storage, to picking point, to shipping was at full capacity on a two-shift basis. During busy periods, the conveyer system was so packed with orders that additional staff had to be hired, over-time was

---

[7] The term "pick" refers to selecting items from stock for shipment to distributors.

required to process orders, and conveyer equipment breakdowns began occurring on a more regular basis.

(4) Delivery Failures. The increased volume of orders and the inability of the system to handle orders efficiently caused deliveries of products to be delayed to distributors anywhere from one to two days. Amway had committed to deliver orders to distributors on time. Because the system was so tightly linked, delays in one day's orders that required overtime and extra work to complete also caused the next day's orders to be delayed.

Facilities

All warehousing and distribution activities for the Amway of Canada business were conducted at the London Regional Distribution Center (RDC) and two additional off-site leased warehouses in the London area. The London RDC facility was approximately 170,000 square feet in size and included warehousing, distribution operations, and corporate offices within this space. This facility was last expanded in 1979/80. In order to address ongoing space shortages at the main facility and to adapt to the growth and increased activity levels, 22,000-and 71,500-square foot warehouses had been leased at an annual cost of approximately CDN$300,000.

In addition to the monthly lease expenses, the off-site warehouses generated additional material handling, truck shuttling, labor and equipment expenses, consumed limited dock space at RDC, and added lead time to the replenishment process.

ALTERNATIVES

Several alternatives were evaluated that were intended to address the changes that occurred within the Amway business environment. In order to address these changes, the Eaches and Direct Fulfillment Programs were suggested. To address the lack of facility space due to sales growth, facility expansion both on-site and off-site was considered.

Eaches Program

Traditionally, Amway products had only been available for purchase by distributors in case lots. An alternative to this was for distributors to purchase the majority of these products in either cases or individual units. This option would have meant additional orders, material handling, and labor. Also the increased activity would place additional pressure on the already stressed facility.

Direct Fulfillment Program

Traditionally, on a weekly basis, distributors had placed one large order for their respective distributors to be delivered to a single destination point. However, an option had been presented that would allow individual distributors to place their own orders that would be delivered to a destination of their choice. This would have increased the number of orders to be fulfilled and shipped each week.

Both the Eaches and Direct Fulfillment Programs presented major challenges for the Canadian distribution operation. Implementation of these programs would mean more skus, order picks, re-orders, material handling, and labor.

Facility Expansion

Three options were being considered to deal with the lack of facility space. First, Amway could expand upon the existing operations facility with an addition of physical space. Second, an off-site location could be purchased and equipped so that the two other leased locations would not be required. Lastly, state-of-the-art picking equipment could be purchased to increase the efficiency of the current operation and thus accommodate the increased number of orders.

On-Site Expansion

A 55,000-square foot expansion of warehouse space was being considered at a cost of CDN$3 million. Benefits of the expansion included additional truck dock space, bulk storage areas for inbound stock, future area for picking, and improvements in material handling and efficiency. Additionally, the 71,500-square foot off-site warehouse could likely be eliminated.

Off-Site Expansion

An off-site option to purchase a 320,000-square foot facility was available at a base cost of CDN$4 million. This off-site location would include 65 acres of land as well as highway access. The off-site location would likely allow the elimination of both off-site warehouses and their associated costs. However, an additional CDN$5 million worth of improvements to raise ceilings, upgrade conditions, and outfit the facility would be required. Some environmental clean-up was required and needed to be considered carefully before choosing this option.

State-of-the-Art Picking Equipment

State-of-the-art picking equipment was being considered to meet the challenges placed on the existing system. The equipment would provide ample capability for the future, increase capacity utilization, result in improved on-time delivery, and provide several productivity improvements. This equipment would cost the company CDN$5 million to purchase and install.

DECISION

Having gathered the key information that he felt was relevant, Tom wondered what action he should take next.

52   CANADIAN NOVELTY PRINTING

Andy Cook, newly appointed President and CEO of Canadian Novelty Printing's Canadian Operations, located in Brampton, Ontario, faced the following problem. Company profits and the number of active distributors that remain with the company had been steadily declining during the last few years. After reviewing the situation, Andy wondered what action he should take next.

INDUSTRY OVERVIEW

The World Federation of Direct Selling Associations estimated that 1998 Canadian retail sales by direct selling sources amounted to $1.6 billion. The percentage of sales by major product groups was as follows: home and family care products (cleaning, cookware, and cutlery, etc.), 11 per cent; personal care products (cosmetics, jewelry, and skin care, etc.), 30 per cent; services and miscellaneous, etc., 14 per cent; wellness products (weight loss, vitamins and nutritional supplements, etc.), 36 per cent; and leisure items (books, toys and games, etc.), 9 per cent. Canadian retail sales by direct selling sources are expected to experience an average annual growth rate of 10 to 15 per cent over the next five years.

The location of these sales that were sold by an estimated 1.3 million distributors reported as a percentage of sales dollars was as follows: in the home, 75 per cent; in the workplace, 10 per cent; over the phone (in a follow-up to a face-to-face solicitation), 11 per cent; and at temporary or other locations (fair, exhibition, shopping mall, etc), 4 per cent.

The sales strategies used to generate sales varied considerably. The methods used to generate sales, as a percentage of sales dollars, was as follows: individual one-to-one selling, 65 per cent; party-plan or group selling, 29 per cent; and customers placing an order directly to the firm (following a face-to-face solicitation), 6 per cent.

CANADIAN NOVELTY PRINTING: GENERAL COMPANY BACKGROUND

In 1946, with a $1000 investment, Canadian Novelty Printing (CNP) was started by a young Canadian entrepreneur by the name of Rick Baily. Mr. Baily was intrigued by the idea of manufacturing and selling personalized business cards and stationery to the expanding market for these products in Canada.

Some of the very first products offered by CNP included personalized business cards and office stationery. Over the years, however, additional products were added to CNP's product line including office furniture, office supplies, personalized apparel, unique value-priced gift items, books, and motivational art work.

CNP was a subsidiary of a publicly traded company incorporated under the laws of the Province of Ontario, Canada. The registered office of CNP was located in Brampton, Ontario, Canada.

CANADIAN OPERATIONS

During 1999, CNP had an established Canadian network of 156,000 active distributors who marketed and sold the company's products to individuals and small businesses across Canada from 44 distribution centres.

PRODUCTS AND NEW PRODUCT DEVELOPMENT

Products

Historically, CNP was known for a product line that focused primarily on quality personalized business cards and stationery. However, over the last few years CNP had expanded its product line to include such items as office furniture, office supplies, personalized apparel, unique value-priced gift items, books, and motivational art work. CNP selected products that were competitively priced for the quality that they offered.

New Product Development

Over the years new products had been added to enrich CNP's product line. These items were added based on management's belief that customers wanted a wider range of products to chose from. New product ideas were derived from a number of sources including existing distributors, customers, management, and various other CNP personnel.

Purchase volumes were based on estimated demand for products according to seasonal market consumption patterns. For instance, business cards and stationery sold more rapidly during the first few months of the year, whereas novelty gift items and personalized apparel sold more rapidly during the busy Christmas season.

COMPANY STRUCTURE

General Workforce

CNP employed approximately 100 people in a variety of general functions including administration, marketing, information systems, and operations. There were no collective bargaining agreements in effect. The company enjoyed excellent ongoing relations with employees. Employees received competitive benefit and compensation packages.

Senior Management

CNP was managed by Andy Cook - President and CEO, Paul Haesler - Senior Vice-President and Chief Financial Officer, Chris Lauterbach - Senior Vice-President Operations, Mary Steeds - Senior Vice-President Marketing and Sales, and Christine Martini - Senior Vice-President Merchandising. CNP senior management had spent most of their careers working in a direct marketing environment. They had come to believe from both their formal education and many years of practical work experience that the success of any direct marketing company was the result of an effective marketing plan. In order to be successful, CNP senior management believed that they needed to continually recruit and retain distributors that were highly motivated towards improving upon their customer base.

Distribution Centre Managers and Staff

Each of CNP's 44 distribution centres employed a manager, an assistant manager, and various general support staff. The people employed within these distribution centres usually had distribution backgrounds. They had acquired their expertise from years of managing the flow of product from suppliers to distributors. Their jobs typically involved stock-keeping and order-filling. The people employed within each distribution centre had little or no marketing experience and could be seen as an operationally focused workforce.

SALES AND MARKETING

Sales
The company's products were sold and distributed through a marketing system consisting of approximately 156,000 active distributors. Distributors were independent contractors who purchased products directly from the company for their own use and for resale to other consumers. Sales revenues were generated from four distinct segments:

Self Buyer - Family Buyer
The self buyer - family buyer segment represented approximately 30 per cent of sales revenues. These distributors were people who shared CNP product catalogues with friends and family members. They used their status as distributors to either take advantage of the discounts offered on purchases for themselves or they passed these discounts along to their friends and family members. The average annual dollar spent by each self buyer - family buyer distributor was $135 per year.

Direct Seller Representative
The direct seller representative segment represented approximately 40 per cent of sales revenues. These distributors were people who saw themselves as independent business owners who actively distributed CNP product catalogues and recruited customers in order to make more sales and earn larger commission incomes for themselves. The average annual dollar spent by each direct seller representative distributor was $1900 per year.

Non-Catalogue Retail
The non-catalogue retail segment represented approximately 19 per cent of sales revenues. These were both distributors and non-distributors who purchased heavily discounted items that were advertised through flyers and various mailings and sold through the 44 retail distribution centres.

Fundraising
The fundraising segment represented approximately 11 per cent of sales revenues. These distributors were people who used the products sold by CNP to support fundraising activities. These items included personalized apparel, pins and key chains, and other similar items such as personalized coffee mugs or cups. The average annual dollar spent by each fundraising distributor was $2000 per year.

Marketing
CNP employed a system that enabled distributors to become involved on a part-or full-time basis. CNP concentrated its efforts on encouraging individuals to develop their own business, at their own pace, without the costly expense inherent to franchise operations or other start-up enterprises. CNP gave individuals the opportunity to go into business without significant risk, yet offered them significant upside potential, albeit wholly dependent upon their own efforts.

The company's ability to increase sales was significantly dependent on its ability to attract, motivate, and retain distributors, and its ability to offer products and services that were well suited to the needs of their customers. Management attempted to do this through a catalogue marketing program which it believed was superior to programs offered by other network marketing companies. Typically, CNP product catalogues were mailed to distributors who circulated these catalogues to small businesses, friends, family members, and the like in order to generate sales. Distributors could advertise through classified ads, hold home parties where information on the company and its products could be disseminated, go door to door, or contact people through phone solicitation.

Customers would place their orders through distributors who would then contact a distribution centre where orders could be filled, picked up and delivered to customers. Money for each order was collected directly from each customer by the respective distributor. This system allowed an individual distributor to leverage his or her time, talent and energy to earn commissions from sales to all of the people that were introduced to company product lines. These methods had proven to be a simple and effective distribution model for CNP.

The marketing program offered by CNP provided financial incentives for distributors to earn income based on the retail mark-up on product sales. Distributors purchased product from the company and resold the product at retail prices to consumers. The difference between the price paid by the distributor and the retail price was a distributor's profit or compensation. As a distributor sold more product the discounts offered would increase accordingly. These discounts ranged from 10 per cent for cumulative sales under $250 to 50 per cent for cumulative sales above $15,000. Three years ago, in an attempt to motivate sales, changes were made to the discount structure for distributors. Level 1 discounts were reduced from 20 to 10 per cent and top level discounts were raised to as high as 50 per cent. (Exhibit 1 provides the new discount structure that corresponded to respective sales levels.)

COMPETITION

Overview
CNP competed with many companies marketing products similar to those marketed and sold by the company. It also competed directly with other direct marketing companies for the recruitment of distributors.

Not all competitors sold all the types of products marketed by CNP. Some competitors had more focused lines - others more varied lines. For example, some competitors were known for and were identified by the personalized stationery that they sold, while others were known for and identified by a wide array of product lines.

Another source of competition in the sale and distribution of CNP products was from direct retail establishments such as large retailers, independents, and non-category stores.

There were also many other companies with which CNP competed for distributors. (Exhibit 2 provides an outline of direct marketing companies with whom CNP competed for product sales and distributors including details on product lines offered, discounts offered, distributor support and new distributor promotional programs.)

FUTURE OUTLOOK

The company believed that its success to date was due to its reputation for quality products and services offered, in-stock first time delivery of items, its familiar quality product line such as personalized business cards and stationery, and its appeal to distributors as a business opportunity for those interested in establishing their own direct sales business.

The company's primary objective for the future was to increase sales and profitability by capitalizing on its operating strengths in order to become a leading distributor of consumer products in each of its markets. The company intended to do this by introducing new products, attracting new distributors, and increasing company awareness and loyalty. (Exhibit 3 provides sales and earnings projections for the next three years.)

CURRENT SITUATION

Sales Trends
Over the last three years the financial performance of the company had shown a steady decline despite attempts to enrich catalogue offerings and adjust discount structures for distributor segments. (Exhibit 4 provides financial results for the past four years.)

Declining Distributor Base
During the last three years the total number of CNP distributors had declined from 180,000 to 156,000 distributors. (Exhibit 4 provides distributor levels for the past four years.)

Stock Outs and Other Inventory Problems
Over the last four years the number of stock-keeping units for CNP products had increased from 3700 to over 7900 units. Management believed that this increase might have contributed to stock-outs and the problems associated with managing the larger inventory levels needed to meet customer demand. During the last two years distribution centers had been unable to provide in-stock first-time delivery of items for 75 per cent of orders.

Mandate for Turnaround
Due to the losses experienced during the last few years, CNP's parent company decided to change CNP's status as an operating subsidiary to a discontinued operation. Unless Andy could find a way to turn the company around, CNP's parent company would be forced to either sell off or close CNP permanently.

Other Problems Encountered
Management believed that there were other factors that might have contributed to the decline in sales and distributor levels over the last few years. These factors included a mail strike that occurred two years ago that prevented the timely delivery of CNP product catalogues and advertisements, and a rise in inflation that caused significant price increases.

DECISION

Having reviewed the key information that he felt relevant, Andy wondered what action he should take next.

Exhibit 1: Revised Distributor Discount Structure

Discount Level	Sales Volume	Old Discount	New Discount
1	$0 - $249	20 per cent	10 per cent
2	$250 - $499	20 per cent	20 per cent
3	$500 - $999	30 per cent	30 per cent
4	$1,000 - $2,999	35 per cent	35 per cent
5	$3,000 - $7,499	40 per cent	40 per cent
6	$7,500 - $14,999	40 per cent	45 per cent
7	Over $15,000	45 per cent	50 per cent

Source: Internal Company Documents

Exhibit 2: CNP Competition and Related Attributes

Company & Attributes	Product Line	Discount Structure	Distributor Support	New Distributor Promotional Programs
CNP	Personalized business cards and stationery, office furniture and supplies, apparel, unique value-priced gift items, books, and motivational art work.	10-50 per cent discounts on cumulative annual sales volumes.	Support was offered through a 1-800 telephone line, and regular non-catalogue flyers, and newsletters.	There was an additional 10 per cent discount offered to new distributors as well free information packages and starter coupons for various products.
Company A	Over 5000 brand name products from over 300 various companies plus thousands of private label products.	30 per cent discounts on items as well as commissions from a distributor's down-line sales network plus 3-25 per cent discounts on certain sales items.	Support was offered through product guarantees, written business plans, brochures, and interviews with successful distributors.	There were no special programs. New distributors had to purchase a sales starter kit for approximately $200.
Company B	Wide range of cosmetic products	10-50 per cent based on current order	Support was offered through district	Occasionally the $20 sign-up fee for new

	including make-up, perfumes, fashion items, jewelry, vitamins, toys, games, compact discs and videos.	volumes plus special discounts on special items.	managers, a contact person who assisted distributors with questions and training, meetings, conferences, and various brochures.	representatives was waived or discounted.
Company C	Various office products including novelty gift items, supplies, and stationery.	30 per cent based on current sales order.	Support was offered through written material, regular sales training from supervisors, and an extensive distributor support network.	There were no special programs. New representatives had to purchase a sales starter kit for approximately $45.
Company D	Plastic household products and toys.	25-35 per cent discounts on current orders.	Support was offered through regular sales and information session meetings, and phone consultation with other distributors.	Many programs existed including product incentives, and new distributor parties. New distributors had to purchase a sales starter kit for approximately $125.
Company E	Office business cards and stationery.	50 per cent discount off retail on all orders.	Support was offered through extensive sales and product-related training sessions.	There were no special programs.
Company F	Household consumable food items, laundry and cleaning products, and	28-48 per cent discounts based on current orders.	Support was offered through local meetings, conferences, and conventions.	There were no special programs. New distributors had to purchase a sales starter kit

	personal health products.		An area supervisor was also available for consultation.	for approximately $99.

Source: Internal Company Documents

Exhibit 3: Three Year Sales Forecast

Canadian Dollars (000,000)	Current Year	1st Year Ended	2nd Year Ended	3rd Year Ended
Sales	$63.0	$69.3	$79.7	$91.7
Earnings Before Tax	(6.7)	(1.0)	5.1	9.8

Assumptions
4. 1st Year Ended: sales grow by 10 per cent; margin at 49 per cent; expenses reduced by $3.4 million.
5. 2nd Year Ended: sales grow by 15 per cent; margin at 50 per cent; expenses grow by 2 per cent.
6. 3rd Year Ended: sales grow by 15 per cent; margin at 51 per cent; expenses grow by 3 per cent.

Source: Internal Company Documents

Exhibit 4: Comparative Results Prior Four Years Ended

Canadian Dollars (000,000)	4th Year Ended	3rd Year Ended	2nd Year Ended	Current Year Ended
Sales	$69.2	$72.3	$70.6	$63.0
Cost of Goods Sold	31.1	35.1	36.1	32.8
Gross Margin	38.1	37.2	34.5	30.2
Operating Expenses	34.1	35.6	41.1	36.9
Earnings Before Taxes	4.0	1.6	(6.6)	(6.7)
Number of Distributors	172,000	180,000	176,000	156,000

Joseph J. Schiele prepared this case for the Direct Selling Education Foundation of Canada, solely to provide material for class discussion. The author did not intend to illustrate either effective or ineffective handling of a managerial situation. The author may have disguised certain names and other identifying information to protect confidentiality.

53   Lifestyle International

INTRODUCTION

In September 1997, Christina Blake, General Manager of Vitality's Canadian Operations, located in Windsor, Ontario, faced the following problem. She had just been notified that her company would be merging with Long-life and Healthy Choice, two other direct selling companies, to form one company known as Lifestyle International. Christina was assigned the task of managing the merger between Vitality and Long-life's Canadian operations. After reviewing the situation, Christina wondered what action she should take next.

DIRECT SELLING

Direct selling involved the sale and distribution of a company's products and services through a network of distributors. Distributors were independent contractors who purchased products directly from a company for their own use and for resale to retail consumers.

Direct selling enabled distributors to become involved on a part or full-time basis. Companies concentrated their efforts on encouraging individuals to develop their own business, at their own pace, without the costly expense inherent in franchise operations or other start-up enterprises. Direct selling gave individuals the opportunity to go into business without significant risk, yet offered them significant upside potential, albeit wholly dependent upon their own efforts.

Direct selling used word-of-mouth advertising to grow and capture market shares. It was people talking to other people, sharing something that they believed in. In addition, direct selling allowed an individual to leverage his or her time, talent and energy to earn commissions from sales to all the people that were introduced to the business.

Compensation plans developed for distributors provided several opportunities for distributors to earn money. Each distributor was required to purchase and sell products in order to earn compensation. Distributors could not simply develop a down-line sales organization or receive payment based upon the recruitment of new distributors.

The first method of earning a commission through a direct selling system was through retail mark-up on product sales. Distributors purchased product from a company and resold the product at retail prices to consumers. The difference between the price paid by the distributor and the retail price was a distributor's profit or compensation.

The second method of earning a commission through a direct selling system was through commissions on sales volumes generated by a distributor's down-line sales organization. This down-line sales organization consisted of additional distributors introduced to the company by the distributor.

A direct selling company's ability to increase sales was significantly dependent on its ability to attract, motivate, and retain distributors. A company did this by utilizing a marketing program which it believed was superior to programs offered by other direct selling companies. Programs provided financial incentives, distributor training and support, low-priced starter kits, little or no inventory requirements, and little or no monthly purchase requirements.

INDUSTRY OVERVIEW

The World Federation of Direct Selling Associations estimated that 1998 Canadian retail sales by direct selling sources would amount to $1.6 billion. The percentage of sales by major product groups was as follows: home and family care products (cleaning, cookware, and cutlery, etc.), 11 per cent; personal care products (cosmetics, jewelry, and skin care, etc.), 30 per cent; services and miscellaneous, 14 per cent; wellness products (weight loss, vitamins and nutritional supplements, etc.), 36 per cent; and leisure items (books, toys and games, etc.), 9 per cent. Canadian retail sales by direct selling sources were expected to experience an average annual growth rate of 10 to 15 per cent over the next five years.

The location of these sales, that were sold by an estimated 1.3 million distributors reported as a percentage of sales dollars, was as follows: in the home, 75 per cent; in the workplace, 10 per cent; over the phone (in a follow-up to a face-to-face solicitation), 11 per cent; and at temporary or other locations (fair, exhibition, shopping mall, etc), 4 per cent.

The sales strategies used by direct selling companies to generate sales varied considerably. These methods, as a percentage of sales dollars, were as follows: individual one-to-one selling, 65 per cent; party-plan or group selling, 29 per cent; and customers placing an order directly to the firm (following a face-to-face solicitation), 6 per cent.

COMPETITION

Vitality, Long-life, and Healthy Choice marketed and sold a variety of products including herbal remedies, vitamins, food supplements, skin and personal care items, household and commercial cleaners, and water purification systems. They competed with many other companies marketing similar products to those that they sold. They also competed directly with other direct selling companies in the recruitment of distributors.

Not all competitors sold all the types of products marketed by Vitality, Long-life, and Healthy Choice. For example, some competitors were known for and were identified with sales of herbal formulations, others with household cleaning and personal care products, while others were known for and identified with sales of nutritional and dietary supplements. Some competitors also marketed products and services in addition to those that Vitality, Long-life, and Healthy Choice sold.

Another source of competition in the sale and distribution of health and nutrition products was from direct retail establishments such as large retailers, independents, and non-category stores (e.g., drug stores). The most prominent retailer was the General Nutrition Center (GNC) which had a number of retail stores located both in the U.S. and in Canada.

There were also many direct selling companies with which the companies competed for distributors. Some of the largest of these were Amway, Herbalife International Inc., Rexall Sundown Inc., Market America Inc., and Relive International Inc. Vitality, Long-life, and Healthy Choice competed for these distributors through marketing programs that included its commission structure, training and support services, and other benefits.

PROPOSED MERGER

Background

In September 1997, Christina Blake was notified that her company, Vitality, would be merging with Long-life and Healthy Choice, two other direct selling companies, to form one company known as Lifestyle International. This merger would form one of the world's largest and most dynamic direct selling companies. With hundreds of thousands of distributors, 600 full-time employees, and 52 distributor servicc centres in over 33 countries around the world, Lifestyle International would be well positioned to serve the market within which it operated.

Exhibit 1 contains summary information for Healthy Choice, Long-life, and Vitality with respect to the dates each company was founded and the countries within which they operated.

As part of this initiative, Christina was assigned the task of managing the merger of Vitality and Long-life's Canadian operations. Both companies were to move into one Canadian location, and conduct business as one company. The proposed merger was intended to take advantage of each other's strengths and established distributor network. Christina's task was to effect this change as efficiently as possible without anyone losing their job from either company.

Exhibit 2 contains a proposed organizational chart for Lifestyle International in Canada.

Lifestyle International Values

Lifestyle International had identified a set of core values that would guide everything that they did. These values included:

People Are Number One

Lifestyle International committed to put people first. They believed that the first step to achieving any goal was to focus on the needs of the individual.

Products That Satisfy

In order to create lifelong customers, Lifestyle International committed to offering only those products that satisfied both the needs and wants of consumers.

Complete Integrity

Lifestyle International committed to conduct themselves with complete integrity in all aspects of their business.

Opportunity for All

Regardless of sex, race, age, politics, religion, education level, or culture, Lifestyle International committed to ensure that all people would have equal access to Lifestyle International products and business opportunities.

Long Range Thinking

Lifestyle International committed to take a long range approach to all company decisions to ensure growth and stability of the company for many years to follow.

Lifestyle International Mission Statement

Lifestyle International's mission was to: provide ongoing opportunity for financial security and independence through the development of a successful Lifestyle International business; provide each person with the support needed in the development and attainment of their full potential; provide a continuous supply of superior health-related products to meet the needs of people everywhere; and cause Lifestyle International to become a household name, recognized for their products, and sought after as a excellent business opportunity.

VITALITY: GENERAL COMPANY BACKGROUND

Company Structure

Vitality was a large U.S.-based company with operations throughout the world. Christina Blake was the General Manager of Vitality's Canadian operations, a separate legal entity, registered within the Province of Ontario. She reported directly to the Vice-President of Operations for the U.S. Christina was educated at York University. She had worked in various progressive positions for several multi-national companies across several industries. Christina had joined Vitality in 1990 as General Manager.

Vitality's Canadian operations, which consisted of one 4,300-square foot office and warehouse facility located in Windsor, Ontario and approximately 1500 square feet in a public warehouse facility located in Western Canada, served as an independent sales, marketing, and distribution company for Vitality products in Canada.

The Windsor location was responsible for managing all aspects of the Canadian operation including inventory control, administration of the company marketing plan, accounting, distributor network management and administration, and commission cheque calculation and issuance. All transactions, inventory control, and record keeping were managed using a sophisticated computerized system.

Management and General Workforce

There were six people employed in Canada who worked from Vitality's Windsor office. These people included: Christina Blake, General Manager; Sharon Newson, Operations Manager; Mary Elise, Distributor Services; Tricia Martin, Inventory Control and Purchasing; Liz Clayson, Order Entry and Distributor Services; and Craig Barnes, Warehousing. Vitality's Western Canada location was staffed by a single individual who performed general shipping and receiving duties for the region.

Exhibit 3 contains an organizational chart for Vitality.

Corporate Culture

The people who worked for Vitality's Canadian operation conducted themselves in a highly professional manner, meeting at scheduled times, and proceeding from day to day in a very formal fashion. In addition, workers were also highly team-orientated, always working together to ensure that corporate goals and objectives were met.

Vitality management continuously challenged employees on a regular basis to ensure personal growth and advancement. Goal-setting and training contributed to the professional advancement of staff. All

Vitality employees continuously looked for ways to improve upon the operation and felt a strong commitment to the work that they did.

In addition, Vitality's Canadian employees had a strong understanding of the corporate marketing plan and operation in general. Christina believed that was the result of the extent to which the Canadian operation was maintained and controlled by the Windsor head office located in Canada.

Products Sold - Description
Vitality sold and marketed a variety of health-related products across various regions in Canada, including Nova Scotia, Ontario, Manitoba, Alberta, and British Columbia. These products included herbal remedies, vitamins, food supplements, skin and personal care items, household and commercial cleaners, and a water purification system that were sourced from a company-owned manufacturer located in the United States.

Shipments of these products were ordered and received monthly and inventory levels were determined by the Windsor head office based upon anticipated sales volumes.

Sales and Marketing
Distributors were supported by a marketing plan that used Vitality's reputation for offering high quality products as a basis to promote the company. This marketing plan provided distributors with discounts on products purchased from the company that were based on the sales volumes of a distributor's personal sales and a distributor's down-line distributor network.

The number of active distributors who sold and marketed Vitality products across Canada during 1993, 1994, 1995, and 1996 was 7.2, 9.1, 8.3, and 9.2 thousand, respectively. These distributors had contributed to the steady increase in sales revenues for the same period.

Sales and Profitability
Vitality (Canada) sales and profitability had remained relatively stable over the last four years. Aside from a slight decrease in 1995, sales levels had increased steadily. Sales levels for 1993, 1994, 1995, and 1996 were $2.3, $2.7, $2.4, and $2.7 million dollars, respectively.

LONG-LIFE: GENERAL COMPANY BACKGROUND

Company Structure
Long-life was a large U.S. based company with operations throughout the United States (U.S.) and Canada. Shelly-Lynn Costa was the Operations Manager for Long-life's Canadian operations. She reported directly to the Vice-President of Operations for the U.S.

Long-life's Canadian operation consisted of one 5,300-square foot office and warehouse facility, located in Windsor, Ontario that served as a distribution centre for Long-life products in Canada. This facility's primary role was to provide Canadian distributors with product and sales support and to warehouse the products sold and marketed in Canada.

Long-life's Canadian operations were heavily dependent upon the U.S. head office for corporate services such as inventory control, accounting, marketing, and commission cheque calculation and issuance. All general day-to-day transactions and record keeping were managed using a manual recording process. An outdated computer terminal that linked Long-life's Canadian operation to the U.S. was used to input current inventory levels from which the U.S. head office would determine how much new inventory would be sent to the Canadian operation. For the most part, computers were not used within Long-life's Canadian operation.

Management and General Workforce

There were four people employed in Canada who worked from Long-life's Windsor office. These people included: Shelly-Lynn Costa, Operations Manager; Lisa Bartow, Distributor Relations; Alice Pistone, Shipper and Receiver; and Dave Milstone, part-time Office Assistant.

Exhibit 4 contains an organizational chart for Long-life.

These people worked collectively to provide the support necessary to Long-life's Canadian distributors. All other Long-life employees worked out of the U.S. head office.

Corporate Culture

The people who were employed at Long-life's Canadian operation worked in a rather casual and relaxed environment. People often met informally and proceeded from day to day in a carefree fashion. Employees generally worked independently of each other, performing the duties that related to their specific jobs.

Employees at Long-life did not feel very challenged by their activities from day to day. There was limited goal setting or planning for personal development. Most of the staff were content on maintaining the roles that they had performed for the company during the last several years.

In addition, aside from senior management, Long-life's Canadian employees had limited knowledge of the corporate marketing plan or operation in general. Christina believed that this was the result of the extent to which the Canadian operation was maintained and controlled by the head office located in the U.S.

Products Sold - Description

Long-life sold and marketed a variety of health-related products across various regions in Canada, including Nova Scotia, Quebec, Ontario, Alberta, and British Columbia. These products included herbal remedies, vitamins, food supplements, skin and personal care items, household and commercial cleaners, and a water purification system that were sourced from the manufacturer that Vitality owned that was located in the United States.
Shipments of these products were ordered and received monthly and inventory levels were determined by the U.S. head office based upon anticipated sales volumes.

Sales and Marketing

Distributors were supported by a marketing plan that used Long-life's reputation as an excellent business opportunity as the basis for promoting the company. This marketing plan provided distributors with discounts on products purchased from the company that were based on the sales volumes of a distributor's personal sales and a distributor's down-line distributor network.

The number of active distributors who sold and marketed Long-life products across Canada during 1993, 1994, 1995, and 1996 was 5.1, 8.2, 3.3, and 1.1 thousand, respectively. During 1995 and 1996, approximately seven thousand distributors left Long-life to join another direct marketing company formed by one of Long-life's senior executives. This decrease in the number of active distributors contributed to the dramatic decline in sales revenues for the same period.

Sales and Profitability
Long-life (Canada) sales and profitability varied over the last four years. Aside from a significant increase in sales for the 1994 period, sales and profitability had dramatically declined. Sales levels for 1993, 1994, 1995, and 1996 were $1.7, $2.5, $.86, and $.31 million dollars, respectively. The company had experienced a net loss for the 1995 and 1996 periods.

DECISION

Having the information that she felt relevant, Christina wondered what action she needed to take next.

Exhibit 1: Summary Information for Healthy Choice, Long-life, and Vitality

Company:	Healthy Choice	Long-life	Vitality
Founded:	1970	1975	1983
Market	Eastern Europe Western Europe Africa	Caribbean Islands Asia Canada United States	United Kingdom Presence: Ireland Eastern Europe Western Europe Canada United States Mexico

Source: Internal company documents

Exhibit 2: Lifestyle International Proposed Organizational Chart

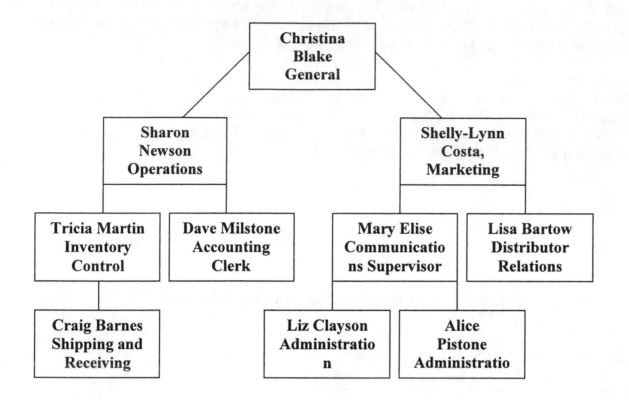

Exhibit 3: Vitality Organizational Chart

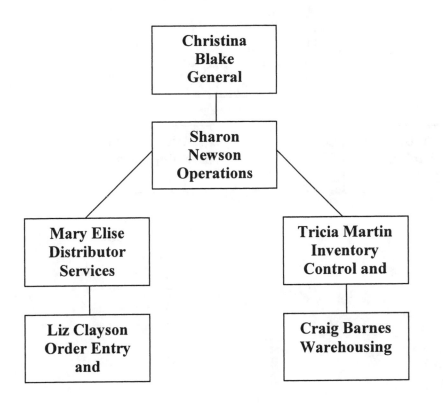

Exhibit 4: Long-life Organizational Chart

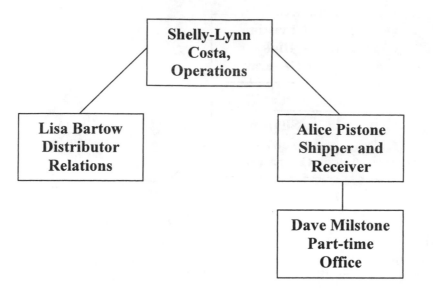

Joseph J. Schiele prepared this case for the Direct Selling Education Foundation of Canada, solely to provide material for class discussion. The author did not intend to illustrate either effective or ineffective handling of a managerial situation. The author may have disguised certain names and other identifying information to protect confidentiality.

54   Amway Launches Quixtar.com

On February 1, 1999, Jim Hunking, General Manager of Amway's Canadian Operations, located in London, Ontario, faced the following problem. Amway had just announced its commitment to launching a fully functioning e-commerce Web site called Quixtar.com on September 1, 1999. He realized that a number of challenges would have to be overcome and a great deal of planning and coordination would have to occur in order for this commitment to be met by the stated date. Jim wondered what action he should take next.

AMWAY CORPORATION

General Company Background
Amway Corporation was one of the world's largest direct selling companies with 1998 estimated retail sales of approximately six billion dollars U.S. More than two and a half million people in 45 countries had embraced the Amway business opportunity. Amway was founded in 1959 by two friends, Jay Van Andel and Rich DeVos, in the basements of their homes in Grand Rapids, Michigan, U.S.A. Amway's very first product was L.O.C.® (Liquid Organic Cleaner), an all-purpose cleaning solution containing biodegradable surfactants.

Ownership and Management
Amway Corporation was privately held by the DeVos and Van Andel families and was governed by the Amway Policy Board (which functioned as the corporation's board of directors), composed of both co-founders and eight second-generation members of the DeVos and Van Andel families. Amway management was led by Chairman Steve Van Andel and President Dick DeVos, who shared management responsibility for the worldwide business and who led a global management team of seasoned Amway executives. Amway's Canadian operation was managed by Jim Hunking, General Manager.

Jim Hunking, General Manager, Amway's Canadian Operations
Jim Hunking was employed as the General Manager of Amway's Canadian Operations. Jim had been with Amway for the past 21 years. Jim began his career with Amway as a Financial Accountant, then moved progressively through various positions including Chief Accountant and Chief Financial Officer to his current position in 1995. In 1990 Jim also obtained his Certified Management Accounting designation from the Certified Management Accounting Association of Ontario.

As General Manager of Amway's Canadian operations, Jim was ultimately responsible for the day-to-day operations for Amway in Canada including activities associated with Distribution, Marketing, Finance, and Customer Service.

Company Vision, Mission, and Values
The founding families believed that it was vital for everyone at Amway to understand the philosophy upon which the business operated and the strategic direction by which it would move forward. This was outlined in the following vision, mission, and values statements.

Vision
To be the best business opportunity in the world.

Mission
Through the partnering of distributors, employees, and the founding families, and the support of quality products and services, Amway set out to offer all people the chance to achieve their goals through the Amway business opportunity.

Values
Amway identified the following six fundamental values as the essential and enduring standards, not to be compromised, by which it operated:

1. Partnership
Amway was built on the concept of partnership, beginning with the partnership between the founders. The partnership that existed among the founding families, distributors, and employees was their most prized possession. They always tried to do what was in the best interest of their partners, in a manner that increased trust and confidence. Amway would reward all who contributed to its success.

2. Integrity
Integrity was essential to Amway's business success. It tried to do what was right, not just whatever "worked." Amway's success was measured not only in economic terms, but by the respect, trust, and credibility it earned.

3. Personal Worth
Amway acknowledged the uniqueness present in each individual. Every person was worthy of respect, and deserved fair treatment and the opportunity to succeed to the fullest extent of his or her potential.

4. Achievement
Amway founders, distributors, and employees were builders and encouragers. They strove for excellence in all that they did. Their focus was on continued improvement, progress, and achievement of individual and group goals. They anticipated change, responded swiftly to it, took action to get the job done, and gained from their experiences. They encouraged creativity and innovation.

5. Personal Responsibility
Each individual at Amway was responsible and accountable for achieving personal goals, as well as for giving 100 per cent effort in helping to achieve corporate or team goals. By helping people help themselves, the company furthered the potential for individual and shared success. Amway also had a responsibility to be a good citizen within the communities where its people lived and worked.

6. Free Enterprise
Amway was a proud advocate of freedom and free enterprise. Human economic advancement was clearly proven to be best achieved in a free market economy.

Taken as a whole, the above six points constituted the foundation upon which Amway felt it could achieve its vision: to be the best business opportunity in the world.

Sister Companies

Amway Japan Limited was the exclusive distribution company for Amway Corporation in Japan. Amway Asia Pacific Limited was the exclusive distribution company for Amway Corporation in Australia, Brunei, New Zealand, Thailand, Taiwan, Malaysia, Macau, Hong Kong, and the People's Republic of China. Certain trusts, foundations, and other entities that were established by or for the benefit of the founders were the majority shareholders of each company. A minority of each company was publicly traded. Both companies were listed on the New York stock exchange: Amway Japan Limited as AJL and Amway Pacific Limited as AAP.

Facilities

Amway of Canada was based in London, Ontario. Manufacturing occurred at the Ada, Michigan, world headquarters; Amway's Nutrilite facilities were in Lakeview and Buena Park, California; and there were facilities in South Korea and China. Amway's ARTISTRY® Cosmetics and Skin Care products were manufactured at the corporation's state-of-the-art manufacturing facility in Ada, Michigan, for distribution on six continents.

Products were delivered to Amway distributors in the United States and Canada through ten Amway Service Centers. Amway had 46 affiliated operations world-wide serving 80 countries and territories. Approximately 70 per cent of Amway's business occurred outside of North America. Amway and its affiliates employed more than 14,000 people worldwide.

Canadian Operations

Amway Corporation's Canadian operations were started as Amway's first foreign affiliate in October 1962, with a 600-square foot facility on Hyman Street in London, Ontario. In 1964, Amway moved to its present location on Exeter Road, into a 4,000-square foot facility that was ultimately expanded to 225,000 square feet. The Canadian headquarters, with approximately 300 employees, provided distribution of Amway's products and services to Amway's 76,000 Canadian distributors across the nation.

The number of new distributors joining the company in Canada had increased 9.5 per cent annually over the past five years. In addition, Amway of Canada's revenues at estimated retail for the fiscal year ended August 31, 1998 were approximately $203 million, up from $170 million the previous year. The average annual growth in Canada over the previous five years was 18 per cent.

During 1998, Amway of Canada processed an average of 41,000 orders per month. These products were generally shipped out within 24 hours of ordering, to various locations across Canada.

Products and Services

Over time, Amway products and services had expanded to include more than 450 personal care, nutrition and wellness, home care, home tech, and commercial products, developed and manufactured by Amway, plus a variety of products and services carrying the Amway name. Based on 1998 sales, Amway was one of the world's largest manufacturers of branded vitamin and mineral supplements in tablet and capsule form.

Amway also offered goods and services from a variety of major companies, including the Amway Food Storage System created exclusively for Amway by Rubbermaid. Other products included thousands of brand name items in Amway of Canada's PERSONAL SHOPPERS® Catalogue and other specialty catalogues, available in both English and French. These products included a wide range of food products, clothing, furniture, jewelry, appliances, televisions and other home entertainment products, plus many other personal and commercial use items.

Amway of Canada Ltd. also marketed a variety of services, including AT&T Canada Long Distance Telephone Service, Cantel cellular phone service, the Franklin Covey Day Planner System, and the Amway Auto Club, administered by the Dominion Automobile Association.

Sales and Marketing

As of 1998, a core force of more than two and a half million distributors world-wide, including more than 76,000 Canadians, represented the primary distribution network for Amway products and services. These distributors were independent business owners, not Amway employees. They were sponsored and trained by active distributors, and they operated their businesses using the Amway Sales and Marketing Plan.

New distributors began by buying a Business Kit, valued at approximately CDN $204, which contained 13 of Amway's most popular products, as well as information on Amway products and programs. The kit was returnable if a distributor chose not to continue.

There were two ways in which an Amway distributor earned income. First, Amway distributors earned income from the mark-up of products and services they sold directly to consumers. Typically, this mark-up was 25 to 30 per cent of the wholesale price, but distributors were entitled to determine independently the prices at which they sold products. In most cases, distributors sold to consumers in their homes; you could not buy Amway-branded products off store shelves.

The second method by which an Amway distributor could earn income was from bonuses earned from the down-line sales of distributors that they sponsored. A distributor would receive bonuses not only from his or her direct sales but also from the sales of those within their respective down-line sales organizations.

Although these distributors were independent entrepreneurs, distributors were not alone in building their business. New distributors were trained by a sponsor to ensure that they knew best how to build their business. The Business Kit came with the Amway Sales and

Marketing Plan that provided information on business principles. Ethical values were outlined in the Amway Code of Ethics, and rules of conduct were also provided to distributors before they were allowed to set out on their own.

Competition

Amway competed with many companies marketing similar products. Few competitors in the direct marketing industry marketed the number of products and services offered by Amway. Another source of competition in the sale and distribution of products was from direct retail establishments such as large retailers, independents and non-category stores (e.g., drug stores).

Amway also competed directly with other network marketing companies in the recruitment of distributors. Some of the largest of these were Avon, Mary Kay Cosmetics, Tupperware, and NuSkin. The company competed for these distributors through its marketing program that included its commission or bonus structure, training and support services, and other benefits.

SITUATION

Changes in the Competitive Business Environment

As electronic commerce (e-commerce) emerged as a dominant way of conducting business, it became increasingly important for companies to utilize e-commerce as a way to maintain existing market share and to expand customer networks.

E-commerce was an electronic means of funds transfer from consumers to a variety of vendors that provided a vast array of goods and services via the Internet. In this new type of economic exchange, value changed hands without the involvement of physical currency, bank notes, cheques, or other type of physical medium. It was estimated that by the year 2003 worldwide sales via e-commerce would reach between $1.3 and $2.3 trillion.

E-commerce via the Internet provided a number of benefits to companies. These benefits included increased revenue streams, improved customer service, reduced internal costs, increased market share through access to new markets, improved order and inventory management, expedited cash flow, improved supply chain management, improved global partnerships, and the opportunity to take advantage of a wealth of information collected about customer spending patterns and preferences. These benefits, however, were also accompanied by a number of significant challenges.

Many direct selling companies had expanded their businesses and increased the level of service to their customers through the introduction of e-commerce company Web sites. These Web sites allowed individuals to gain more flexibility from the options they had for both ordering and receiving products. In addition, company Web sites allowed individuals to expand upon their direct marketing businesses, purchase products on-line, and gain wider access to a customer base that would otherwise not be available through traditional direct selling methods.

The Announcement of Quixtar.com

On February 1, 1999, as a response to changes in the competitive business environment, Amway announced that it would launch a fully functioning e-commerce Web site, effective September 1, 1999, called Quixtar.com.

Quixtar.com would be a new Internet-based business featuring the unique convergence of e-commerce, member benefits, business ownership, and office services. Quixtar Incorporated would be based in Grand Rapids, Michigan. The Canadian subsidiary, Quixtar Canada Corporation, would be based in London, Ontario.

Ownership and Management

Quixtar.com was owned by the families of Rich DeVos and Jay Van Andel, who also owned the Amway Corporation. Quixtar.com would be contracting many services from the Amway Corporation, including programming, warehousing, distribution, and product development. Quixtar.com's core management team would be assembled from numerous individuals who have led key functional areas for the Amway Corporation.

A Quixtar.com Business

Quixtar.com would allow entrepreneurs in the United States and Canada to start their own Internet-based business without the burden of having to invest in the necessary infrastructure or product lines generally required of new start-up Internet companies. These Independent Business Owners (IBOs) would direct their Clients to Quixtar to purchase a wide variety of products, earning income on the retail mark-up for those products. In addition, IBOs would recruit Members and other IBOs and earn bonuses based on the overall monthly sales volume of those individuals in their group.

Products, Services and More

Quixtar.com would feature a wide variety of products and services similar to those already offered by Amway. A "Quixtar Exclusives" store would feature "My Home", "My Health", and "My Self" sections offering skin care and cosmetics, nutrition and wellness products, laundry care products, cookware products, as well as other various high quality product lines. In addition to these high quality products, this section would also feature personalized information providing solutions to everyday challenges plus a "Ditto Delivery" service that would offer shipments to customers automatically when they needed them.

A "Store For More" would feature hundreds of products from leading brand name companies in many product categories. These categories would include apparel and athletic shoes for men and women, beauty care, over-the-counter medications, cameras, electronics, appliances, furniture, and many more. A "Hot Buys" section would contain many of these brand name products offered at very special prices.

Finally, there would be dozens of links to partner stores, other e-commerce sites that would provide benefits to Quixtar.com Clients, Members, and IBOs. These were yet to be determined and would be announced just prior to Quixtar.com's launch on September 1, 1999. The categories that these stores would fall into would include sporting goods, apparel, jewelry, collectable toys, gifts, designer eye-wear, high-end luxury products, specialty foods, entertainment, flowers, art, gardening, music, tools, office supplies, computer hardware and software, and much more.

Independent Business Owners (IBOs), Members, and Clients
Quixtar.com would feature three basic levels of participation – IBOs, Members, and Clients. As of February 1, 1999, an overwhelming number of people across North America expressed an interest in joining Quixtar.com as either an IBO, Member, or Client.

Independent Business Owners (IBOs)
Quixtar.com IBOs would build businesses that allowed them to earn income based on the business sales volume from their down-line networks. These down-line networks would comprise other IBOs, Members, and Clients that a particular IBO would recruit. IBOs would also be able to take advantage of special business services, including a Virtual Office where they would be able to access detailed volume inquiries showing the invoices that made-up the total sales of their down-line network. Some IBOs would qualify for, based on individual sales volumes, access to Business Profile reports that would provide detailed and trending information about their businesses such as product line movement and sponsoring activity. To become an IBO, a start-up fee of $149 would be required. This fee would include $90 worth of products that could be selected by the new IBO.

Members
Quixtar Members would be preferred customers that were recruited by or were affiliated with IBOs, who obtained products at special discount prices and received special benefits through their association with Quixtar. Members would be able to earn Q-Credits for many Quixtar.com purchases. Q-Credits would be earned in a number of ways and would be redeemable for a number of items, including small appliances, gifts, and other household items. There would also be a special option allowing Members to convert Q-Credits into frequent Flyer Miles on an airline of their choice. To become a Member, a minimal start-up fee of $30 would be required. In addition to the initial start-up fee, a $15 annual renewal fee would also be required to maintain a Member's current status.

Clients
Clients would be individuals that were recruited by or affiliated with IBOs, who would be able to shop from a large selection of high-quality products and learn more about what they needed through expert advice on health, personal care, home maintenance and more. There were no fees associated with becoming a Client. Clients needed only to be recruited by and be associated with an individual IBO.

Delivery to IBOs, Members, and Clients
Products purchased by IBOs, Members, and Clients would be shipped directly to an individual's home, and in most cases, Members and Clients would know the particular IBOs who would be benefiting from each of their individual purchases.

DECISION

Amway had made a significant commitment to the public regarding Quixtar.com and the services that it would offer starting September 1, 1999. Nothing had been done to date to provide the infrastructure needed to support these commitments. Jim realized that a number of challenges would have to be overcome and a great deal of planning and coordination would have to occur in order for this commitment to be met. Jim wondered what action he should take next.

55   Cortech Provides Access to the Internet

On April 12, 2000, Tony Nichols, Internet Product Manager of Cortech's Canadian operations, faced the following problem. During the last two weeks the company had received more than a hundred complaints from customers regarding their inability to log onto the Internet using Cortech's newly launched Internet Access Service. With 50 to 100 new customers subscribing to the newly launched service each day, Tony wondered what action he should take next.

CORTECH COMMUNICATIONS INCORPORATED

General Company Background

Cortech Communications Incorporated (Cortech U.S.) was founded in 1988 by President and CEO Daniel McGuigan. In 1989 Paul Jereau joined the company and introduced the network marketing business model upon which the company was based. In 1996, Cortech U.S. became a public corporation trading on the New York Stock Exchange. In 1997, Cortech U.S. generated more than $1.7 billion in revenues becoming the fourth largest long distance company in the United States, in terms of revenues.

In 1998, Cortech U.S. merged with Canacomm Incorporated, a large Canadian company, creating a global telecommunications company with the capability to serve residential, business, wholesale voice and data customers around the world.

Cortech's success was fueled by the power of personal relationships. Cortech combined a strong line of telecommunications products and services with the network marketing business model.

CANADIAN OPERATIONS

In 1999, following the merger between Cortech U.S. and Canacomm Incorporated, Cortech Canada was formed to serve the Canadian telecommunications market.

Cortech Canada positioned itself to provide residential customers a variety of telecommunications products and services, including calling cards, reduced rate long-distance services, and a digital alternative to cable and direct-to-home satellite television.

Cortech Canada's corporate head office was located in Markham, Ontario from which the majority of administrative activities were conducted.

Tony Nichols, Internet Product Manager

Tony Nichols was Cortech Canada's Internet Product Manager and worked at Cortech's corporate head office in Markham, Ontario. Tony was responsible for ensuring that all products and services related to the Internet were offered by Cortech in an effective and efficient manner. Tony's responsibilities also included managing the successful launch of any new Internet related products.

Tony had more than 12 years of experience in various product management positions with some of Canada's largest technology companies. Tony received his Bachelor of Arts in Economics in 1985 from York University, and his Master of Business Administration in 1988 from Concordia University.

Sales and Marketing
Cortech Canada was supported by a network of more than 20,000 Independent Representatives (IRs) who utilized a network marketing strategy to both recruit their sales force and serve more than 100,000 customers. Sixty per-cent of these IRs were based in rural areas with the other forty per-cent centered in Canada's ten largest cities.

IRs were independent business owners who sold and marketed Cortech products and services to their family, friends, business associates, and acquaintances.

Cortech offered a home based equal opportunity business to any willing person regardless of sex, race, origin, or education. Cortech representatives were not required to purchase any products, nor meet any sales quotas in order to earn income. IRs could earn income from their personal sales as well as from their down-line sales network. This allowed IRs to earn both immediate and long-term residual income.

There were two ways in which to join Cortech. The first was to become an IR by purchasing a basic materials kit for $65 which provided the marketing materials needed to start a Cortech business.

The second was to become a Managing Representative by purchasing a Cortech management services kit for $255 including an annual renewal fee of $165 that provided home office support materials, monthly down-line reports, newsletter subscription and training by a certified Cortech trainer.

Many Representatives also chose to earn income as trainers, earning $30 each time they trained a new Managing Representative. The cost to become a Trainer was $500, with an annual renewal fee of $150.

SITUATION

Changes in the Competitive Business Environment
Since the early 1990's the Internet's growth rate had surpassed that of any other technology in its pervasiveness and acceptance on a worldwide scale. In Canada, by the end of 1998, there were over 2.3 million residential Internet users that generated over $500 million in revenues. This figure represented a 280 per-cent increase from 1996.

In the U.S., over a four year period, there had been more than 50 million new Internet users. It took radio 38 years, television 13 years, and PCs 16 years to reach the same penetration levels. A March 1999 report showed that 29 per-cent of Canadian adults had connected to the Internet from their home during a three month period (Comquest Research – March 1999).

In 1998, Internet traffic doubled every 100 days, with an annual growth rate of more than 700 percent. It was estimated that Internet transactions worldwide would surpass $450 billion (Canadian) by 2002. The number of global Internet users soared to more than 100 million in 1997, and the number of web pages increased to over 300 million by early 1998 (up from 200 million in late 1997).

According to a 1999 survey conducted by the International Data Corporation (Canada) Limited (IDC), a computer consulting company located in Toronto, Ontario exactly 50 per-cent of all Canadian households included at least one person with regular access to the Internet at home, work, school or another location. Seventy-two percent of those had access in their homes while 56 per-cent were connected at work or at school.

Other studies showed that 48 per-cent of the U.S. population used the Internet as their primary news source and 36 per-cent used e-mail as their primary communications tool. The number of U.S. Web users surpassed 57 million in late April 1998, up 1.6 million from January that same year.

1999 surveys of Americans indicated that 44 percent of Internet users were female, 77 percent between the ages of 18 and 49, and 51 percent had college degrees (compared to 24 per-cent of the general population). People spent approximately 24 hours per month on the Web in ten separate sessions, during which they viewed 348 pages. There were approximately 98 million U.S. consumer households, with 40 million owning personal computers. Only 50 percent of these PC households had access to the Internet at year-end 1997.

According to Statistics Canada, the percentage of households actually connected to the Internet at the end of 1998 was as follows:

Province	%
BC	28
Alberta	28
Manitoba	18
Saskatchewan	20
Ontario	26
Quebec	16
New Brunswick	18
Nova Scotia	24
Newfoundland	15

*Source: CCTA, Statistics Canada, 1999

Competition

Consumer use of the Internet and its explosive growth rates had led to a market serviced by a multitude of fragmented competitors. The Canadian Association of Internet Providers (CAIP) estimated that in 1999 there was in excess of 400 different Internet Service Providers. These ranged from small mom-and-pop companies to large national companies such as Sympatico or AT&T Canada. They were as follows.

Internet Service Provider	Market Share %	Number of Customers
Independents	38	874,000
Sympatico	18	414,000
Telus & BCTel	9	207,000
AOL Canada	6	138,000
Sprint Canada	6	138,000
Internet Direct	5	115,000
PSINet	4	92,000
Other	14	322,000
Total	100	2,300,000

*Source: Yankee Group 1999

A 1999 Yankee Group Report predicted that there would be a considerable reduction in the number of independent Internet Service Provider's as they were acquired by larger competitors. However, it was predicted that this phenomenon would likely occur only in large metropolitan areas, as larger Internet Service Provider's would be unlikely to see the value of acquiring Internet Service Provider's in non-metropolitan areas distant from corporate head offices located in large city centers.

Population centers outside the metropolitan areas would likely continue to be served by smaller Internet Service Provider's that have the advantage of existing relationships with a rural customer base.

The Announcement of *CortechOnline*

In October 1998, as the Internet emerged as a dominant way of conducting business, Cortech U.S. launched its own Internet Access Service called *CortechOnline*. By September 1999, *CortechOnline* had more than 23,000 subscribers.

CortechOnline provided a high performance, high availability remote Internet Access Service that provided residential and business customers local dial-up services to intranets, extranets, and the Internet. The offering was national in scope covering approximately 95 per-cent of U.S. households.

Each customer was entitled to either 150 hours or unlimited online service per-month and one or three e-mail addresses. Additional e-mail addresses could be purchased for $1 per month. Hours over 150 were billed at $1 each.

Most of the functions associated with providing the Internet Access Service including local Internet access numbers, back-office services including billing, user verification, and email administration, and customer service and technical support was provided to Cortech customers through an independent Internet Service Provider located in the U.S. This independent Internet Service Provider was one of the largest companies providing such services and was well positioned to meet the needs of Cortech customers in the United States.

An independent Internet Service Provider provided the infrastructure necessary for an Internet Access Service customer to dial up a local access number and sign onto the Internet. They also provided the necessary customer service and technical support required to assist customers with problems as they may have arose. In addition a full service Internet Service Provider would have also kept track of billing, would have been responsible for verifying and authenticating users, and the administration of e-mail services.

Cortech Canada Launches its Own Internet Access Service
Recognizing the success of *CortechOnline* in the U.S., Cortech Canada decided to launch its own branded version of the Internet Access Service.

Cortech Canada took several steps to launch its own Internet Access Service. The first thing that management did was estimate the volume of new subscribers that would likely subscribe to the service in each month following the launch. Management estimated that approximately 1000 new customers would subscribe to the service in the first few months. This number was used to estimate the service levels needed to provide the Internet Access Service.

The next thing that management did was decide on a means by which to provide the service. They looked at two options. First, they considered using an independent Internet Service Provider to launch their own branded version of an Internet Access Service, second they considered marketing the services of an existing company that already provided this type of service. After careful consideration management decided to launch its own branded version of the Internet Access Service.

After evaluating proposals from four independent Internet Service Providers, Cortech Canada management decided to use the same vender that Cortech U.S. had used. While this company was very well positioned to serve the U.S. market they had only just entered the Canadian marketplace.

Once Cortech management decided on an independent Internet Service Provider they began the process of producing the necessary registration CD-ROM and training and support materials required to launch the service. They also provided extensive training to Cortech representatives that was necessary to support and sell the new Internet Access Service to Canadian consumers.

At the end of March 2000, Cortech Canada formally launched its own branded Internet Access Service in seven cities including Montreal, Ottawa, Toronto, Kitchener, Edmonton, Calgary, and Vancouver.

Service Problems
During the first two weeks that the Canadian Internet Access Service was launched between 50 and 100 new customers were subscribing to the service each day. This was considered a tremendous success considering that initial estimates were in the 25 to 50 new customer range.

However, during the same period the Cortech Canadian customer service centers received more than a hundred complaints from customers regarding their inability to log onto the Internet using Cortech's newly launched service. Customers were repeatedly encountering busy signals each time they attempted to log onto the Internet.

Upon closer examination it was determined that the U.S. Internet Service Provider chosen, was not equipped to provide the number of access lines necessary to service the rapidly increasing number of new service subscribers.

This problem was first reported in busier city centers like Vancouver and Toronto.

DECISION

After numerous and extensive conversations with the independent Internet Service Provider, that failed to remedy the current service failure, Tony realized that he had a serious problem to solve. Tony wondered what action he should take next.

Joseph J. Schiele prepared this case for the Direct Selling Education Foundation of Canada, solely to provide material for class discussion. The author did not intend to illustrate either effective or ineffective handling of a managerial situation. The author may have disguised certain names and other identifying information to protect confidentiality.